D0773112

KidbitS

KidbitS

Illustrated by
Bob Italiano and Tamia Dowlatabadi

Text by
Jenny Tesar and Kathleen Rocheleau

Executive Editor
Bruce S. Glassman

BLACKBIRCH PRESS
An imprint of Thomson Gale, a part of The Thomson Corporation

THOMSON
★
GALE

Detroit • New York • San Francisco • San Diego • New Haven, Conn. • Waterville, Maine • London • Munich

For more information, contact
Blackbirch Press
27500 Drake Rd.
Farmington Hills, MI 48331-3535
Or you can visit our Internet site at http://www.gale.com

Special thanks to my wife Joan, without whom
this project would not have been possible.
–B.I.

LIBRARY OF CONGRESS CATALOGING-IN-PUBLICATION DATA

Tesar, Jenny
  Kidbits / illustrated by Bob Italiano; text by Jenny Tesar
     p. cm.
  Includes index.
  Summary: more than 1,500 eye-popping charts, graphs, maps, and visuals that instantly show you everything you want to know about your world!
  ISBN 1-4103-0492-2 (pbk. : alk. paper) — ISBN 1-4103-0527-9 (lib. : alk. paper)

Printed in China
10 9 8 7 6 5 4 3 2 1

Table of Contents

Top NFL Team Salaries • Top NFL Earners • All-Time Home Run Hitters • Pitchers with Most Career Games • MLB Players with Most Career Games • All-Time RBI Leaders • All-Time Base Stealers • All-Time Run Scorers • Top MLB Earners • Largest Baseball Stadiums • Top Teams in All-Time World Series Wins • Top NHL Goal Scorers • Top Point Scorers in Stanley Cup Playoff Games • NHL Teams with Highest Payroll • Fastest Kentucky Derby Horses • NASCAR Winners • Women's Top Tennis Players • Tennis Leading Money Winners • U.S. Open Singles Champions • PGA/LPGA Tour Total Birdies • PGA/LPGA Money Leaders • America's Favorite Sports Stars • Top Payroll in Top Pro Sports • Average Professional Sports Franchise Values

Who Are We?

By 2001, more than 287 million people lived in the United States. About 73 million were kids—that is, under age 18. Their ancestors came from every part of the world. They represented nearly every race and ethnic background. Most of them lived in cities and suburbs, and a growing number lived in the South and West.

Every ten years since 1790, the Census Bureau has made an official count of the U.S. population. It asks people about their place of birth, age, race, marital status, home, and other aspects of their lives. In 2000 the Census Bureau estimated that 75% of the population was white and 12% was black. The population also included Asians, Pacific Islanders, American Indians, Eskimos, and other people. According to the Census Bureau, Hispanics—people of Spanish or Spanish American heritage—can be of any race; they made up 12.5% of the 2000 population.

The 2000 population included 28 million people who were born in other countries. About 28% had been born in Mexico and 18% in Asia. California had the largest foreign-born population, followed by New York, Florida, and Texas.

Kidbits Tidbits

- In 2001, there were 96.4 males for every 100 females in the United States. Among young people, there are more males than females. But men die earlier than women, and among older people there are more women than men.
- In 1900, a newborn baby could expect to live to the age of 45. Today, a newborn can expect to live to age 77.
- About 4 million babies were born in the United States in 2002.
- Families are getting smaller. In 1970, the average size of a family was 3.58 people. By 2000, it was 3.17 people.

The population is expected to grow during the coming decades. By the year 2010, the Census Bureau predicts the United States will have 299.9 million people, including more than 72.3 million under age 18.

Each year, some 2.3 million marriages take place in the United States May through October are the most popular months for "getting hitched," with June ranking number 1. In 1998, about 7% of the women and 3% of the men who got married were under age 20.

In 2002, 4 million babies were born in the United States They included 7,315 babies born to girls under age 15 and 425,493 born to girls ages 15 to 19. Those babies, like all babies born in America, could expect

to live to an average age of 77. Most of them will grow up in middle- and upper-class families. But some will live in poverty. Today, about 16% of American children live in poverty. This means their families do not have enough income to buy adequate food and clothing.

There were 72 million families in the United States in 2000. About 50% of the families did not have any children. About 20% had one child, 19% had two children, and 11% had three or more children. Nearly one-third of all families with children were headed by a single parent.

Kidbits Tidbits

- 9.3 million kids (people under age 18) lived in California in 2000—more than in any other state. In comparison, Wyoming only had 129,000 residents under age 18.
- In Mississippi, over 36.3% of the population is black—more than in any other state.
- More than 32% of the population of California and Texas is Hispanic.
- Most U.S. Hispanics are of Mexican origin.
- In 2000, almost 16.1% of Americans under age 18 lived in poverty.
- In 2000, more than 19% of the people in New Mexico lived below the poverty level—more than in any other state.
- In 1790, about 5% of U.S. people lived in cities and 95% lived in rural areas. In 2000, some 79% lived in cities and 21% lived in rural areas.

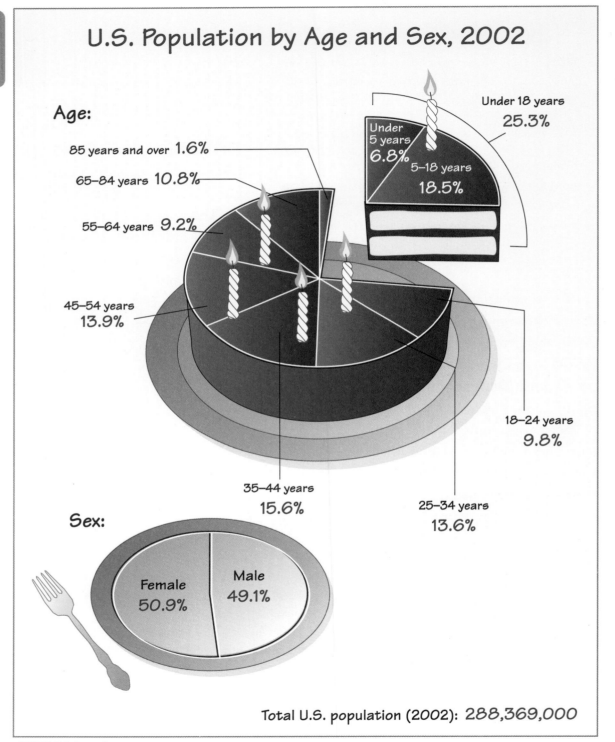

U.S. Population by Age and Sex, 2002

Age:

85 years and over 1.6%

65–84 years 10.8%

55–64 years 9.2%

45–54 years 13.9%

35–44 years 15.6%

25–34 years 13.6%

18–24 years 9.8%

Under 18 years 25.3%

Under 5 years 6.8%

5–18 years 18.5%

Sex:

Female 50.9%

Male 49.1%

Total U.S. population (2002): 288,369,000

SOURCE: U.S. Census Bureau

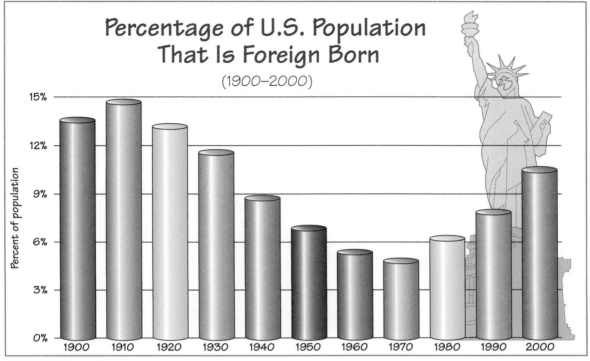

Percentage of U.S. Population That Is Foreign Born
(1900–2000)

SOURCE: U.S. Census Bureau

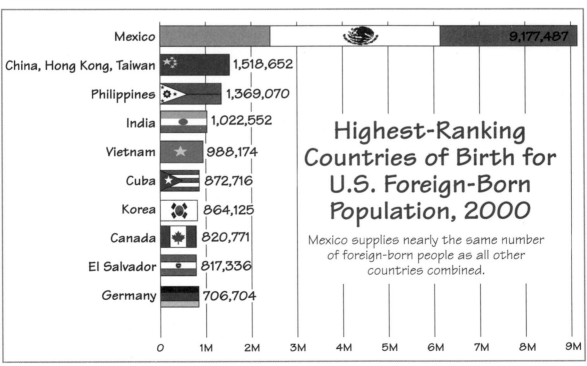

Highest-Ranking Countries of Birth for U.S. Foreign-Born Population, 2000

Mexico supplies nearly the same number of foreign-born people as all other countries combined.

Mexico	9,177,487
China, Hong Kong, Taiwan	1,518,652
Philippines	1,369,070
India	1,022,552
Vietnam	988,174
Cuba	872,716
Korea	864,125
Canada	820,771
El Salvador	817,336
Germany	706,704

SOURCE: U.S. Census Bureau

Total U.S. Population by Region, 2000

The South is the region with the highest combined population.

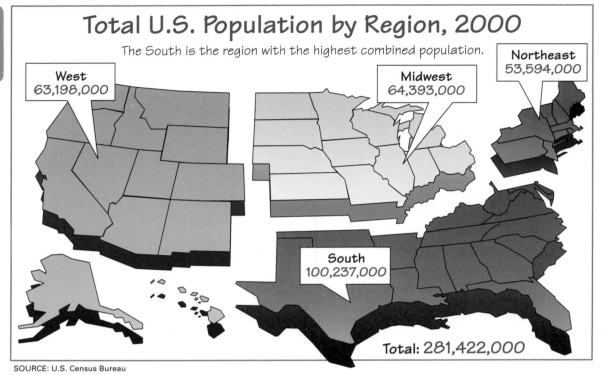

West
63,198,000

Midwest
64,393,000

Northeast
53,594,000

South
100,237,000

Total: 281,422,000

SOURCE: U.S. Census Bureau

U.S. Child and Teenage Population by Region, 2000

The South has the most kids and teens.

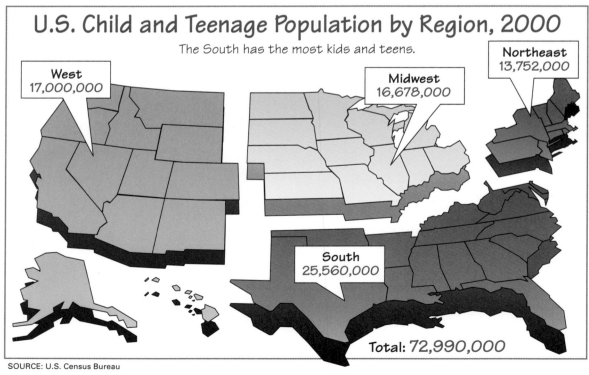

West
17,000,000

Midwest
16,678,000

Northeast
13,752,000

South
25,560,000

Total: 72,990,000

SOURCE: U.S. Census Bureau

U.S. Population by Region and Race, 2000

(In millions)

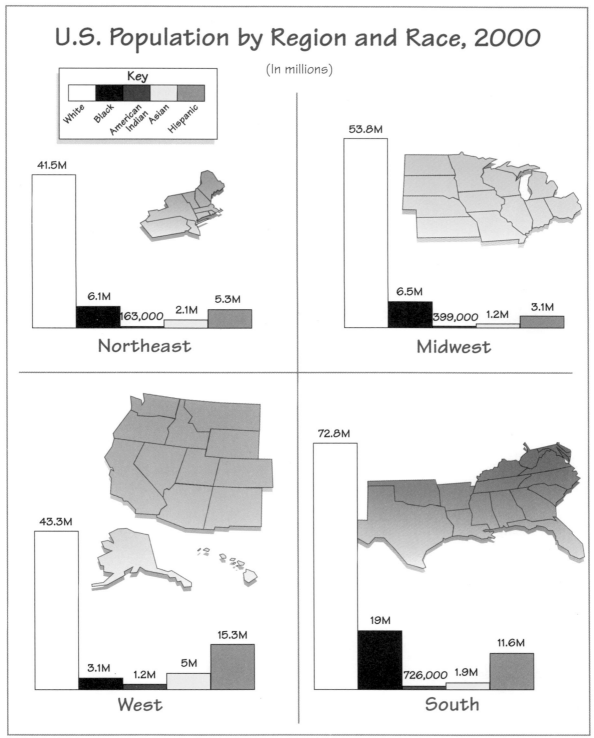

Key

White Black American Indian Asian Hispanic

Northeast
41.5M
6.1M
163,000
2.1M
5.3M

Midwest
53.8M
6.5M
399,000
1.2M
3.1M

West
43.3M
3.1M
1.2M
5M
15.3M

South
72.8M
19M
726,000
1.9M
11.6M

SOURCE: U.S. Census Bureau

Who Are We?

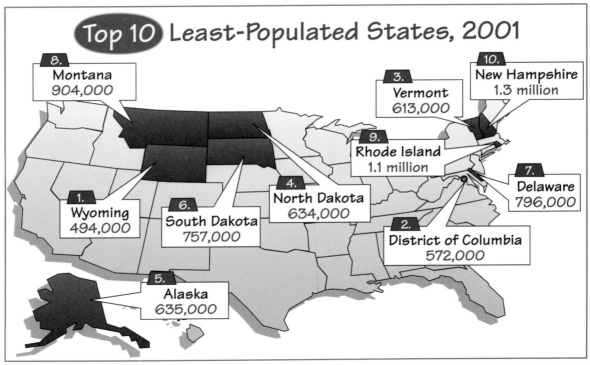

Top 10 Least-Populated States, 2001

8. Montana
904,000

3. Vermont
613,000

10. New Hampshire
1.3 million

9. Rhode Island
1.1 million

7. Delaware
796,000

1. Wyoming
494,000

6. South Dakota
757,000

4. North Dakota
634,000

2. District of Columbia
572,000

5. Alaska
635,000

SOURCE: U.S. Census Bureau

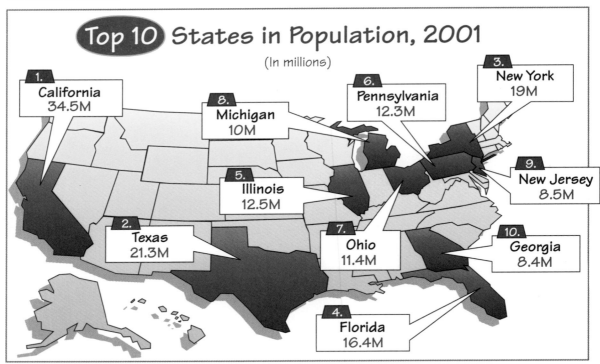

Top 10 States in Population, 2001

(In millions)

1. California
34.5M

8. Michigan
10M

6. Pennsylvania
12.3M

3. New York
19M

9. New Jersey
8.5M

5. Illinois
12.5M

2. Texas
21.3M

7. Ohio
11.4M

10. Georgia
8.4M

4. Florida
16.4M

SOURCE: U.S. Census Bureau

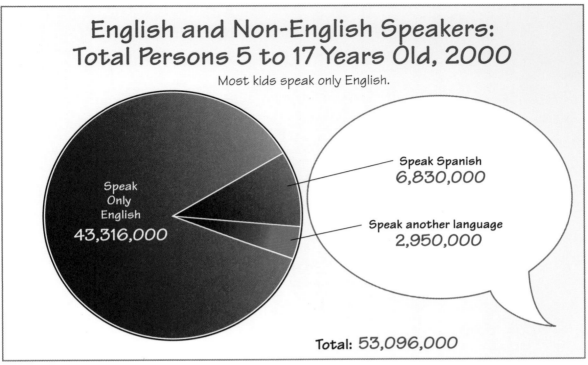

English and Non-English Speakers: Total Persons 5 to 17 Years Old, 2000

Most kids speak only English.

Speak Only English
43,316,000

Speak Spanish
6,830,000

Speak another language
2,950,000

Total: 53,096,000

SOURCE: U.S. Census Bureau

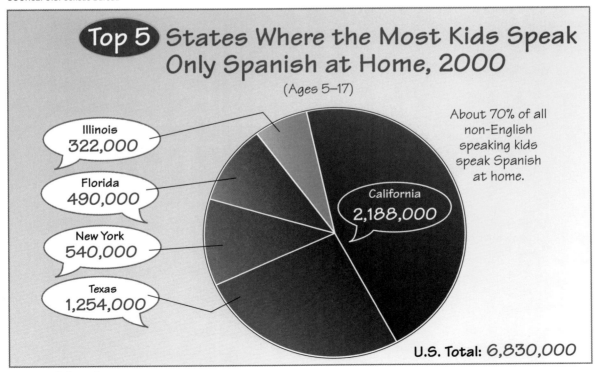

Top 5 States Where the Most Kids Speak Only Spanish at Home, 2000

(Ages 5–17)

Illinois
322,000

Florida
490,000

New York
540,000

Texas
1,254,000

California
2,188,000

About 70% of all non-English speaking kids speak Spanish at home.

U.S. Total: 6,830,000

SOURCE: U.S. Census Bureau

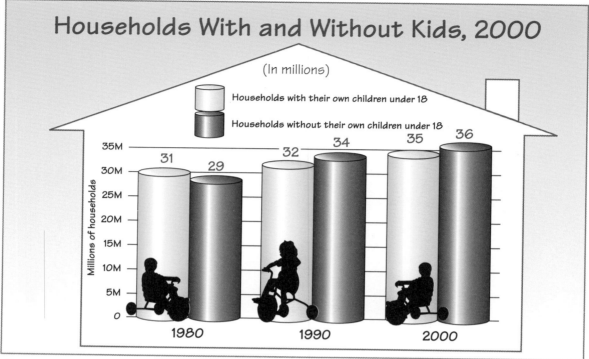

Households With and Without Kids, 2000

(In millions)

Households with their own children under 18

Households without their own children under 18

SOURCE: U.S. Census Bureau

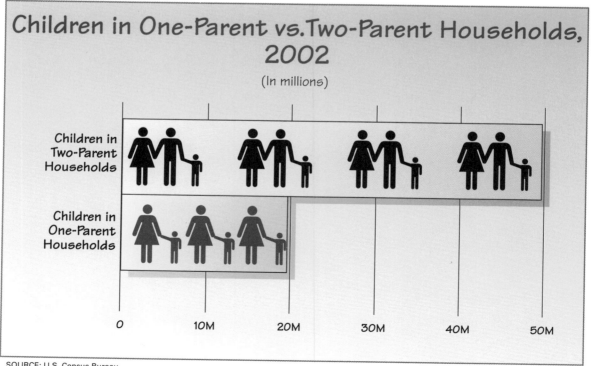

Children in One-Parent vs.Two-Parent Households, 2002

(In millions)

Children in Two-Parent Households

Children in One-Parent Households

SOURCE: U.S. Census Bureau

Size of U.S. Families, 1980 vs. 2000

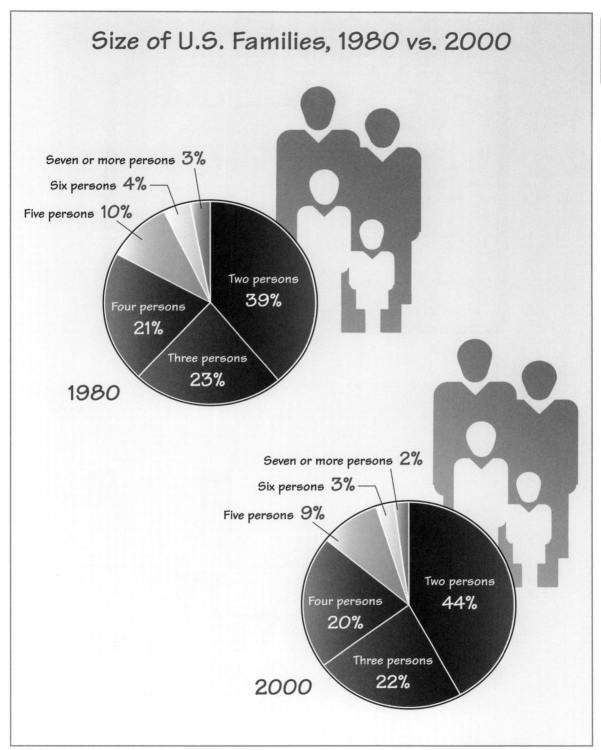

Seven or more persons 3%

Six persons 4%

Five persons 10%

Two persons
39%

Four persons
21%

Three persons
23%

1980

Seven or more persons 2%

Six persons 3%

Five persons 9%

Two persons
44%

Four persons
20%

Three persons
22%

2000

SOURCE: U.S. Census Bureau

Religions of the Believers, 2001

(Percentage of U.S. population affiliated with certain religions)

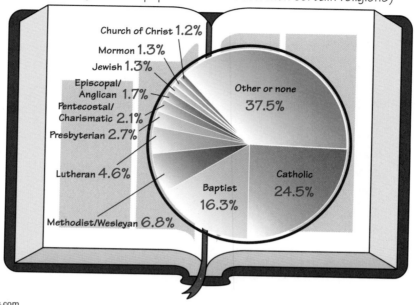

Church of Christ 1.2%

Mormon 1.3%

Jewish 1.3%

Episcopal/Anglican 1.7%

Pentecostal/Charismatic 2.1%

Presbyterian 2.7%

Lutheran 4.6%

Methodist/Wesleyan 6.8%

Other or none 37.5%

Catholic 24.5%

Baptist 16.3%

SOURCE: adherents.com

Marriage and Divorce Rates, 1950 to 2002

Marriage and divorce have declined since 1980.
(Rate per 1,000 population)

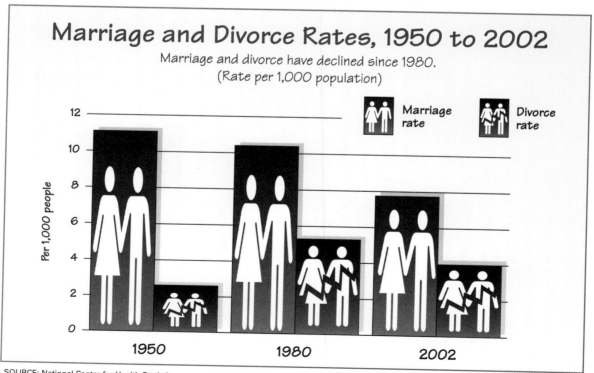

Marriage rate

Divorce rate

Per 1,000 people

1950   1980   2002

SOURCE: National Center for Health Statistics

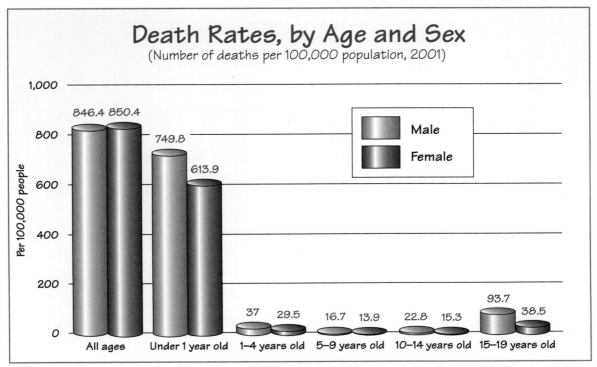

Death Rates, by Age and Sex

(Number of deaths per 100,000 population, 2001)

Per 100,000 people

Male
Female

	Male	Female
All ages	846.4	850.4
Under 1 year old	749.8	613.9
1–4 years old	37	29.5
5–9 years old	16.7	13.9
10–14 years old	22.8	15.3
15–19 years old	93.7	38.5

SOURCE: National Center for Health Statistics

Life Expectancy in 2001

Age at death

Boy
Girl

	Boy	Girl
Born in 2001	74.4	79.8
5 years old	72.8	75.4
10 years old	65.2	70.4
15 years old	60.2	65.5

SOURCE: National Center for Health Statistics

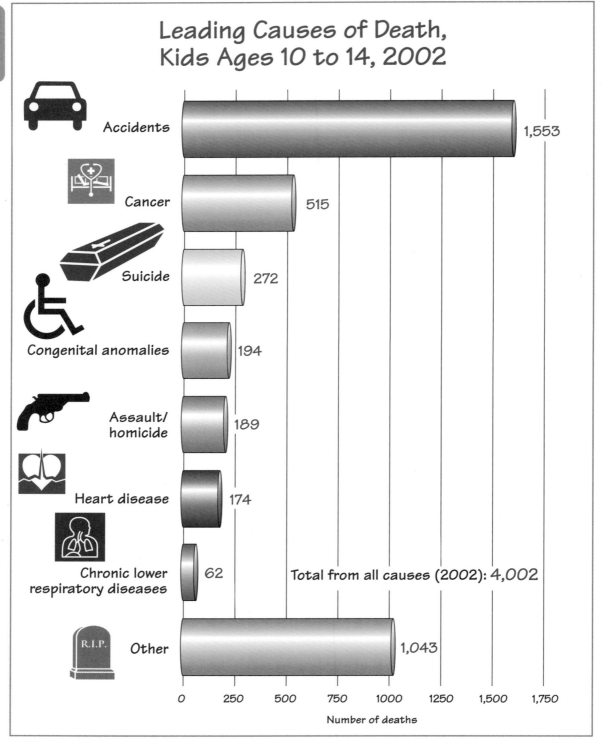

Leading Causes of Death, Kids Ages 10 to 14, 2002

Cause	Number of deaths
Accidents	1,553
Cancer	515
Suicide	272
Congenital anomalies	194
Assault/homicide	189
Heart disease	174
Chronic lower respiratory diseases	62
Other	1,043

Total from all causes (2002): 4,002

Number of deaths

SOURCE: National Center for Health Statistics

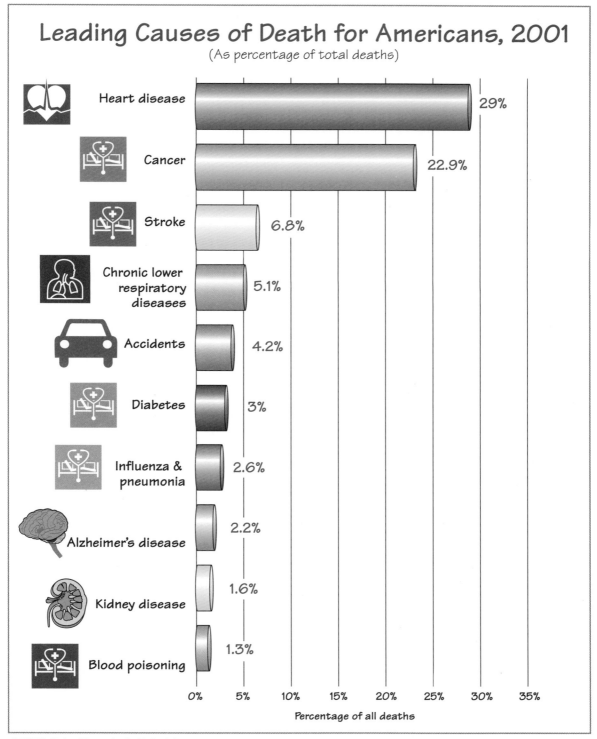

Leading Causes of Death for Americans, 2001
(As percentage of total deaths)

Cause	Percentage
Heart disease	29%
Cancer	22.9%
Stroke	6.8%
Chronic lower respiratory diseases	5.1%
Accidents	4.2%
Diabetes	3%
Influenza & pneumonia	2.6%
Alzheimer's disease	2.2%
Kidney disease	1.6%
Blood poisoning	1.3%

Percentage of all deaths

SOURCE: National Center for Health Statistics

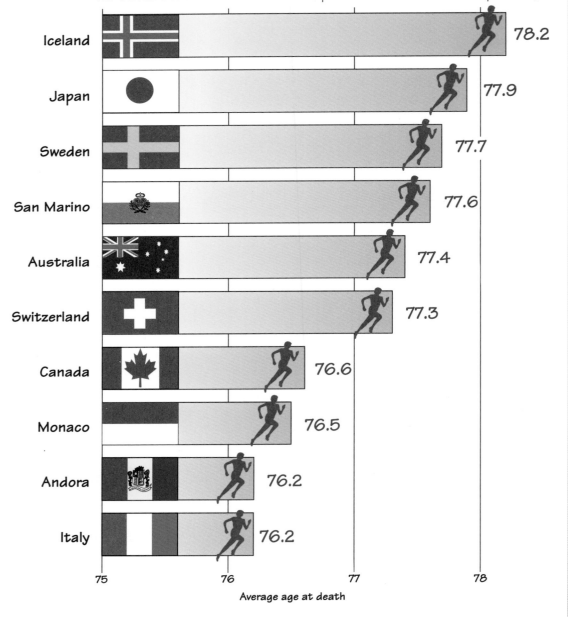

Top 10 Countries with the Highest
Male Life Expectancy, 2002

(U.S. = 74.3 years)
The United States is far behind the top 10 countries in male life expectancy.

Country	Average age at death
Iceland	78.2
Japan	77.9
Sweden	77.7
San Marino	77.6
Australia	77.4
Switzerland	77.3
Canada	76.6
Monaco	76.5
Andora	76.2
Italy	76.2

Average age at death

SOURCE: World Health Organization, World Health Report 2002

Who Are We?

Top 10 Countries with the Highest Female Life Expectancy, 2002

(U.S. = 79.5 years)

The United States is far behind the top 10 countries in female life expectancy.

Country	Average age at death
Japan	84.7
Monaco	84
San Marino	83.9
Andorra	82.9
France	82.9
Switzerland	82.8
Australia	82.6
Spain	82.6
Sweden	82.3
Italy	82.2

Average age at death

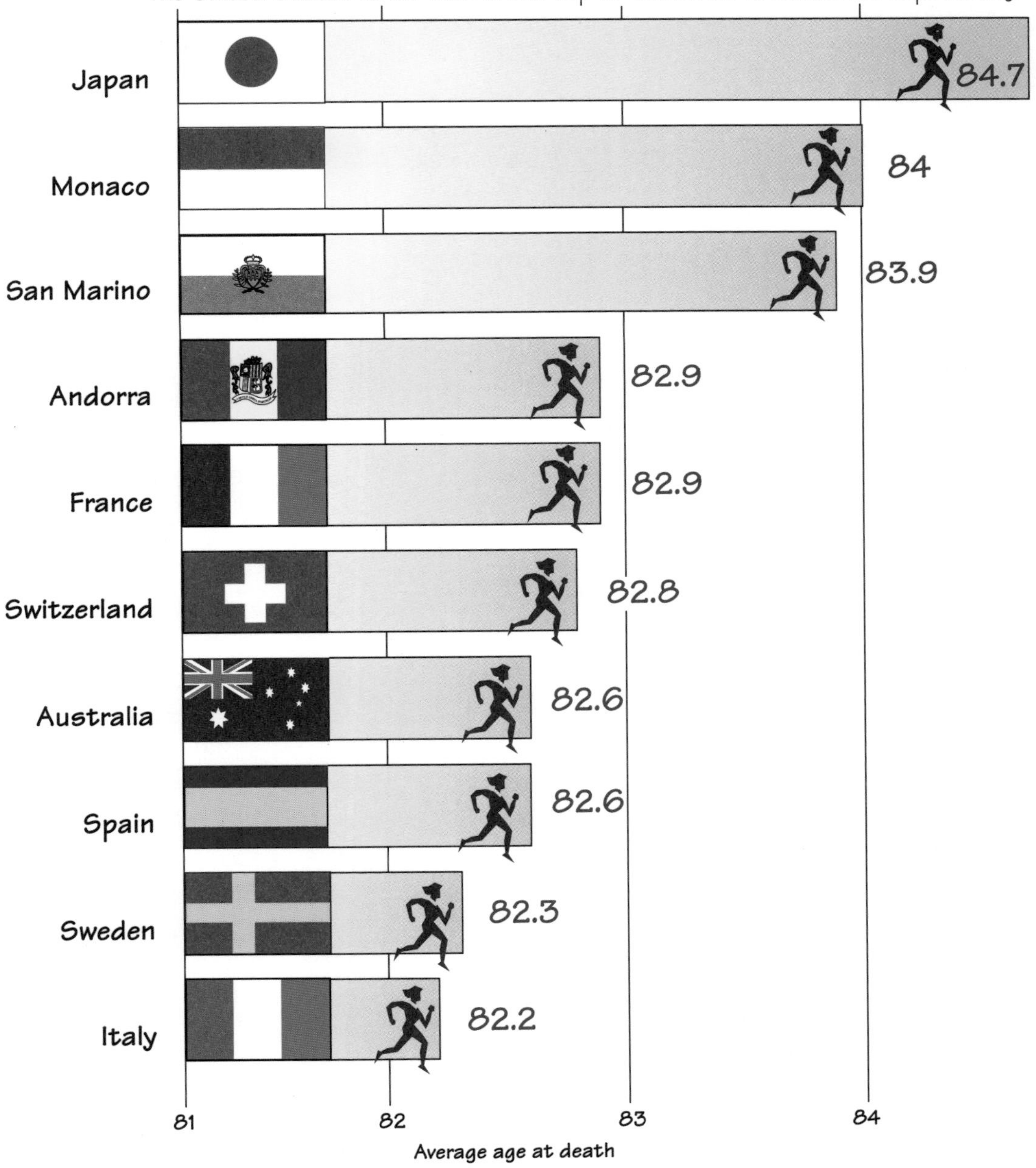

SOURCE: World Health Organization, World Health Report 2002

Who Are We?

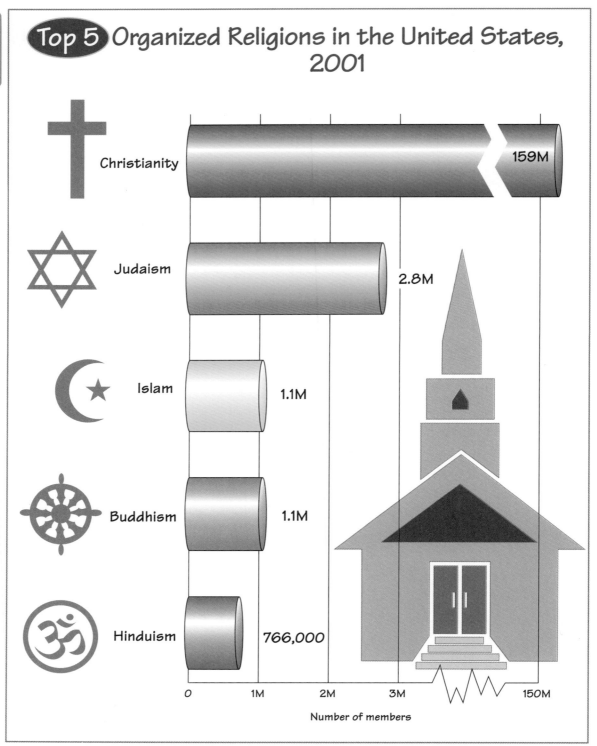

Top 5 Organized Religions in the United States, 2001

Christianity — 159M

Judaism — 2.8M

Islam — 1.1M

Buddhism — 1.1M

Hinduism — 766,000

0   1M   2M   3M   150M

Number of members

SOURCE: adherents.com

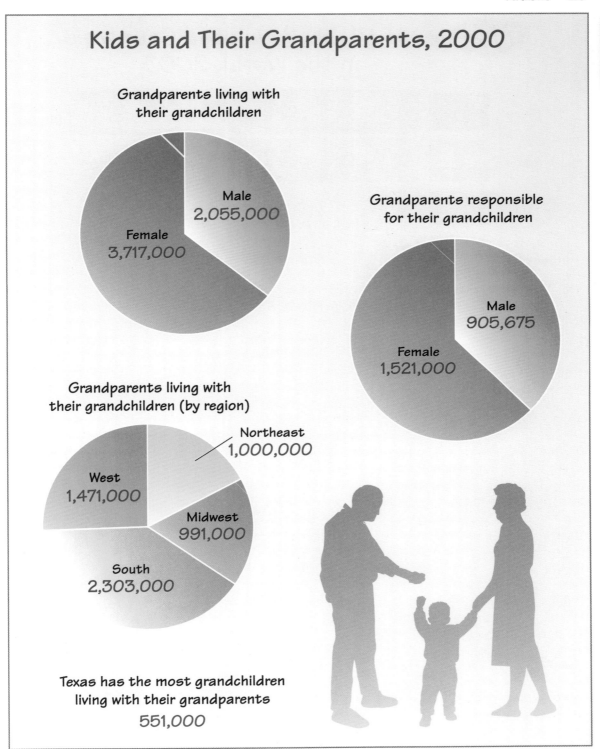

Kids and Their Grandparents, 2000

Grandparents living with their grandchildren

Male 2,055,000

Female 3,717,000

Grandparents responsible for their grandchildren

Male 905,675

Female 1,521,000

Grandparents living with their grandchildren (by region)

Northeast 1,000,000

West 1,471,000

Midwest 991,000

South 2,303,000

Texas has the most grandchildren living with their grandparents
551,000

SOURCE: U.S. Census Bureau

Who Are We?

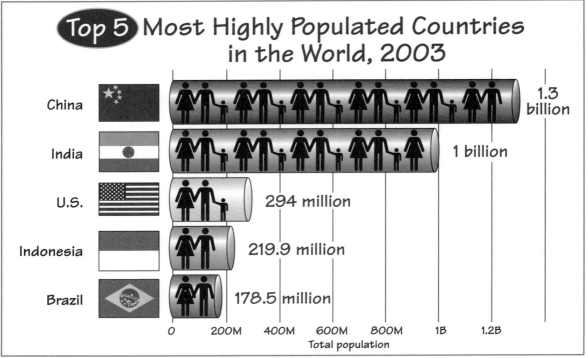

Top 5 Most Highly Populated Countries in the World, 2003

China — 1.3 billion

India — 1 billion

U.S. — 294 million

Indonesia — 219.9 million

Brazil — 178.5 million

0   200M   400M   600M   800M   1B   1.2B

Total population

SOURCE: United Nations World Polulation Prospects

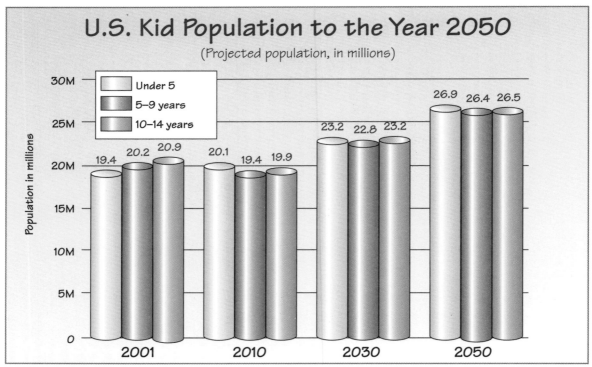

U.S. Kid Population to the Year 2050

(Projected population, in millions)

Under 5
5–9 years
10–14 years

Population in millions

30M
25M
20M
15M
10M
5M
0

2001: 19.4 20.2 20.9
2010: 20.1 19.4 19.9
2030: 23.2 22.8 23.2
2050: 26.9 26.4 26.5

SOURCE: U.S. Census Bureau

Top 10 Largest Cities in the World*, 2001
(In millions)

City	Population
Seoul, South Korea	10.2 million
São Paulo, Brazil	10 million
Bombay, India	9.9 million
Jakarta, Indonesia	9.4 million
Karachi, Pakistan	9.3 million
Moscow, Russia	8.3 million
Istanbul, Turkey	8.3 million
Mexico City	8.2 million
Shanghai, China	8.2 million
Tokyo, Japan	8.1 million

Total population

* cities with legally defined boundaries—does not include suburbs or area outside city boundaries

SOURCE: City Mayors World Cities Report

Who Are We?

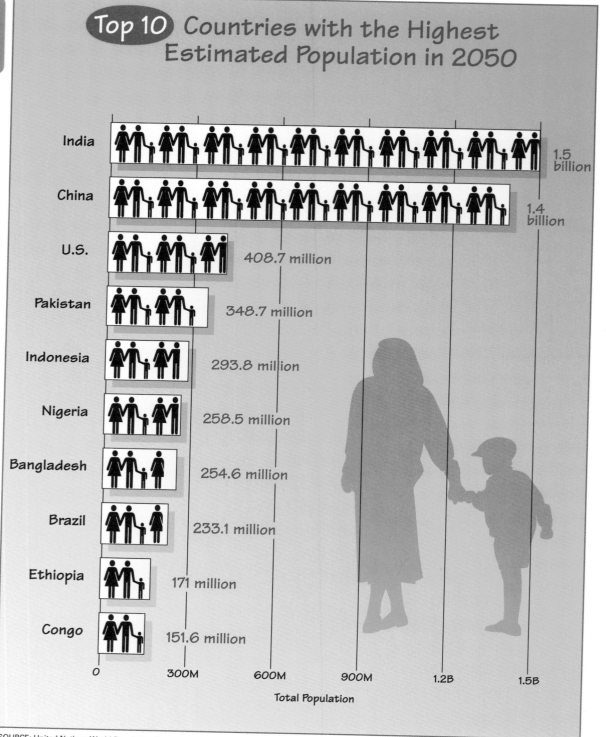

Top 10 Countries with the Highest Estimated Population in 2050

India — 1.5 billion
China — 1.4 billion
U.S. — 408.7 million
Pakistan — 348.7 million
Indonesia — 293.8 million
Nigeria — 258.5 million
Bangladesh — 254.6 million
Brazil — 233.1 million
Ethiopia — 171 million
Congo — 151.6 million

0   300M   600M   900M   1.2B   1.5B

Total Population

SOURCE: United Nations World Population Prospects

More American Kids Are Overweight, 2000

Almost 9 million kids ages 6–19 are overweight (15%).
This is triple what the proportion was in 1980.

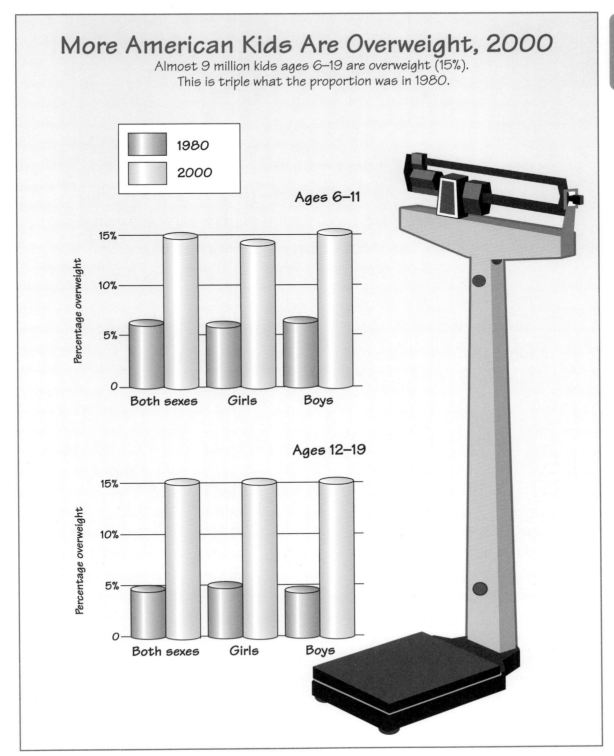

1980
2000

Ages 6–11

Percentage overweight

15%

10%

5%

0

Both sexes   Girls   Boys

Ages 12–19

Percentage overweight

15%

10%

5%

0

Both sexes   Girls   Boys

SOURCE: National Center for Health Statistics.

Money

Everyone can use money, which is one good reason why people work. Adults aren't the only workers. Many kids work, too. They earn money mowing lawns, babysitting, delivering newspapers, walking dogs, washing cars, and creating computer Web sites. The older they are, the more likely they are to have a job. More than one-quarter of people ages 15 to 18 have part- or full-time jobs. Millions more pick up money doing odd jobs for family, neighbors, and other people.

When the United States first set a minimum wage, in 1938, it was 25 cents an hour. By 2004, it was $5.15 an hour! But while wages have increased, so has the cost of living. A comic book, a pair of jeans, a bicycle—they all cost a lot more today than they did when your parents and grandparents were your age.

Of course, jobs aren't the only source of money. Most kids also get money from their parents. Many receive allowances and gifts of money, especially on birthdays and at other special times of the year. Combine all those sources of income and kids have a lot of

Kidbits Tidbits

● In 2003, some 7.6 million teenagers ages 16 to 19 worked. About 20% of those workers worked in the evenings or at night.

● In 1998, an *Amazing Fantasy* comic book that included the first appearance of Spider Man, sold for $2,000.

● American consumers owe more than $1.7 trillion. In 2002, most of this—some $713 billion—was on credit card accounts. One trillion was for loans, automobiles, education, vacations, boats, etc.

spending power! American teenagers alone have more than $100 billion to spend each year!

The number 1 item on kids' shopping lists is candy. Kids spend their own money on candy more often than on anything else. Other foods are also popular. Surveys show that teenagers visit supermarkets more often than any other kind of store. Convenience stores, which stock tempting arrays of sodas and junk food, aren't far behind.

Kids also spend lots of money on clothes, sporting goods, music, movies, toys, and books. They like to spend money on collecting stuff, too. Some 37-cent stamps, packs of stickers, or new comic books don't cost very much. But save them for a decade or two and they may be great investments as well as sources of pleasure. Over the years, they

can become very valuable. For instance, a Mickey Mantle rookie-year baseball card has sold for as much as $50,000!

The main way that kids invest money for the future is to save some of their income. On average, American kids save about 21 cents of every dollar they get. They save it for big purchases, such as a car or a computer. They also save money for college. And they see saving money as a first step toward becoming wealthy. Eighty percent of American kids dream about becoming rich one day!

If you're dreaming about getting rich, you should probably dream about the computer business and related businesses. In 2004, four of America's Top 10 richest people made their billions in the computer industry. Together, the four tycoons are worth more than 120 billion!

Kidbits Tidbits

● There are about 16,000 savings-banks in the United States.

● The occupations with the most job growth between 2002 and 2012 are teaching, health care, and software engineering.

● The unemployment rate in June 2004 was 6.3%, the highest rate since April 1994. By February 2003, it was back down to 5.6%.

Teens and Spending Money

How much money teens have to spend in a typical week

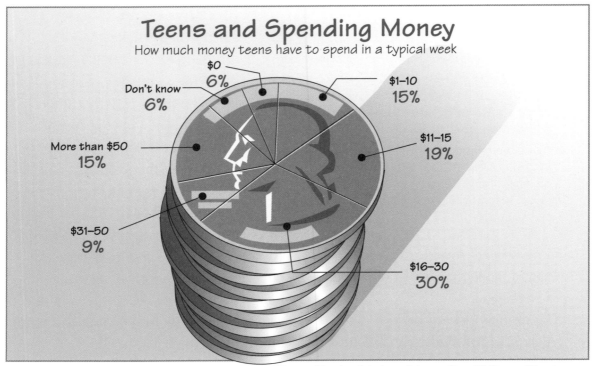

$0
6%

Don't know
6%

$1–10
15%

More than $50
15%

$11–15
19%

$31–50
9%

$16–30
30%

SOURCE: National Center on Addiction and Substance Abuse, *National Survey of American Attitudes on Substance Abuse VIII: Teens and Parents*

Top 5 Worst Jobs for Teens

Every 30 seconds, an American teen worker is injured on the job.

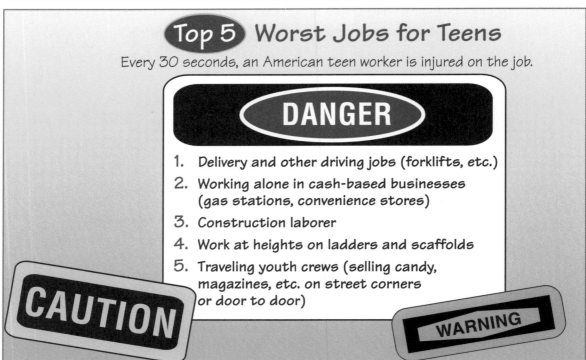

DANGER

1. Delivery and other driving jobs (forklifts, etc.)
2. Working alone in cash-based businesses (gas stations, convenience stores)
3. Construction laborer
4. Work at heights on ladders and scaffolds
5. Traveling youth crews (selling candy, magazines, etc. on street corners or door to door)

CAUTION

WARNING

SOURCE: National Consumers League

Money

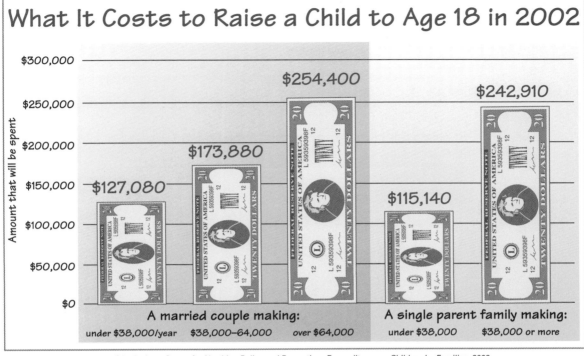

What It Costs to Raise a Child to Age 18 in 2002

$254,400

$242,910

$173,880

$127,080

$115,140

Amount that will be spent

$300,000
$250,000
$200,000
$150,000
$100,000
$50,000
$0

A married couple making:

under $38,000/year $38,000–64,000   over $64,000

A single parent family making:

under $38,000 $38,000 or more

SOURCE: U.S. Department of Agriculture Center for Nutrition Policy and Promotion, *Expenditures on Children by Families, 2002*

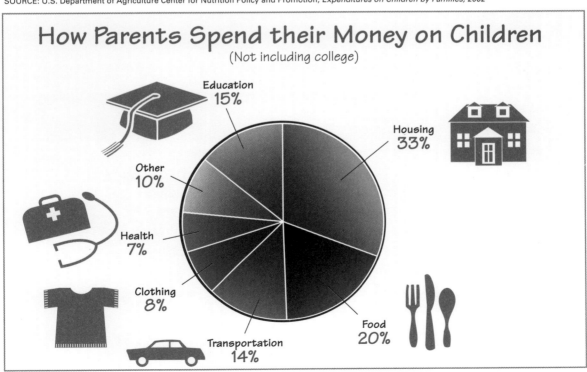

How Parents Spend their Money on Children
(Not including college)

Education
15%

Housing
33%

Other
10%

Health
7%

Clothing
8%

Transportation
14%

Food
20%

SOURCE: U.S. Department of Agriculture Center for Nutrition Policy and Promotion, *Expenditures on Children by Families, 2002*

Money

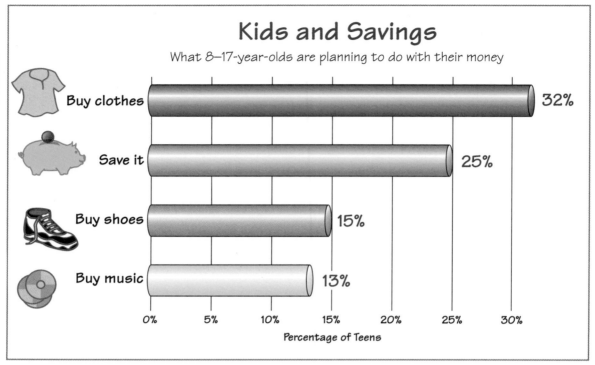

Kids and Savings
What 8–17-year-olds are planning to do with their money

Buy clothes	32%
Save it	25%
Buy shoes	15%
Buy music	13%

0% 5% 10% 15% 20% 25% 30%

Percentage of Teens

SOURCE: Roper ASW 2003 Youth Report

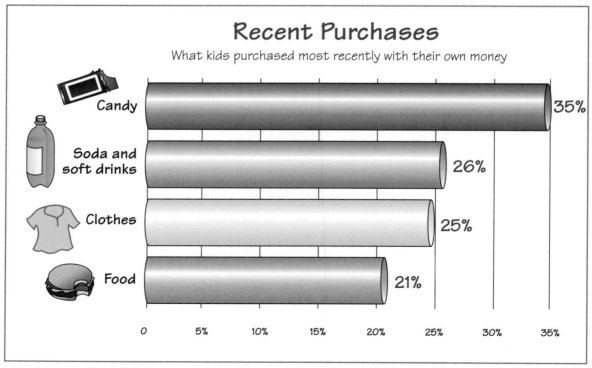

Recent Purchases
What kids purchased most recently with their own money

Candy	35%
Soda and soft drinks	26%
Clothes	25%
Food	21%

0 5% 10% 15% 20% 25% 30% 35%

SOURCE: Roper ASW 2003 Youth Report

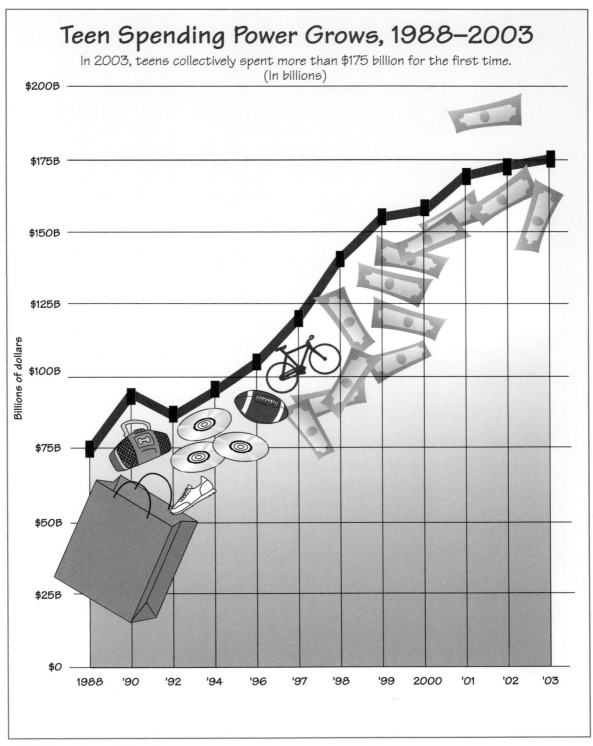

Teen Spending Power Grows, 1988–2003

In 2003, teens collectively spent more than $175 billion for the first time.
(In billions)

Billions of dollars

$200B
$175B
$150B
$125B
$100B
$75B
$50B
$25B
$0

1988 '90 '92 '94 '96 '97 '98 '99 2000 '01 '02 '03

SOURCE: Teenage Research Unlimited, Inc.

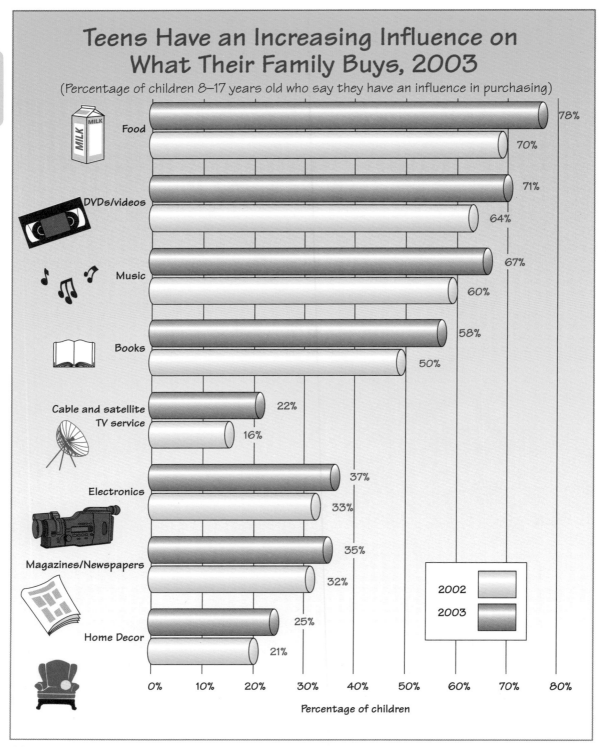

Teens Have an Increasing Influence on What Their Family Buys, 2003

(Percentage of children 8–17 years old who say they have an influence in purchasing)

Food — 78% / 70%

DVDs/videos — 71% / 64%

Music — 67% / 60%

Books — 58% / 50%

Cable and satellite TV service — 22% / 16%

Electronics — 37% / 33%

Magazines/Newspapers — 35% / 32%

Home Decor — 25% / 21%

2002
2003

Percentage of children

SOURCE: Roper ASW 2003 Youth Report

Money

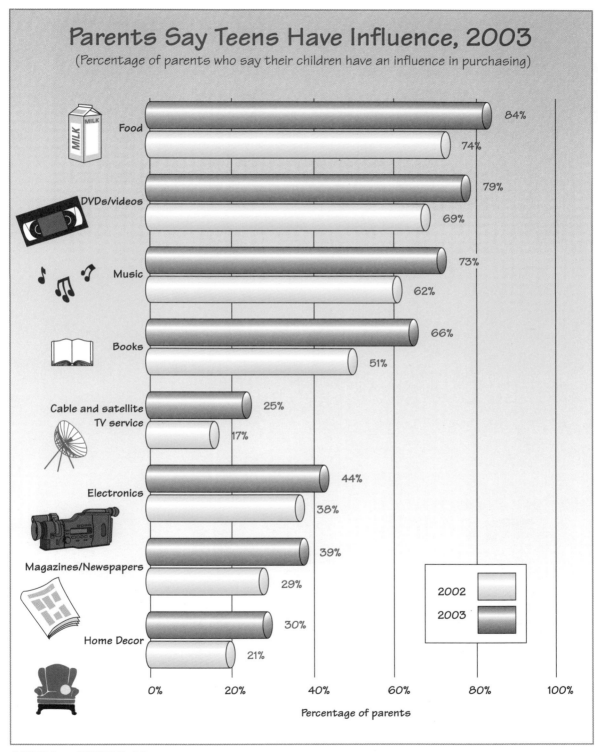

Parents Say Teens Have Influence, 2003

(Percentage of parents who say their children have an influence in purchasing)

Food — 84%, 74%

DVDs/videos — 79%, 69%

Music — 73%, 62%

Books — 66%, 51%

Cable and satellite TV service — 25%, 17%

Electronics — 44%, 38%

Magazines/Newspapers — 39%, 29%

Home Decor — 30%, 21%

0% 20% 40% 60% 80% 100%

Percentage of parents

2002
2003

SOURCE: Roper ASW 2003 Youth Report

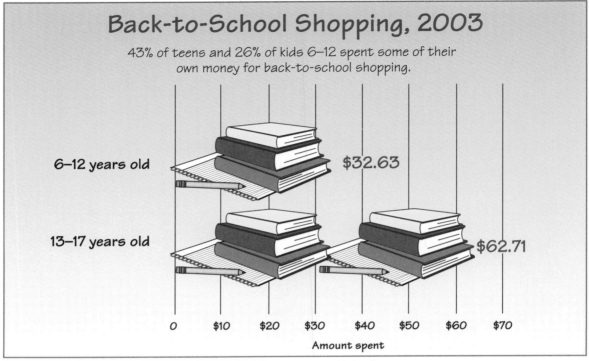

Back-to-School Shopping, 2003

43% of teens and 26% of kids 6–12 spent some of their own money for back-to-school shopping.

6–12 years old $32.63

13–17 years old $62.71

0    $10 $20 $30 $40 $50 $60 $70

Amount spent

SOURCE: National Retail Federation, *NRF 2003 Back-to-School Consumer Intentions and Actions Survey*

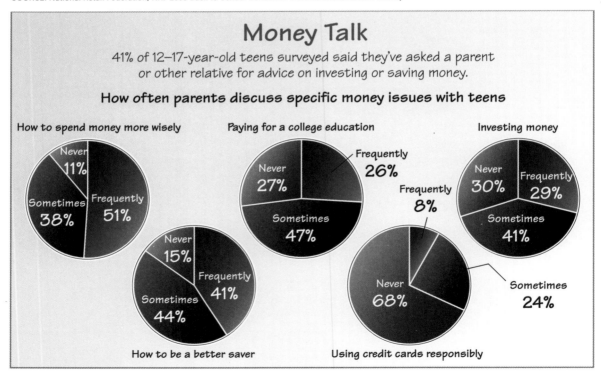

Money Talk

41% of 12–17-year-old teens surveyed said they've asked a parent or other relative for advice on investing or saving money.

How often parents discuss specific money issues with teens

How to spend money more wisely
- Never 11%
- Sometimes 38%
- Frequently 51%

Paying for a college education
- Frequently 26%
- Never 27%
- Sometimes 47%

Investing money
- Never 30%
- Frequently 29%
- Sometimes 41%

How to be a better saver
- Never 15%
- Frequently 41%
- Sometimes 44%

Using credit cards responsibly
- Frequently 8%
- Never 68%
- Sometimes 24%

SOURCE: Merrill Lynch annual survey of teens

Kid Costs, 2001

Estimated yearly spending per child for middle-income families ($39,100–$65,800)

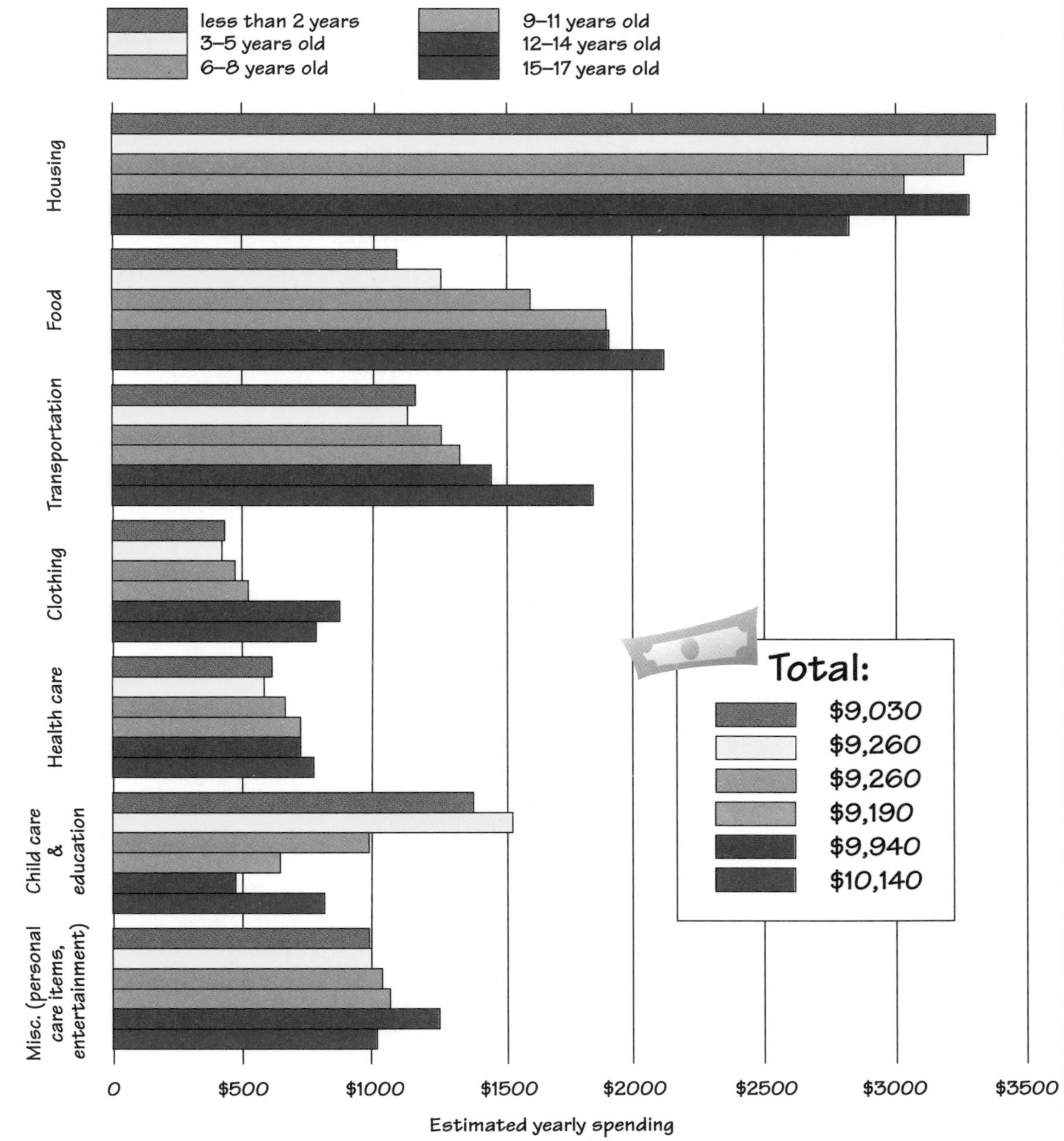

less than 2 years
3–5 years old
6–8 years old
9–11 years old
12–14 years old
15–17 years old
Housing
Food
Transportation
Clothing
Health care
Child care & education
Misc. (personal care items, entertainment)
0
$500
$1000
$1500
$2000
$2500
$3000
$3500
Estimated yearly spending
Total:
$9,030
$9,260
$9,260
$9,190
$9,940
$10,140

SOURCE: U.S. Department of Agriculture Center for Nutrition Policy and Promotion, *Expenditures on Children by Families, 2001*

Money

America's (Top 10) Richest People, 2004

Name	Source	Worth in billions of $
William Gates III	Computers	$46.6
Warren Buffett	Investment	$42.9
Paul Allen	Computers	$21.0
Alice Walton	Inheritance	$20
Helen Walton	Inheritance	$20
Jim Walton	Inheritance	$20
John Walton	Inheritance	$20
S. Robson Walton	Inheritance	$20
Lawrence Ellison	Computers	$18.7
Michael Dell	Computers	$13

SOURCE: *Forbes*

Money

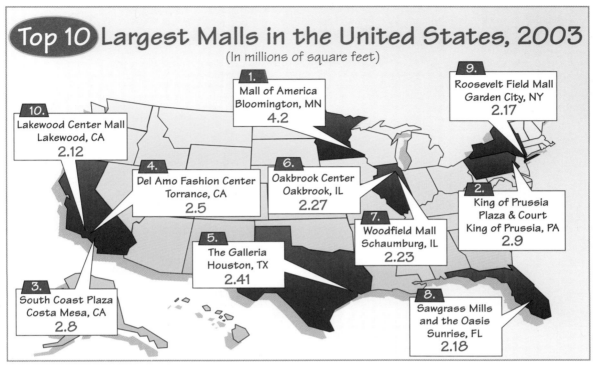

Top 10 Largest Malls in the United States, 2003

(In millions of square feet)

1. Mall of America
Bloomington, MN
4.2

9. Roosevelt Field Mall
Garden City, NY
2.17

10. Lakewood Center Mall
Lakewood, CA
2.12

4. Del Amo Fashion Center
Torrance, CA
2.5

6. Oakbrook Center
Oakbrook, IL
2.27

2. King of Prussia
Plaza & Court
King of Prussia, PA
2.9

7. Woodfield Mall
Schaumburg, IL
2.23

5. The Galleria
Houston, TX
2.41

3. South Coast Plaza
Costa Mesa, CA
2.8

8. Sawgrass Mills
and the Oasis
Sunrise, FL
2.18

SOURCE: International Council of Shopping Centers

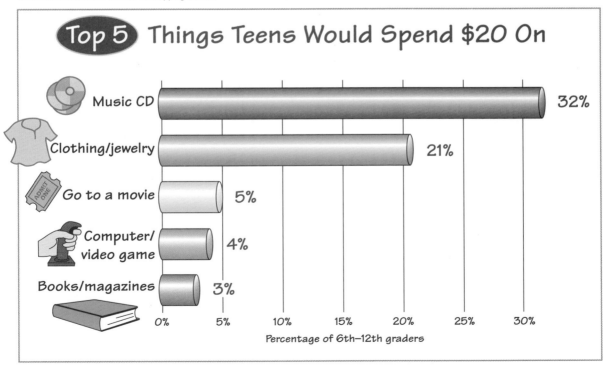

Top 5 Things Teens Would Spend $20 On

Item	Percentage
Music CD	32%
Clothing/jewelry	21%
Go to a movie	5%
Computer/video game	4%
Books/magazines	3%

Percentage of 6th–12th graders

SOURCE: *USA Weekend* "Tunes & 'Tudes Survey"

Money

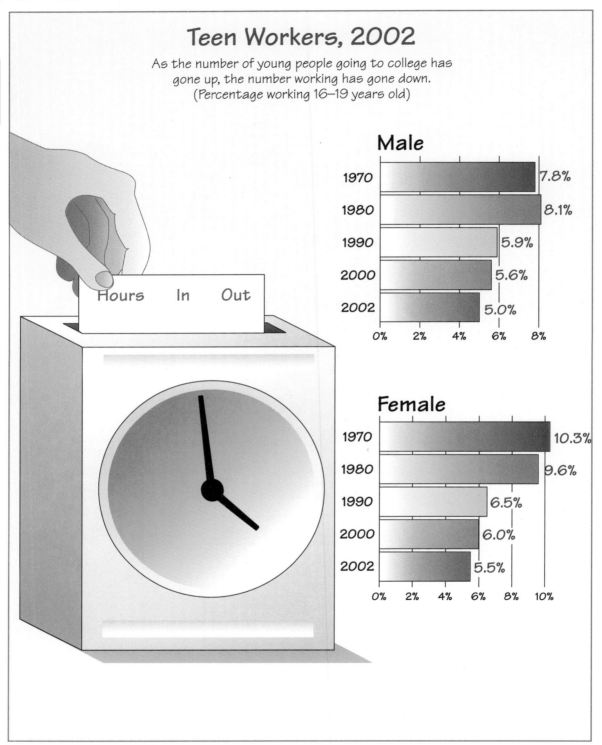

Teen Workers, 2002

As the number of young people going to college has
gone up, the number working has gone down.
(Percentage working 16–19 years old)

Male

Year	Percentage
1970	7.8%
1980	8.1%
1990	5.9%
2000	5.6%
2002	5.0%

Female

Year	Percentage
1970	10.3%
1980	9.6%
1990	6.5%
2000	6.0%
2002	5.5%

Hours   In   Out

SOURCE: U.S. Bureau of Labor Statistics, *Employment and Earnings*

Money

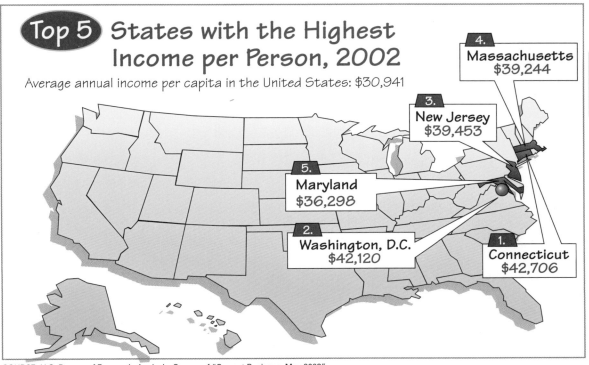

Top 5 **States with the Highest Income per Person, 2002**

Average annual income per capita in the United States: $30,941

4.
Massachusetts
$39,244

3.
New Jersey
$39,453

5.
Maryland
$36,298

2.
Washington, D.C.
$42,120

1.
Connecticut
$42,706

SOURCE: U.S. Bureau of Economic Analysis, Survey of "Current Business, May 2003"

Top 5 **States with the Lowest Income per Person, 2002**

Average annual income per capita in the United States: $30,941

3.
West Virginia
$23,688

5.
Utah
$24,306

4.
New Mexico
$23,941

2.
Arkansas
$23,512

1.
Mississippi
$22,372

SOURCE: U.S. Bureau of Economic Analysis, Survey of "Current Business, May 2003"

Sports for Fun

Kids are sports crazy! They kick soccer balls, take jump shots, swing bats, tumble, run, swim, and skate. While some prefer team sports such as soccer and basketball, others are into one-on-one sports such as tennis and golf. Activities that can be pursued by oneself, such as running and bicycling, also are popular. And so are new twists on old sports, such as snowboarding and ultimate frisbee.

As years pass, some sports become more popular among kids while others attract fewer participants. Soccer in America is one sport that has grown in popularity. (It's about time—soccer is by far the most popular sport throughout the rest of the world!) Track and field has declined, in part because many kids prefer to play soccer.

Some kids commit a lot of time to their sports, training to become eligible for national teams and even for professional competitions. Michelle Kwan was only 15 in 1996 when she won both the U.S. and world women's figure-skating championships.

Kidbits Tidbits

- Basketball is the top high school sport for women in the United States In the 2002–2003 school year, a total of 457,165 girls played. Football tops boys sports with just more than 1 million players.
- Girls' participation in U.S. high school sports has risen dramatically from 294,015 in 1971 to 2.86 million in 2003.
- Americans spent $22.2 billion on sports equipment in 2003, a 1% increase from 2002.

Since then she has won seven more gold medals in the U.S. figure skating championships and five in the world championships. Tiger Woods won his first world golfing title at age 8—and, in 1997, at age 21, he became the youngest person ever to win the Masters. These and other young athletes have become top role models for America's aspiring athletes. They have also greatly increased interest and participation in their sports.

Whether on or off the playing fields, kids like to wear sports attire. For example, people under age 18 account for 40% of all athletic shoe purchases. They also bought 66% of all team sports equipment in 2001.

Kids play sports because it's fun. But they also want to be physically fit. Sports help kids build muscle strength, improve posture and balance, and develop agility and endurance.

When playing sports, it's important to try to avoid injuries and accidents. Each year, more than 300,000 kids are injured riding their bikes; about 78,000 are injured playing soccer; and about 200,000 are injured playing basketball. (In fact, basketball is one of the top causes of injury in America.) So wear a helmet on your bike, strap on a life jacket when in a boat, and be sure to use the right equipment when playing sports!

Kidbits Tidbits

- Americans of all ages list walking as their number 1 sports activity. Camping is number 2 and swimming is number 3.
- Americans spent almost $80 billion on sporting goods in 2003. This included approximately $10 billion on clothing, $14.4 billion on footwear, $22.2 billion on equipment, and $33 billion on transport (boats, bicycles, snowmobiles, etc.).
- It's definitely "cool" to play on the ice and snow. In 2002, a total of 7.4 million Americans reported that they downhill ski. About 5.3 million said they ice or figure skate, and 2.2 million reported cross-country skiing. A total of 2.1 million people play ice hockey, and 5.6 million snowboarded two or more times during the year.

Sports for Fun

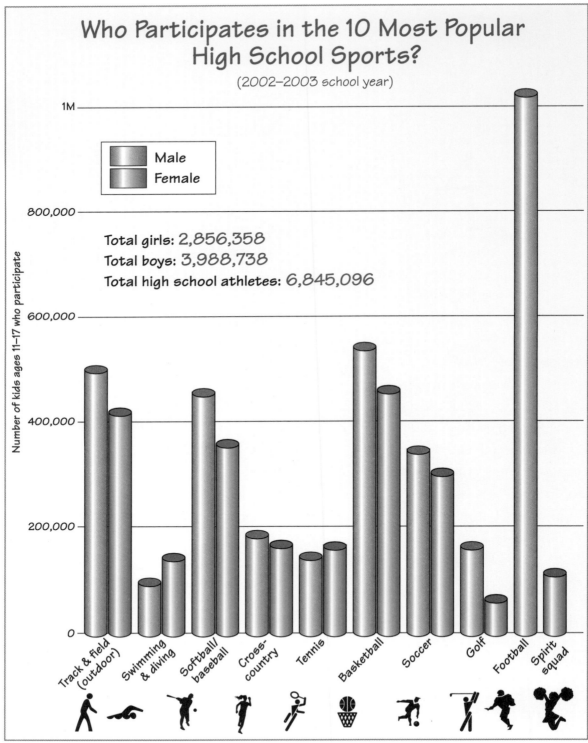

Who Participates in the 10 Most Popular High School Sports?

(2002–2003 school year)

Male
Female

Total girls: 2,856,358
Total boys: 3,988,738
Total high school athletes: 6,845,096

Number of kids ages 11–17 who participate

1M

800,000

600,000

400,000

200,000

0

Track & field (outdoor)
Swimming & diving
Softball/baseball
Cross-country
Tennis
Basketball
Soccer
Golf
Football
Spirit squad

SOURCE: National Federation of State High School Associations

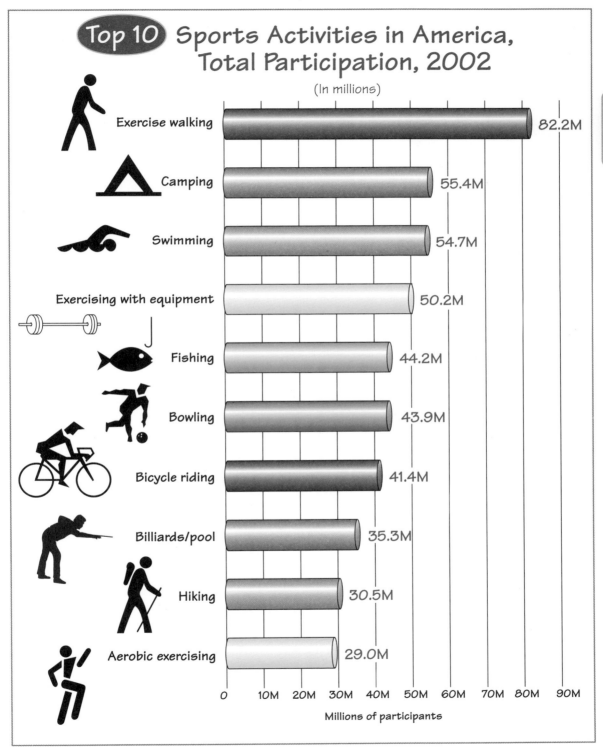

Top 10 Sports Activities in America, Total Participation, 2002

(In millions)

Activity	Participants
Exercise walking	82.2M
Camping	55.4M
Swimming	54.7M
Exercising with equipment	50.2M
Fishing	44.2M
Bowling	43.9M
Bicycle riding	41.4M
Billiards/pool	35.3M
Hiking	30.5M
Aerobic exercising	29.0M

Millions of participants

0 10M 20M 30M 40M 50M 60M 70M 80M 90M

Sports for Fun

SOURCE: National Sporting Goods Association

Sports for Fun

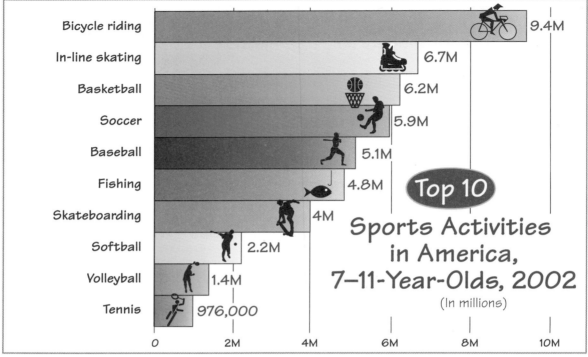

Top 10

Sports Activities in America, 7–11-Year-Olds, 2002

(In millions)

Bicycle riding	9.4M
In-line skating	6.7M
Basketball	6.2M
Soccer	5.9M
Baseball	5.1M
Fishing	4.8M
Skateboarding	4M
Softball	2.2M
Volleyball	1.4M
Tennis	976,000

SOURCE: National Sporting Goods Association

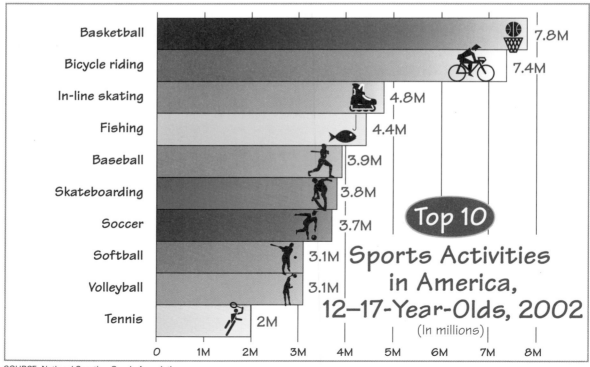

Top 10

Sports Activities in America, 12–17-Year-Olds, 2002

(In millions)

Basketball	7.8M
Bicycle riding	7.4M
In-line skating	4.8M
Fishing	4.4M
Baseball	3.9M
Skateboarding	3.8M
Soccer	3.7M
Softball	3.1M
Volleyball	3.1M
Tennis	2M

SOURCE: National Sporting Goods Association

Sports for Fun

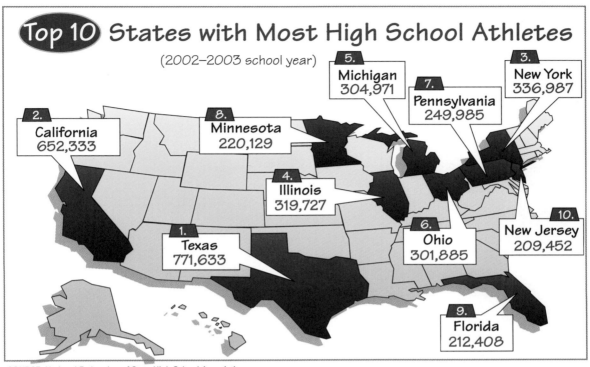

Top 10 States with Most High School Athletes

(2002–2003 school year)

5. Michigan 304,971

7. Pennsylvania 249,985

3. New York 336,987

2. California 652,333

8. Minnesota 220,129

4. Illinois 319,727

1. Texas 771,633

6. Ohio 301,885

10. New Jersey 209,452

9. Florida 212,408

SOURCE: National Federation of State High School Associations

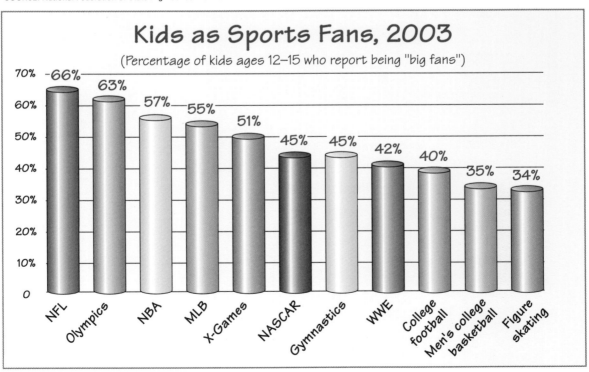

Kids as Sports Fans, 2003

(Percentage of kids ages 12–15 who report being "big fans")

- NFL 66%
- Olympics 63%
- NBA 57%
- MLB 55%
- X-Games 51%
- NASCAR 45%
- Gymnastics 45%
- WWE 42%
- College football 40%
- Men's college basketball 35%
- Figure skating 34%

SOURCE: Taylor Kids Pulse 2003

Sports for Fun

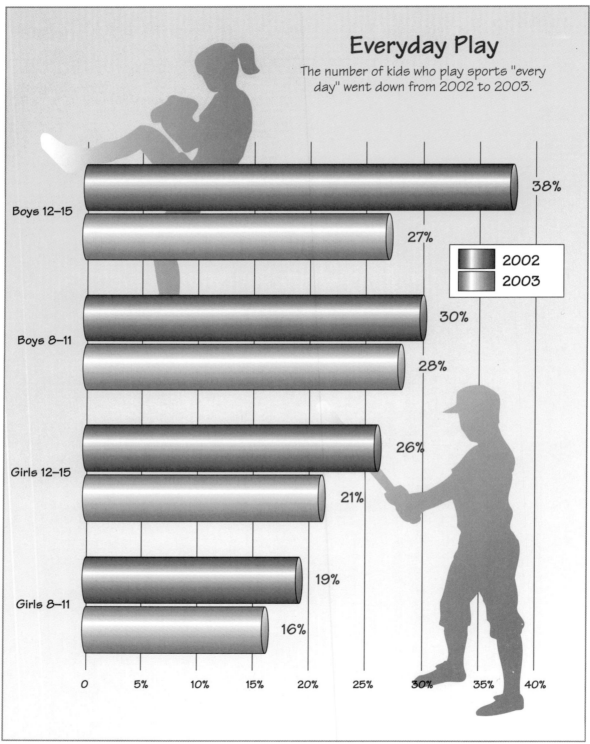

Everyday Play

The number of kids who play sports "every day" went down from 2002 to 2003.

Boys 12–15 — 38% (2002), 27% (2003)

Boys 8–11 — 30% (2002), 28% (2003)

Girls 12–15 — 26% (2002), 21% (2003)

Girls 8–11 — 19% (2002), 16% (2003)

Legend: 2002, 2003

0 5% 10% 15% 20% 25% 30% 35% 40%

Boys Want to Be Athletes

In your school, what would you rather be?

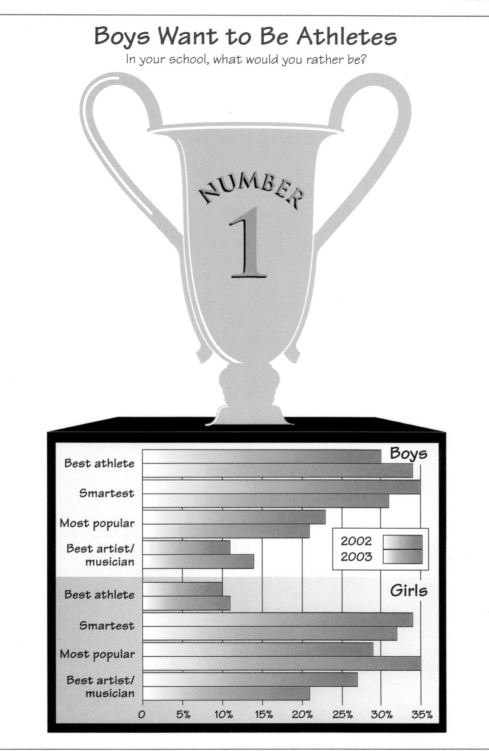

NUMBER 1

Boys

- Best athlete
- Smartest
- Most popular
- Best artist/ musician

2002
2003

Girls

- Best athlete
- Smartest
- Most popular
- Best artist/ musician

0   5%   10%   15%   20%   25%   30%   35%

SOURCE: Taylor Kids Pulse 2003

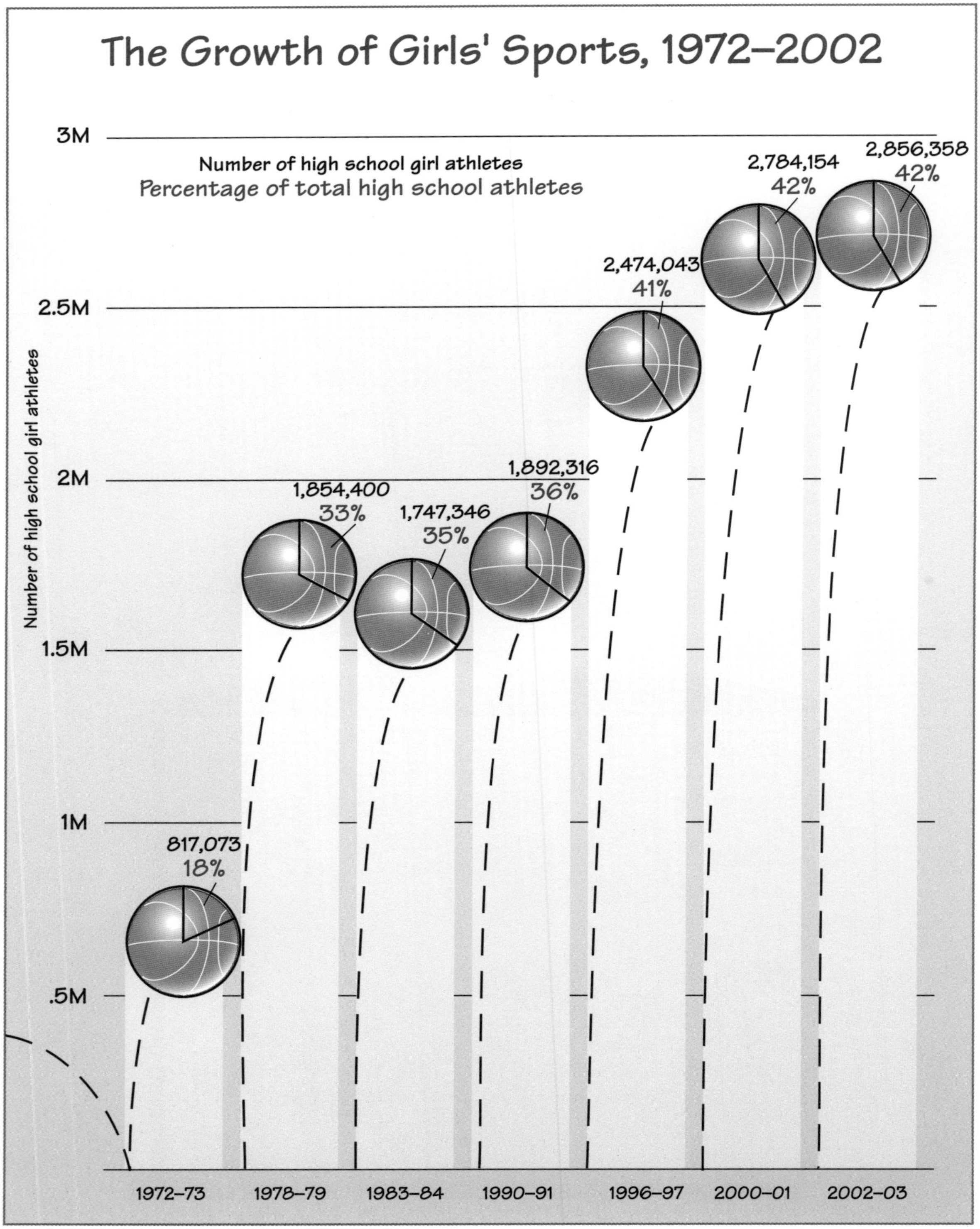

Sports for Fun

The Growth of Girls' Sports, 1972–2002

Number of high school girl athletes
Percentage of total high school athletes

Number of high school girl athletes

3M

2.5M

2M

1.5M

1M

.5M

817,073
18%

1,854,400
33%

1,747,346
35%

1,892,316
36%

2,474,043
41%

2,784,154
42%

2,856,358
42%

1972–73   1978–79   1983–84   1990–91   1996–97   2000–01   2002–03

SOURCE: National Federation of State High School Associations

Sports for Fun

Sneaker Specs
Who bought athletic shoes in 2002?

Gender

Men 46.9%
Women 53.1%

Age

65+ 6.1%
45–64 19.1%
35–44 13.6%
25–34 15%
18–24 6.3%
14–17 8.5%
Under 14 31.4%

SOURCE: National Sporting Goods Association

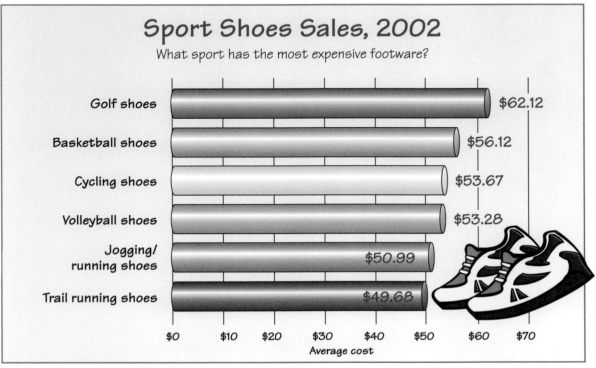

Sport Shoes Sales, 2002
What sport has the most expensive footware?

	Average cost
Golf shoes	$62.12
Basketball shoes	$56.12
Cycling shoes	$53.67
Volleyball shoes	$53.28
Jogging/ running shoes	$50.99
Trail running shoes	$49.68

$0 $10 $20 $30 $40 $50 $60 $70

SOURCE: National Sporting Goods Association

Sports for Fun

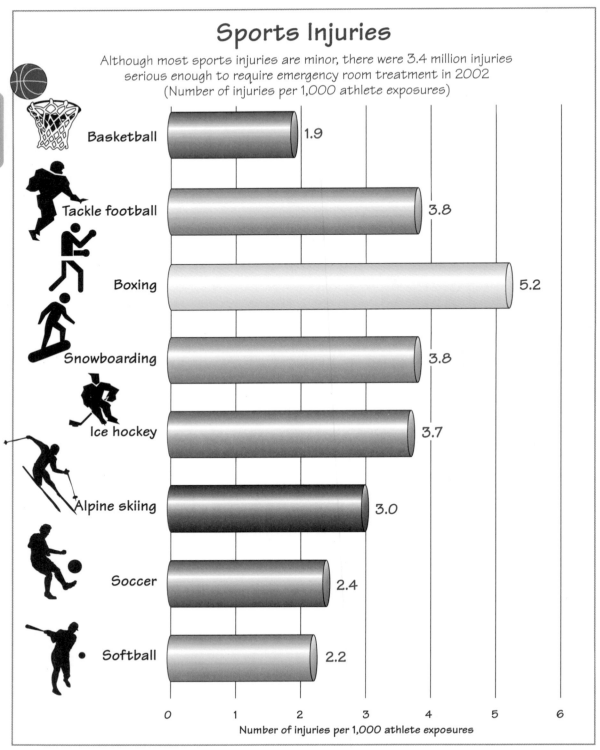

Sports Injuries

Although most sports injuries are minor, there were 3.4 million injuries
serious enough to require emergency room treatment in 2002
(Number of injuries per 1,000 athlete exposures)

Basketball — 1.9

Tackle football — 3.8

Boxing — 5.2

Snowboarding — 3.8

Ice hockey — 3.7

Alpine skiing — 3.0

Soccer — 2.4

Softball — 2.2

0 1 2 3 4 5 6

Number of injuries per 1,000 athlete exposures

SOURCE: American Sports Data

We Want to Play Too!

Number of girls in male-dominated high school sports, 2002–2003

	Number of girls	Total participants (boys and girls)
Baseball	1,622	455,414
Wrestling	3,769	243,614
Ice hockey	6,628	41,864
Football	1,477	1,024,619

SOURCE: National Federation of State High School Associations

Alternative Sports

Sometimes called extreme sports, these activities have exploded among young people in the last few years.

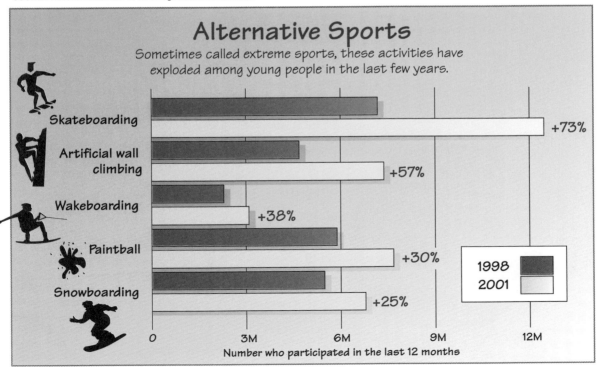

- Skateboarding +73%
- Artificial wall climbing +57%
- Wakeboarding +38%
- Paintball +30%
- Snowboarding +25%

1998
2001

0   3M   6M   9M   12M

Number who participated in the last 12 months

SOURCE: American Sports Data, Inc., *Superstudy of Sports*

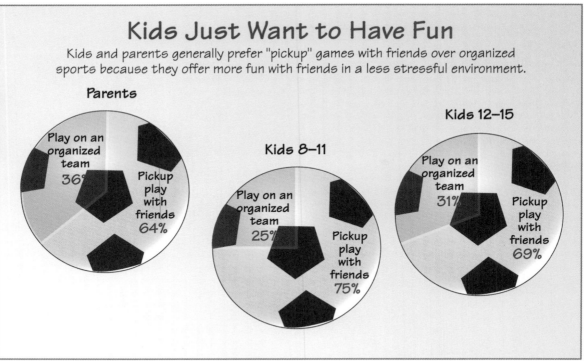

Kids Just Want to Have Fun

Kids and parents generally prefer "pickup" games with friends over organized sports because they offer more fun with friends in a less stressful environment.

Parents
- Play on an organized team 36%
- Pickup play with friends 64%

Kids 8–11
- Play on an organized team 25%
- Pickup play with friends 75%

Kids 12–15
- Play on an organized team 31%
- Pickup play with friends 69%

SOURCE: Taylor Kids Pulse 2003

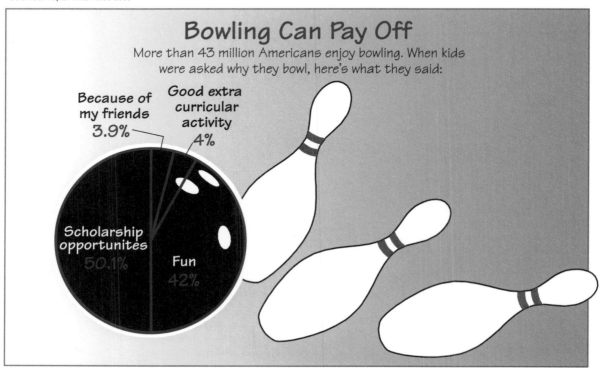

Bowling Can Pay Off

More than 43 million Americans enjoy bowling. When kids were asked why they bowl, here's what they said:

- Because of my friends 3.9%
- Good extra curricular activity 4%
- Scholarship opportunites 50.1%
- Fun 42%

SOURCE: Young American Bowling Alliance

Not Board in the Snow

A total of 5.6 million Americans went
snowboarding more than once in 2002.
Here's a profile of the snowboarding

Age:

- 35–44 **7.9%**
- 45–54 **5%**
- 25–34 **17.8%**
- 55–64 **.4%**
- 18-24 **20.6%**
- 7–11 **17.3%**
- 65+ **1.3%**
- 12–17 **29.7%**

Sex:

- Female **23%**
- Male **77%**

SOURCE: SnowSports Industries America

Spending Dough in the Snow

2001–2002 Season:

- Accessories $662.7M 32%
- Apparel $666.9M 31%
- Equipment $787.4M 37%

2002–2003 Season:

- Accessories $724.5M 33%
- Apparel $666.4M 30%
- Equipment $810.3M 37%

SOURCE: SnowSports Industries America, "SIA Retail Audit"

Clothes

Mission: wearing stuff that's fashionable, "cool," practical, exactly like everyone else's clothing—except for the fact that it is a part of your unique identity. When it comes to clothing, kids are the ultimate consumers. They know what they like, and they'll spend time and money to get it. They haunt the malls, sneaker superstores, vintage clothing shops, even tag sales and thrift shops. And if they can't find what they want, some kids will buy fabric and sew up their own clothes.

Casual wear, such as T-shirts, sweaters, jeans, and sports shoes form the basis of most kids' wardrobes. But not just any T-shirt or sweater will do. Brand names are very important among kids—even for the most ordinary attire. And a brand that's "in" one year may be "out" the next. Kids say that quality is the most important criterion when choosing brand-name clothing. But their parents may question the value of that brand-name label, particularly if it's the parents who are forking over $50 for jeans or $100 for sneakers that are likely to be outgrown in a few months.

Kidbits Tidbits

- In 2002, there were more than 46,000 shopping centers in the United States with a total of 5.8 billion square feet of retail area.
- More than 10.7 million people worked in shopping centers in 2002.
- The Mall of America in Bloomington, Minnesota, is the nation's largest mall, with some 500 stores.
- In 2003, malls devoted almost 9% of their retail space to teen concepts, almost double that of four years before.

It's not just what you wear, it's how you wear it. Kids notice who's wearing caps backwards, jeans artfully ripped, or tees too tight. They get inspiration for new trends from their peers, from models in teen magazines, and from their favorite TV, movie, music, and sports personalities.

Some adults feel that kids place too much importance on clothing. They suspect that kids are more interested in what's being worn at school than in what's being taught there. Parochial and private schools have long used school uniforms to provide a more serious approach to learning. They feel this also removes some of the distractions and other problems connected with clothing fashions and fads. Requiring uniforms in public schools is a matter of much debate, though the trend gained momentum during the 1990s and more school districts are requiring uniforms each year. There is some evidence that wearing uniforms has improved students' lives. For example, beginning in 1994, Long Beach, California, required uniforms for its 70,000 students in kindergarten through grade 8. In the first year of the program there was a 43% reduction in suspensions, 54% fewer fights, and more than 20% fewer cases of weapons possession and robbery. Is there a connection? You be the judge.

Kidbits Tidbits

- Forty-two percent of 16–19-year-olds prefer to shop at specialty stores compared to 12% of people 20–55 years old.
- Between 1999 and 2003, teens spent $70 billion on clothes.
- Nike's "Swoosh" logo represents the wing of the Greek goddess Nike.
- Each year, Nike recycles over 2 million athletic shoes into basketball courts and other sports courts.
- In 2002, Gap, the largest retail clothing store, sold more than $14 billion worth of clothes. Limited was next with $8.4 billion in sales.
- December is the busiest shopping month. Americans spent $27 billion in clothing stores during December 2003 and about $3.8 billion for clothing online.
- In a typical shopping month, more than 201 million people shop at shopping centers.

Clothes

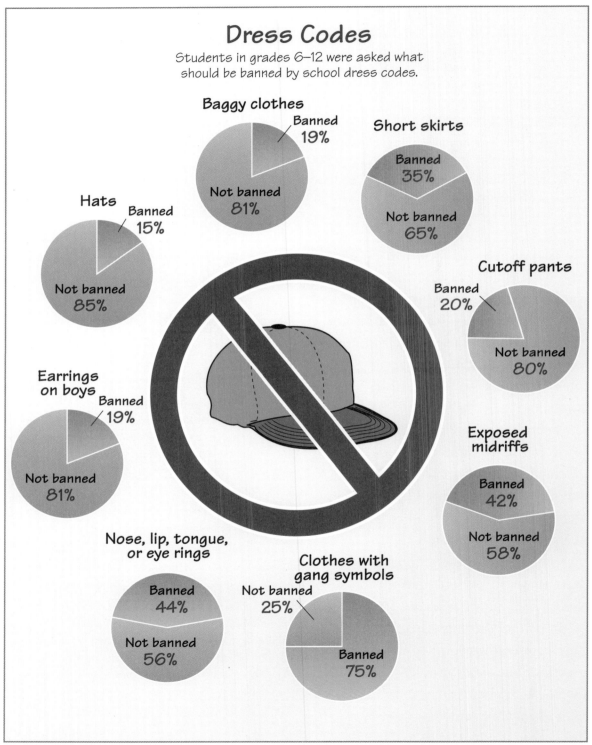

Dress Codes

Students in grades 6–12 were asked what should be banned by school dress codes.

Baggy clothes
Banned 19%
Not banned 81%

Short skirts
Banned 35%
Not banned 65%

Hats
Banned 15%
Not banned 85%

Cutoff pants
Banned 20%
Not banned 80%

Earrings on boys
Banned 19%
Not banned 81%

Exposed midriffs
Banned 42%
Not banned 58%

Nose, lip, tongue, or eye rings
Banned 44%
Not banned 56%

Clothes with gang symbols
Not banned 25%
Banned 75%

SOURCE: *USA Weekend,* "Teens & Freedom Survey"

Clothes

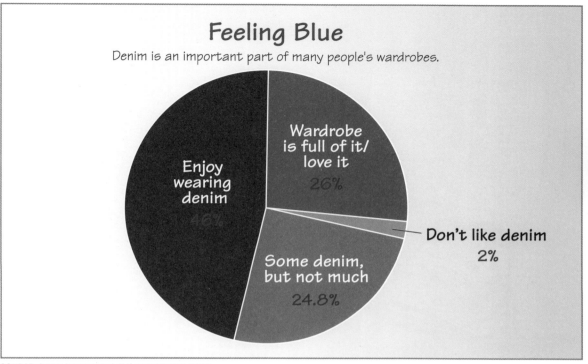

Feeling Blue

Denim is an important part of many people's wardrobes.

- Enjoy wearing denim 46%
- Wardrobe is full of it/ love it 26%
- Some denim, but not much 24.8%
- Don't like denim 2%

SOURCE: Cotton Incorporated, "Lifestyle Monitor 2003"

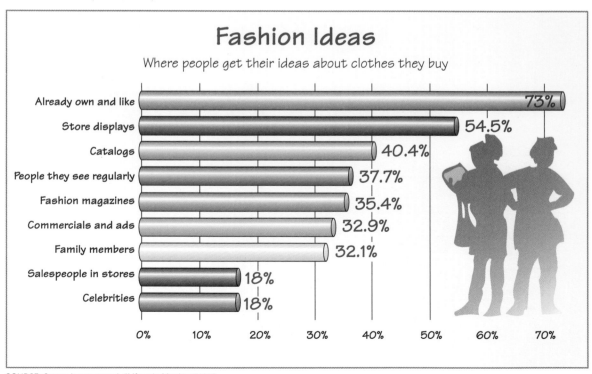

Fashion Ideas

Where people get their ideas about clothes they buy

- Already own and like — 73%
- Store displays — 54.5%
- Catalogs — 40.4%
- People they see regularly — 37.7%
- Fashion magazines — 35.4%
- Commercials and ads — 32.9%
- Family members — 32.1%
- Salespeople in stores — 18%
- Celebrities — 18%

0%   10%   20%   30%   40%   50%   60%   70%

SOURCE: Cotton Incorporated, "Lifestyle Monitor 2003"

Kids' Shoes

Made in the U.S.

Year	Value
2000	1.4M
2001	778,000
2002	491,000

0 .3M .6M .9M 1.2M 1.5M

Imported

Year	Value
2000	228M
2001	219M
2002	234M

0 50M 100M 150M 200M 250M

SOURCE: American Apparel & Footwear Association, "ShoeStats 2003"

Impulse Buying

What garment girls and women are most likely to buy on impulse

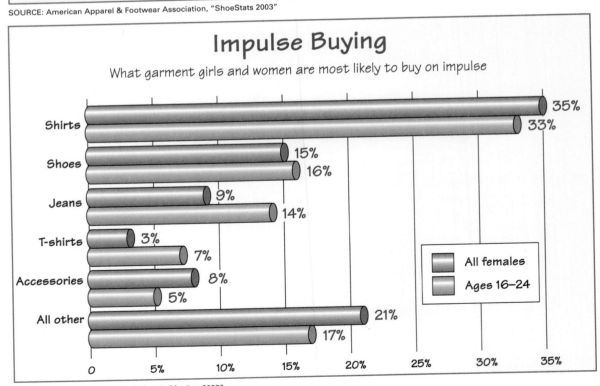

Garment	All females	Ages 16–24
Shirts	35%	33%
Shoes	15%	16%
Jeans	9%	14%
T-shirts	3%	7%
Accessories	8%	5%
All other	21%	17%

0   5%   10%   15%   20%   25%   30%   35%

All females
Ages 16–24

SOURCE: Cotton Incorporated, "Lifestyle Monitor 2003"

Celebrities Influence Fashion

(Percentage of women who get fashion ideas from celebrities)

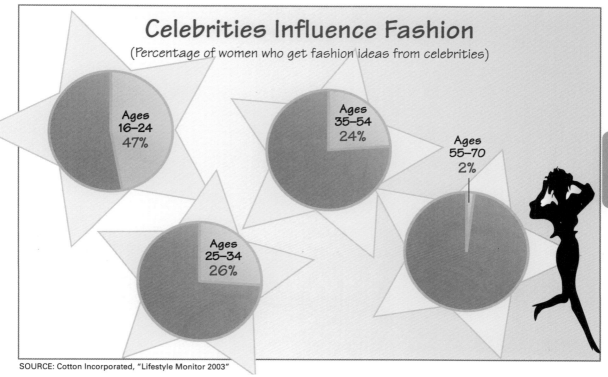

Ages
16–24
47%

Ages
35–54
24%

Ages
55–70
2%

Ages
25–34
26%

Clothes

SOURCE: Cotton Incorporated, "Lifestyle Monitor 2003"

At Your Service

At what point do you prefer a salesperson's help when buying clothing?
(Females 16–70)

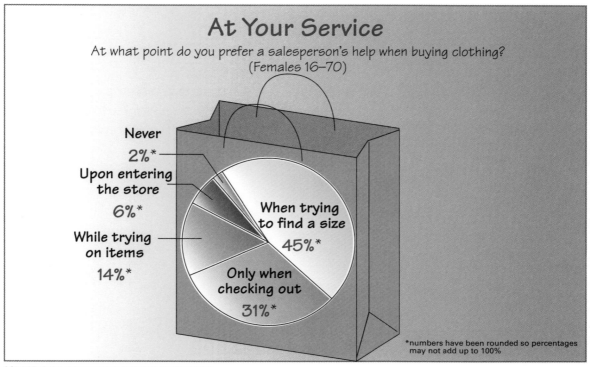

Never
2%*

Upon entering
the store
6%*

While trying
on items
14%*

When trying
to find a size
45%*

Only when
checking out
31%*

*numbers have been rounded so percentages
may not add up to 100%

SOURCE: Cotton Incorporated, "Lifestyle Monitor 2004"

Clothes

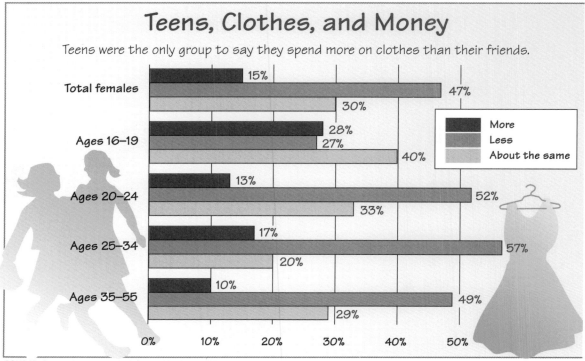

Teens, Clothes, and Money

Teens were the only group to say they spend more on clothes than their friends.

	More	Less	About the same
Total females	15%	47%	30%
Ages 16–19	28%	27%	40%
Ages 20–24	13%	52%	33%
Ages 25–34	17%	57%	20%
Ages 35–55	10%	49%	29%

SOURCE: Cortton Incorporated, "Lifestyle Monitor 2003"

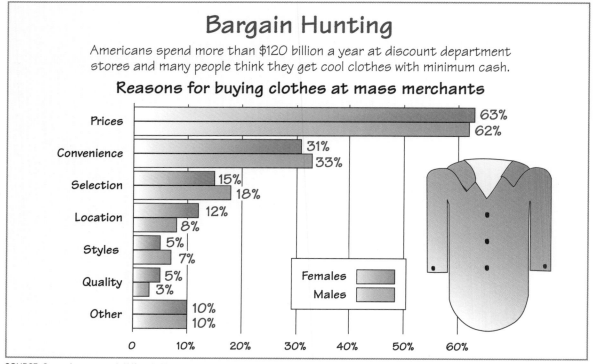

Bargain Hunting

Americans spend more than $120 billion a year at discount department stores and many people think they get cool clothes with minimum cash.

Reasons for buying clothes at mass merchants

	Females	Males
Prices	63%	62%
Convenience	31%	33%
Selection	15%	18%
Location	12%	8%
Styles	5%	7%
Quality	5%	3%
Other	10%	10%

SOURCE: Cotton Incorporated, "Lifestyle Monitor 2003"

Clothes

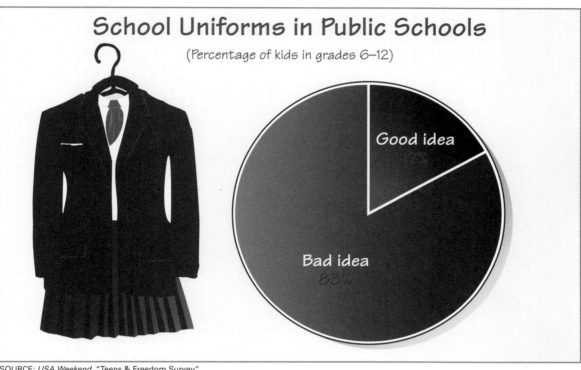

School Uniforms in Public Schools

(Percentage of kids in grades 6–12)

Good idea
17%

Bad idea
83%

SOURCE: *USA Weekend,* "Teens & Freedom Survey"

Top 5 Who Rules Cool, 2003

What teens think are the coolest brands of clothes

1. Nike
2. Abercrombie & Fitch
3. Adidas
4. American Eagle
5. Old Navy

SOURCE: Teenage Research Unlimited, *Getting Wiser to Teens*

Clothes

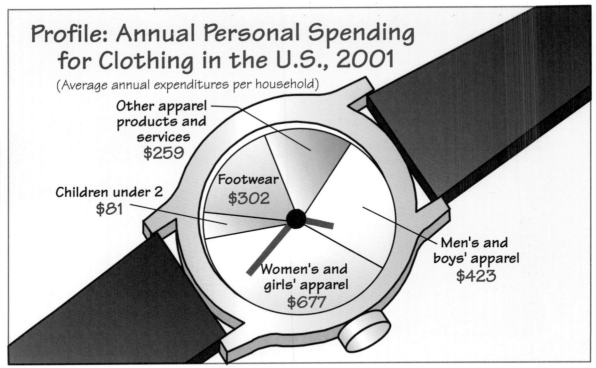

Profile: Annual Personal Spending for Clothing in the U.S., 2001
(Average annual expenditures per household)

Other apparel products and services $259

Footwear $302

Children under 2 $81

Women's and girls' apparel $677

Men's and boys' apparel $423

SOURCE: Bureau of Labor Statistics, Consumer Expenditures in 2001

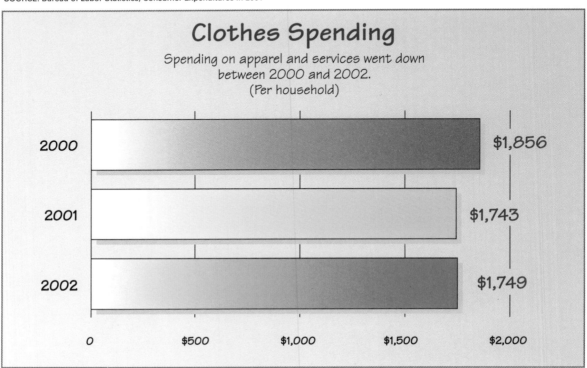

Clothes Spending
Spending on apparel and services went down between 2000 and 2002.
(Per household)

2000 $1,856
2001 $1,743
2002 $1,749

0   $500 $1,000 $1,500 $2,000

SOURCE: Bureau of Labor Statistics, Consumer Expenditures in 2001

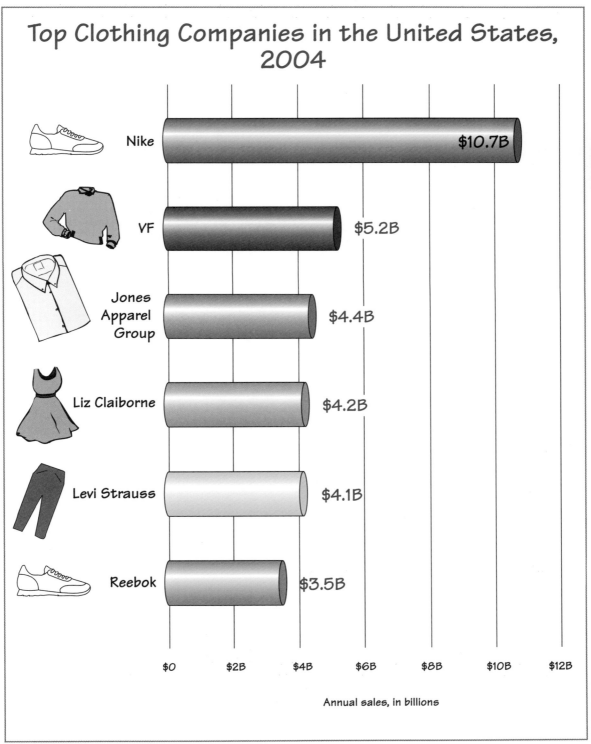

Top Clothing Companies in the United States, 2004

Nike $10.7B

VF $5.2B

Jones Apparel Group $4.4B

Liz Claiborne $4.2B

Levi Strauss $4.1B

Reebok $3.5B

$0 $2B $4B $6B $8B $10B $12B

Annual sales, in billions

Clothes

SOURCE: *Fortune*

Entertainment

Screaming on scary rides at the amusement park, checking out the latest models at an auto show, putting together a jigsaw puzzle, attacking aliens in an arcade game, curling up with a good book, visiting a sports hall of fame—the list of ways to be entertained goes on and on!

Video games are especially popular with many young people. They let you fly an airplane, visit spooky caves, battle fierce robots, and maneuver a hang glider through the canyons of a crowded city. Lots of other types of toys and games are popular, too. Some are silly and easy to learn. Others require lots of practice if you want to be really, really good at them. Etienne Bacrot of France started playing the game of chess when he was only four years old. He practiced every day. Determined to be among the world's best players, he got a professional chess coach. In 1997, Etienne became the youngest chess grandmaster ever—he was only 14!

Some kinds of entertainment are fads that are quickly replaced by new pleasures. Others remain popular for many, many years.

Kidbits Tidbits

- The longest-running musical in history is *Cats* (7,485 performances).
- About 1,450 daily newspapers and 6,700 weekly newspapers are published in the U.S.
- The very first newspaper comic strip, "Hogan's Alley," appeared in 1895.
- The world's best-selling fiction author is British mystery writer Agatha Christie, who died in 1976. More than 2 billion copies of her books have been sold so far.

A metal coil called the Slinky was first sold in 1945. By the time it celebrated its 50th birthday in 1995, some 250 million of these bouncy gizmos had been sold. A big hit in 2003 was the Hokey Pokey Elmo, an electronic version of the Sesame Street character, who performs the well-known dance.

Some popular toys will become collectibles, like Barbie and G.I. Joe dolls. Some collectibles become very valuable—if they are rare and if there is a big demand for them. A recent example of this was bean-bag animals known as Beanie Babies. The first Beanie Babies were introduced in 1994, but they were soon "retired." That is, the company stopped making those designs. By 1997, many collectors were willing to pay thousands of dollars for retired Beanie Babies.

The fad faded, though, and by 2004, the price of retired Beanie Babies had dropped considerably.

Despite all the new toy and game fads that come and go, a few forms of entertainment remain consistent favorites. Reading, watching television, and listening to music are still the most popular means by which kids and adults entertain themselves. In fact, nearly every home in America has at least one color television and one radio, and 92% of all U.S. households now have a VCR. But, even with all those electronics, the majority of people in America still rank reading as their favorite leisure and entertainment activity.

Kidbits Tidbits

- J.K. Rowling's Harry Potter books have sold more copies than any other kids' books.
- In 2003, Americans spent more than $27 billion on books. The majority of books bought were adult fiction and mass market paperbacks.
- State parks and recreational areas had more than 758 million visitors in 2002. National parks had about 64 million visitors.
- About 324 million people visited amusement parks in the United States in 2002. The parks took in $9.9 billion.
- *Seventeen* magazine is read by 2.4 million people every month; 1.3 million people read *Boys' Life*.

Entertainment

TOTY (Toy of the Year) Awards, 2004

Every year the Toy Industry Association presents awards to the best toys developed for North American consumers, as voted by retailers, media, and sales data.

Toy of the Year	Hokey Pokey Elmo by Fisher-Price
Vehicle of the Year	Regenerator R/C by Spin Master, Ltd.
Game of the Year	Cranium Hullabaloo by Cranium, Inc.
Girl Toy of the Year	Bratz Formal Funk Runway Disco by MGA Entertainment
Boy Toy of the Year	Electronic Hulk Hands by Toy Biz Worldwide

SOURCE: Toy Industry Association

Top-Selling Toys of 2002
(By dollar sales)

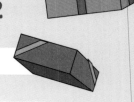

1. LeapPad Books
2. LeapPad
3. Bratz dolls
4. Hot Wheels Basic Cars
5. Trivial Pursuit, 20th edition
6. Spider-Man Dual Web Blaster
7. Star Wars Episode II Assortment
8. My 1st LeapPad
9. Rapunzel Barbie
10. Yu-Gi-Oh! Collector Tin

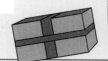

SOURCE: The NPD Group

Entertainment

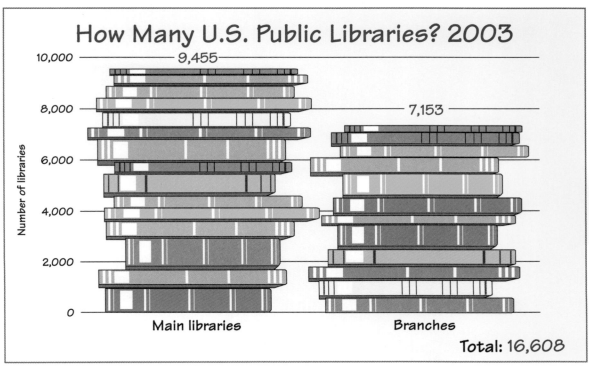

How Many U.S. Public Libraries? 2003

Number of libraries

10,000 — 9,455 —

8,000 — 7,153 —

6,000

4,000

2,000

0

Main libraries   Branches

Total: 16,608

SOURCE: American Library Association

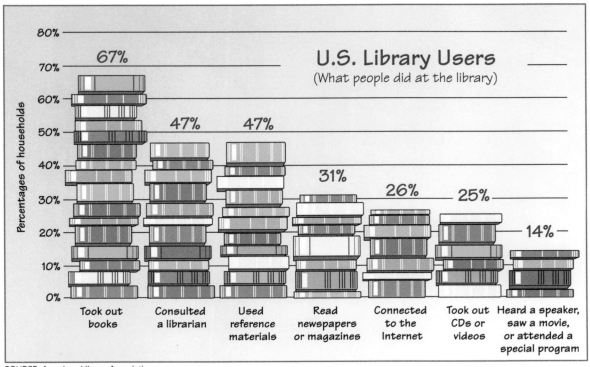

Percentages of households

80%

70% — 67%

60%

50% — 47%   47%

40%

30% — 31%   26%   25%

20% — 14% —

10%

0%

U.S. Library Users
(What people did at the library)

Took out books | Consulted a librarian | Used reference materials | Read newspapers or magazines | Connected to the Internet | Took out CDs or videos | Heard a speaker, saw a movie, or attended a special program

SOURCE: American Library Association

Entertainment

Time Crunch

Many kids, especially older ones, feel their lives are overscheduled, but their parents generally feel they have the right balance.

Kids and their parents were asked how much free time kids have.

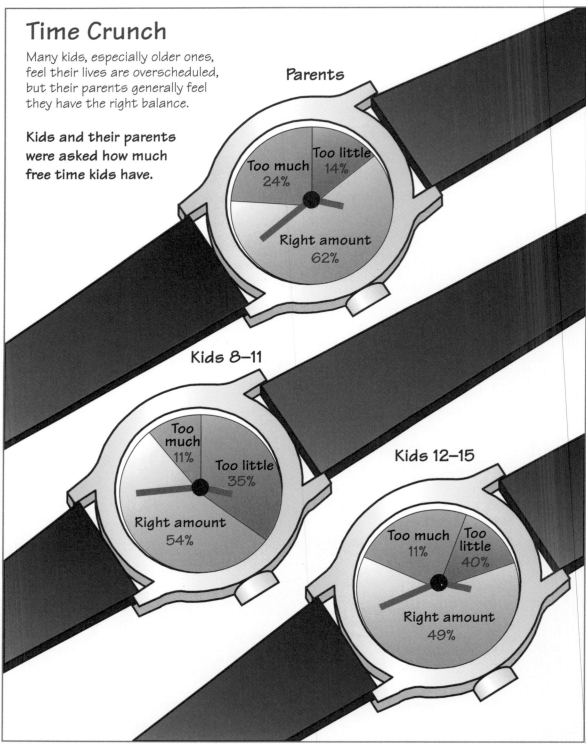

Parents

Too much
24%

Too little
14%

Right amount
62%

Kids 8–11

Too much
11%

Too little
35%

Right amount
54%

Kids 12–15

Too much
11%

Too little
40%

Right amount
49%

SOURCE: Taylor Kids Pulse 2003

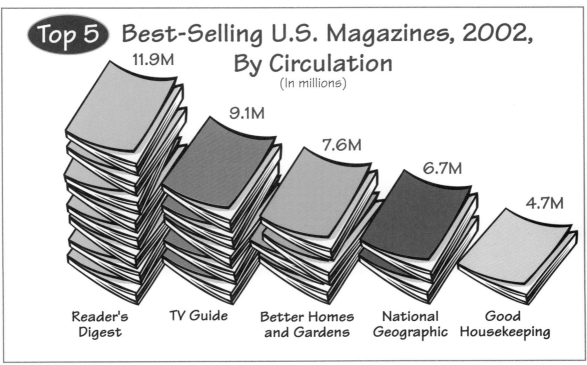

Top 5 Best-Selling U.S. Magazines, 2002, By Circulation
(In millions)

11.9M — Reader's Digest
9.1M — TV Guide
7.6M — Better Homes and Gardens
6.7M — National Geographic
4.7M — Good Housekeeping

SOURCE: Audit Bureau of Circulations

Entertainment

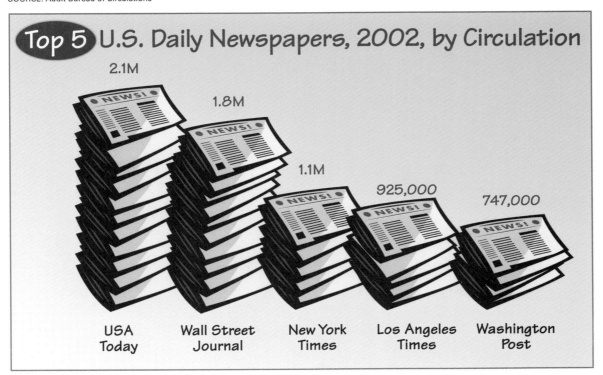

Top 5 U.S. Daily Newspapers, 2002, by Circulation

2.1M — USA Today
1.8M — Wall Street Journal
1.1M — New York Times
925,000 — Los Angeles Times
747,000 — Washington Post

SOURCE: *Editor & Publisher International Yearbook, 2003*

Entertainment

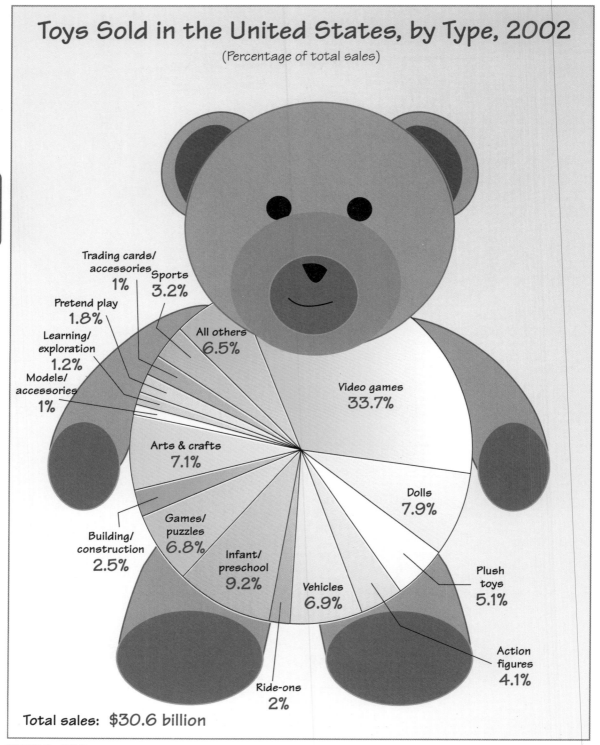

Toys Sold in the United States, by Type, 2002
(Percentage of total sales)

Trading cards/
accessories
1%

Sports
3.2%

Pretend play
1.8%

Learning/
exploration
1.2%

Models/
accessories
1%

All others
6.5%

Video games
33.7%

Arts & crafts
7.1%

Dolls
7.9%

Building/
construction
2.5%

Games/
puzzles
6.8%

Infant/
preschool
9.2%

Vehicles
6.9%

Plush
toys
5.1%

Action
figures
4.1%

Ride-ons
2%

Total sales: $30.6 billion

SOURCE: The NPD Group

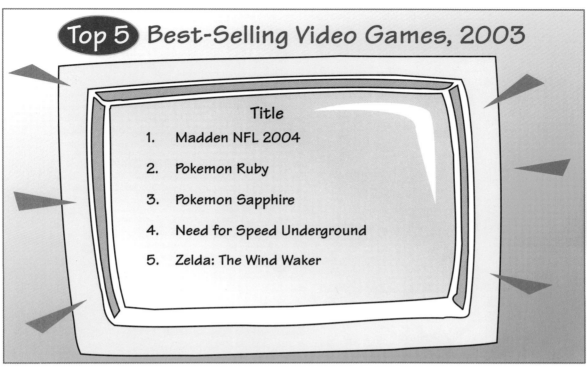

Top 5 Best-Selling Video Games, 2003

Title

1. Madden NFL 2004

2. Pokemon Ruby

3. Pokemon Sapphire

4. Need for Speed Underground

5. Zelda: The Wind Waker

SOURCE: The NPD Group

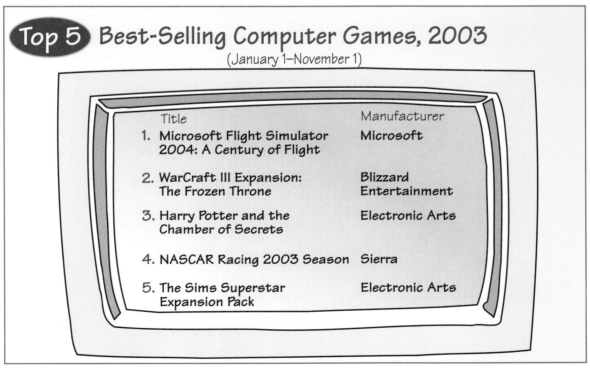

Top 5 Best-Selling Computer Games, 2003
(January 1–November 1)

Title	Manufacturer
1. Microsoft Flight Simulator 2004: A Century of Flight	Microsoft
2. WarCraft III Expansion: The Frozen Throne	Blizzard Entertainment
3. Harry Potter and the Chamber of Secrets	Electronic Arts
4. NASCAR Racing 2003 Season	Sierra
5. The Sims Superstar Expansion Pack	Electronic Arts

SOURCE: Amazon.com

Entertainment

Entertainment

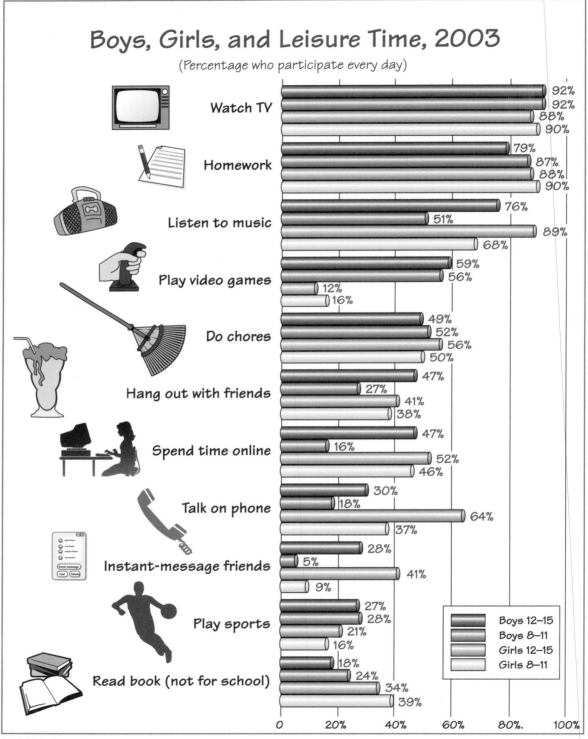

Boys, Girls, and Leisure Time, 2003

(Percentage who participate every day)

Watch TV — 92%, 92%, 88%, 90%

Homework — 79%, 87%, 88%, 90%

Listen to music — 76%, 51%, 89%, 68%

Play video games — 59%, 56%, 12%, 16%

Do chores — 49%, 52%, 56%, 50%

Hang out with friends — 47%, 27%, 41%, 38%

Spend time online — 47%, 16%, 52%, 46%

Talk on phone — 30%, 18%, 64%, 37%

Instant-message friends — 28%, 5%, 41%, 9%

Play sports — 27%, 28%, 21%, 16%

Read book (not for school) — 18%, 24%, 34%, 39%

Legend:
- Boys 12–15
- Boys 8–11
- Girls 12–15
- Girls 8–11

0   20%   40%   60%   80%.   100%

SOURCE: Taylor Kids Pulse 2003

Some Toys Have Been Around a Long Time

(Toy and first year on market)

- Crayola Crayons 1903
- Tinkertoys 1914
- Yo-Yo 1929
- LEGO Building Sets 1930
- Chutes and Ladders 1943
- Tonka Trucks 1946
- Scrabble 1948
- Candy Land 1949
- Silly Putty 1950
- Mr. Potato Head 1952
- Play-Doh 1955
- Barbie 1959
- The Game of Life 1960

SOURCE: Toy Industry Association

Top 5 Most Popular Paperbacks for Kids 2002

- 2.8M — Harry Potter and the Goblet of Fire — J.K. Rowling
- 1.2M — Harry Potter and the Chamber of Secrets — J.K. Rowling
- 585,000 — Chicken Soup of the Teenage Soul: On Tough Stuff — Jack Canfield
- 512,000 — The Adventures of Super Diaper Baby — Dav Pilkey
- 491,000 — Good Morning, Gorillas — Mary Pope Osborne

SOURCE: Bowker Annual 2003 with data from *Publishers Weekly*

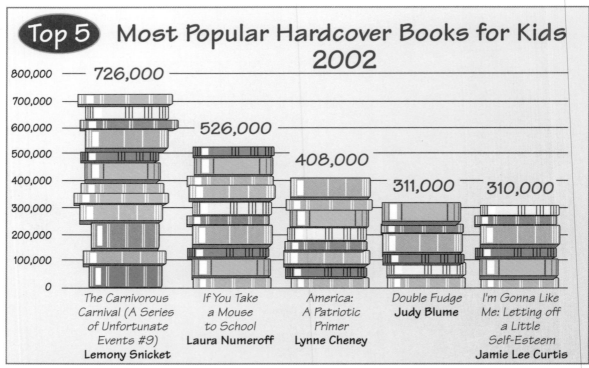

Top 5 Most Popular Hardcover Books for Kids 2002

- 726,000 — The Carnivorous Carnival (A Series of Unfortunate Events #9) — Lemony Snicket
- 526,000 — If You Take a Mouse to School — Laura Numeroff
- 408,000 — America: A Patriotic Primer — Lynne Cheney
- 311,000 — Double Fudge — Judy Blume
- 310,000 — I'm Gonna Like Me: Letting off a Little Self-Esteem — Jamie Lee Curtis

SOURCE: Bowker Annual 2003 with data from *Publishers Weekly*

Family Time

Parents with two children spend an average of 57,661 hours raising them to age 18. About half of that time is spent sharing leisure time and meals.

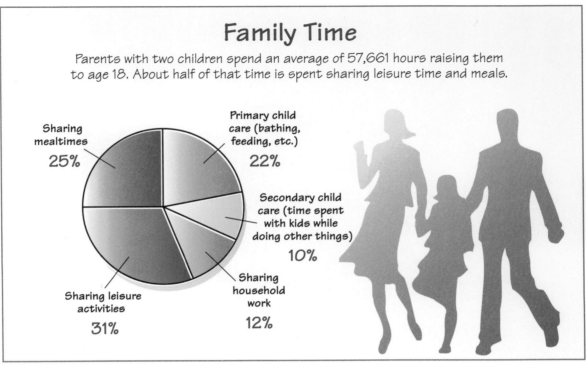

Sharing mealtimes
25%

Primary child care (bathing, feeding, etc.)
22%

Secondary child care (time spent with kids while doing other things)
10%

Sharing household work
12%

Sharing leisure activities
31%

Entertainment

SOURCE: Cornell University, "Child Rearing Time by Parents"

Teens and Boredom

Rarely bored
25%

Never bored
9%

Occasionally bored
49%

Often bored
17%

SOURCE: National Center on Addiction and Substance Abuse, *National Survey of American Attitudes on Substance Abuse VIII: Teens and Parents*

Entertainment

Game Crazy

(Top-selling board games in the United States, 2003, ranked by dollars)

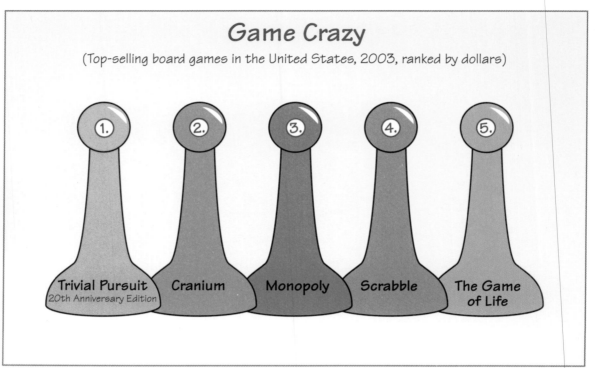

1. Trivial Pursuit 20th Anniversary Edition
2. Cranium
3. Monopoly
4. Scrabble
5. The Game of Life

SOURCE: The NPD Group / NPD Funworld / TRSTS

Harry Potter Magic

When kids were asked how long it would take them to read all 255,000 words of the fifth Harry Potter book, *Harry Potter and the Order of the Phoenix*, almost a quarter said they'd read it in a day.

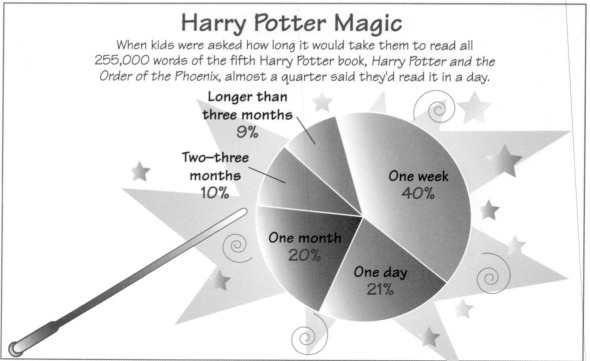

Longer than three months 9%

Two–three months 10%

One month 20%

One day 21%

One week 40%

SOURCE: infoplease.com

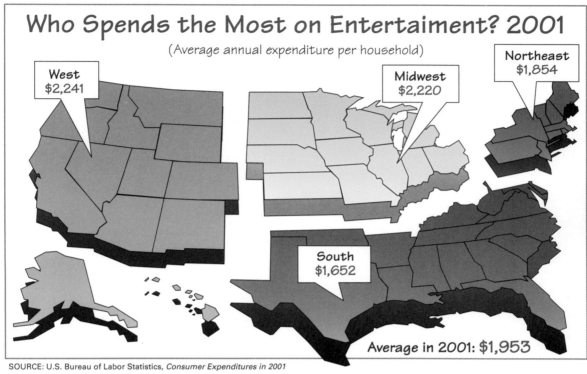

Who Spends the Most on Entertaiment? 2001

(Average annual expenditure per household)

West
$2,241

Midwest
$2,220

Northeast
$1,854

South
$1,652

Average in 2001: **$1,953**

SOURCE: U.S. Bureau of Labor Statistics, *Consumer Expenditures in 2001*

Entertainment

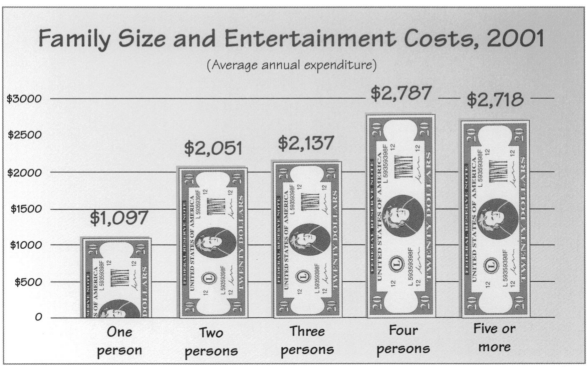

Family Size and Entertainment Costs, 2001

(Average annual expenditure)

$2,787 — $2,718

$2,051 $2,137

$1,097

| One person | Two persons | Three persons | Four persons | Five or more |

SOURCE: U.S. Bureau of Labor Statistics, *Consumer Expenditures in 2001*

School

More than 53.7 million kids attend school—38.2 million in grades K through 8, and 15.4 million in grades 9 through 12. Most of them—47.7 million—attend public schools. About 6 million students attend private schools, the majority of which are affiliated with a religion. In 2002, each teacher had an average of 15.9 students per class. In general, elementary school classes were larger than high school classes, and classes in public schools were larger than classes in private schools.

The United States has about 80,600 elementary schools, 24,900 high schools, and 12,200 schools that cover grades K through 12. Total spending on K–12 education is more than $450 billion a year! The average spent on each student in the 1999–2000 school year was $6,642. The amount varied greatly from state to state, and from one school district to another. New Jersey spent the most—an average of $11,471 per student. Utah spent the least—an average of $5,278 per student.

School

Kidbits Tidbits

- About 9% of public schools have fewer than 100 students; 9.2% have 1,000 or more students.
- Most private schools are affiliated with a religion.
- In 2000, the average elementary school classroom had 21.1 students. The average high school classroom had 23.6 students.
- More than 25.4 million children eat lunch in school, and more than 6 million eat breakfast there.

Most kids graduate from high school, though almost 11% of 16- and 17-year-olds are dropouts. Getting a high school diploma and doing well in school can pay off in many ways. For example, it makes it easier to get a good job or go to college. It can mean money, too! When Sai Gunturi won the National Spelling Bee in 2003, he took home $12,000, among other prizes. James Williams got a $25,000 scholarship when he won the 2003 National Geography Bee.

Today, record numbers of high school graduates continue their education at the college level. More than 15.5 million people are currently enrolled in college, the great majority of them in public institutions. More women than men are enrolled in college. Attending college can be very expensive. The average yearly cost of tuition and fees at 4-year colleges in 2003 was $4,694 at public colleges and $19,710 at private colleges. But there's a financial payoff: the greater the amount of education people have, the better their chances of getting jobs—and earning good salaries. In 2001, only 58.2% of people with less than a high school diploma had jobs, but about 90% of college graduates had jobs. The average earnings of people age 18 and older who did not have high school degrees was $21,897. Earnings of people with a bachelor's degree were $46,463; with a master's degree it was $57,605.

Kidbits Tidbits

- College graduates can expect to earn about $600,000 more during their lifetimes than high school graduates can expect to earn.
- Twenty-eight percent of college students in 2000 were minorities. California had 1.3 million minority college students and Vermont had 1,797.
- In 2003, the cost of tuition and fees for an average year at a private college was nearly 4.2 times more than a public college.
- In 2000, the average salary of public school teachers was $42,949—up from $15,913 in 1980.
- A study of 12th graders in 23 countries found that U.S. students scored close to the international average in math and science.

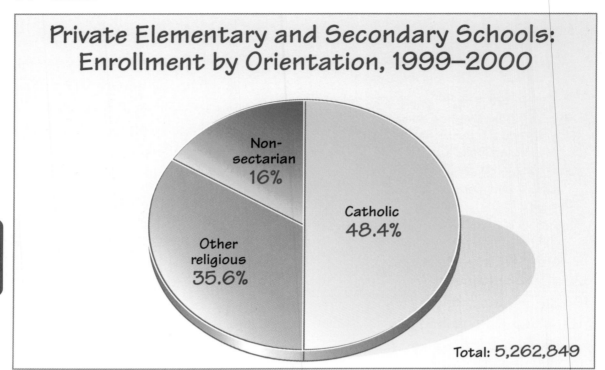

Private Elementary and Secondary Schools: Enrollment by Orientation, 1999–2000

Non-sectarian 16%

Catholic 48.4%

Other religious 35.6%

Total: 5,262,849

SOURCE: National Center for Education Statistics, *Digest of Education Statistics, 2002*

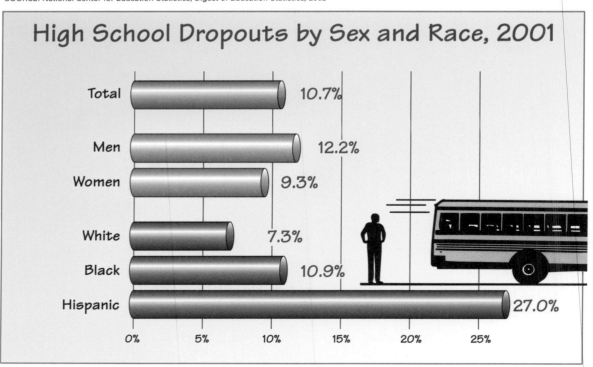

High School Dropouts by Sex and Race, 2001

Total — 10.7%

Men — 12.2%

Women — 9.3%

White — 7.3%

Black — 10.9%

Hispanic — 27.0%

0%   5%   10%   15%   20%   25%

SOURCE: National Center for Education Statistics

School

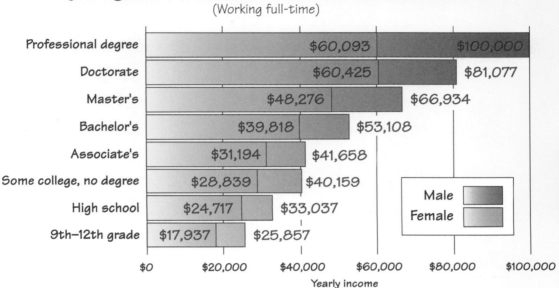

Median Yearly Income of People over 25 by Highest Education Achieved, 2001

(Working full-time)

Education	Female	Male
Professional degree	$60,093	$100,000
Doctorate	$60,425	$81,077
Master's	$48,276	$66,934
Bachelor's	$39,818	$53,108
Associate's	$31,194	$41,658
Some college, no degree	$28,839	$40,159
High school	$24,717	$33,037
9th–12th grade	$17,937	$25,857

$0 $20,000 $40,000 $60,000 $80,000 $100,000

Yearly income

SOURCE: College Board

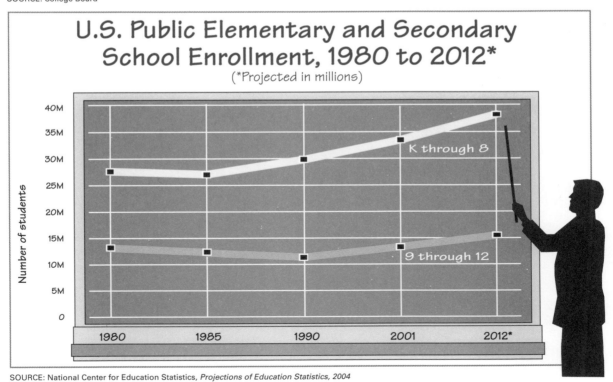

U.S. Public Elementary and Secondary School Enrollment, 1980 to 2012*

(*Projected in millions)

Number of students

40M
35M
30M
25M
20M
15M
10M
5M
0

K through 8

9 through 12

1980   1985   1990   2001   2012*

SOURCE: National Center for Education Statistics, *Projections of Education Statistics, 2004*

School

Student Use of Computers in School, 2001

(By average percentage of population per category)

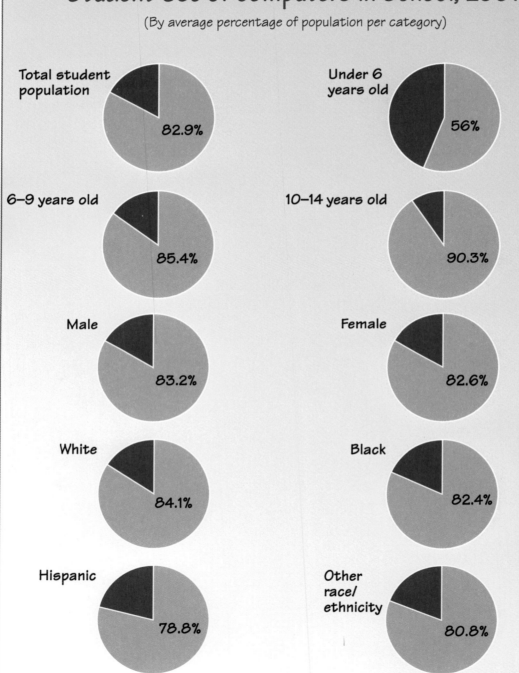

Total student population — 82.9%

Under 6 years old — 56%

6–9 years old — 85.4%

10–14 years old — 90.3%

Male — 83.2%

Female — 82.6%

White — 84.1%

Black — 82.4%

Hispanic — 78.8%

Other race/ethnicity — 80.8%

SOURCE: National Center for Education Statistics, *Digest of Education Statistics, 2002*

Student Use of Computers at Home for Schoolwork, 2001

(By average percentage of population per category)

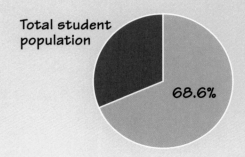

Total student population
68.6%

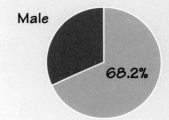

Male
68.2%

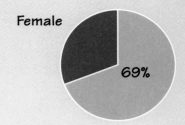

Female
69%

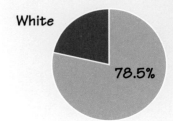

White
78.5%

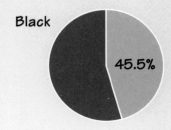

Black
45.5%

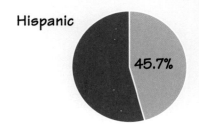

Hispanic
45.7%

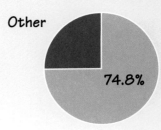

Other
74.8%

School

SOURCE: National Center for Education Statistics, *Digest of Education Statistics, 2002*

School

The Internet and Education

The Internet has become an important classroom tool for students ages 12–17.

Percentage of students who:

Use Internet for school research

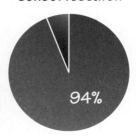

94%

Believe Internet helps with schoolwork

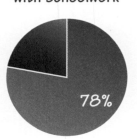

78%

Have downloaded an online study guide

34%

Used Internet as major source for most recent school project or report

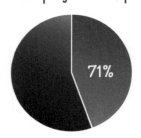

71%

Know someone who has used Internet to cheat on paper or test

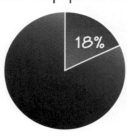

18%

Use Web sites specifically set up for their school or class

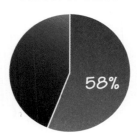

58%

Use e-mail and instant messaging to contact teachers or classmates about schoolwork

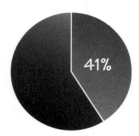

41%

Have created Web page for a school project

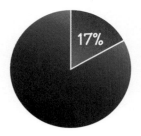

17%

SOURCE: Pew Research Center, *The Internet and Education: Findings of the Pew Internet and American Life Project 2001*

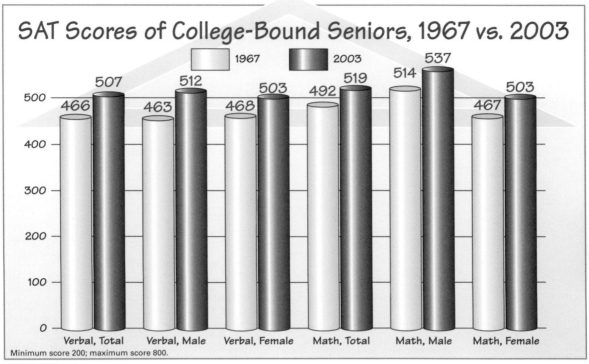

SAT Scores of College-Bound Seniors, 1967 vs. 2003

1967   2003

	Verbal, Total	Verbal, Male	Verbal, Female	Math, Total	Math, Male	Math, Female
1967	466	463	468	492	514	467
2003	507	512	503	519	537	503

Minimum score 200; maximum score 800.

SOURCE: College Board

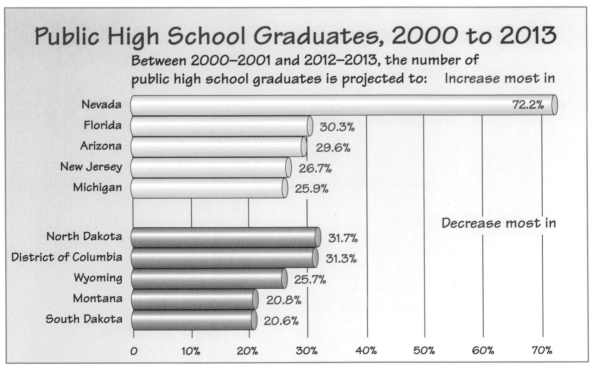

Public High School Graduates, 2000 to 2013

Between 2000–2001 and 2012–2013, the number of
public high school graduates is projected to: Increase most in

Nevada	72.2%
Florida	30.3%
Arizona	29.6%
New Jersey	26.7%
Michigan	25.9%

Decrease most in

North Dakota	31.7%
District of Columbia	31.3%
Wyoming	25.7%
Montana	20.8%
South Dakota	20.6%

0   10%   20%   30%   40%   50%   60%   70%

SOURCE: National Center for Education Statistics, *Projection of Education Statistics 2003*

School

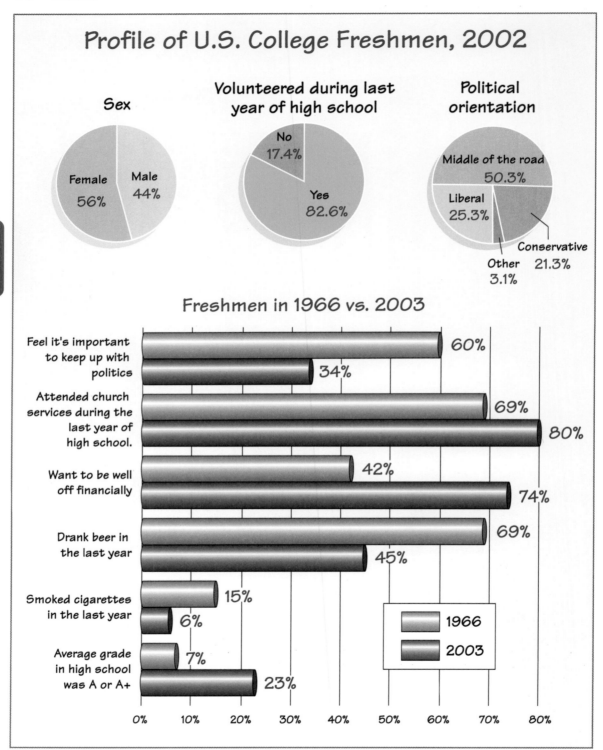

Profile of U.S. College Freshmen, 2002

Sex

Female 56%
Male 44%

Volunteered during last year of high school

No 17.4%
Yes 82.6%

Political orientation

Middle of the road 50.3%
Liberal 25.3%
Conservative 21.3%
Other 3.1%

Freshmen in 1966 vs. 2003

Feel it's important to keep up with politics — 60% / 34%

Attended church services during the last year of high school. — 69% / 80%

Want to be well off financially — 42% / 74%

Drank beer in the last year — 69% / 45%

Smoked cigarettes in the last year — 15% / 6%

Average grade in high school was A or A+ — 7% / 23%

1966
2003

0% 10% 20% 30% 40% 50% 60% 70% 80%

School

SOURCE: *USA Today* with statistics from Higher Education Research Institute and National Center for Education Statistics, *Digest of Education Statistics 2003*

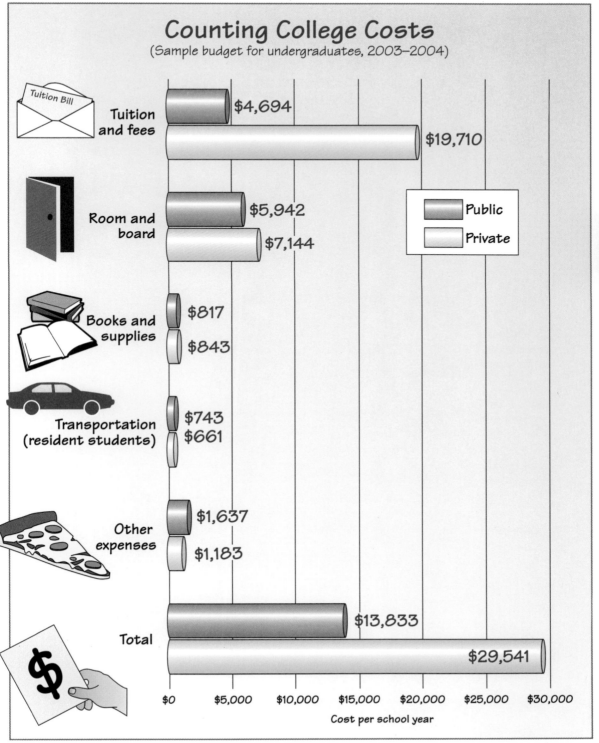

Counting College Costs
(Sample budget for undergraduates, 2003–2004)

Tuition and fees
- $4,694
- $19,710

Room and board
- $5,942
- $7,144

Books and supplies
- $817
- $843

Transportation (resident students)
- $743
- $661

Other expenses
- $1,637
- $1,183

Total
- $13,833
- $29,541

Public
Private

$0 $5,000 $10,000 $15,000 $20,000 $25,000 $30,000

Cost per school year

SOURCE: College Board

School

School

Top 10 Most Popular Undergraduate Majors 2000–2001

Major	Degrees
Business	265,746
Education	185,566
Social Science and History	128,036
Psychology	73,534
Health professions and related sciences	73,490
Visual and performing arts	61,148
Biological/life sciences	60,553
Engineering	58,098
Communications	58,013
English language and literature	51,419

Total bachelor's degrees: 1,244,171

0   50,000   100,000   150,000   200,000   250,000

SOURCE: National Center for Education Statistics, *Digest of Education Statistics, 2002*

Service Learning in High Schools, 1999

Service learning combines community service with academic study. Incorporating service learning into K–12 schools has become very popular over the last decade: 64% of all public schools and 83% of public high schools had students participating in 1999.

Why public schools that offer service learning encourage their students to do it:

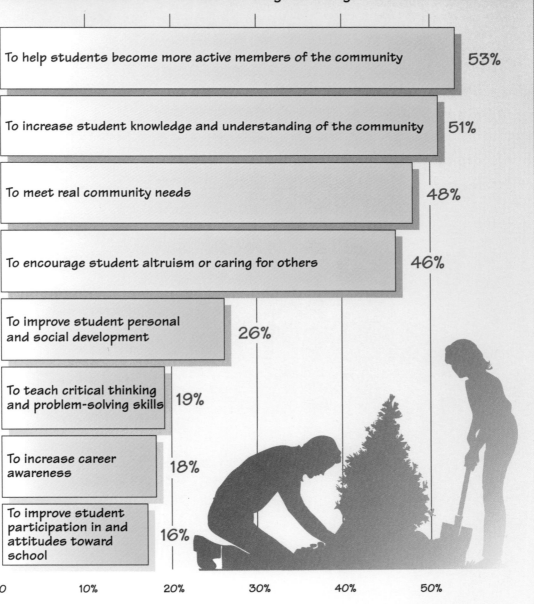

To help students become more active members of the community — 53%

To increase student knowledge and understanding of the community — 51%

To meet real community needs — 48%

To encourage student altruism or caring for others — 46%

To improve student personal and social development — 26%

To teach critical thinking and problem-solving skills — 19%

To increase career awareness — 18%

To improve student participation in and attitudes toward school — 16%

0   10%   20%   30%   40%   50%

SOURCE: National Center for Education Statistics, *Service Learning and Community Service*

School

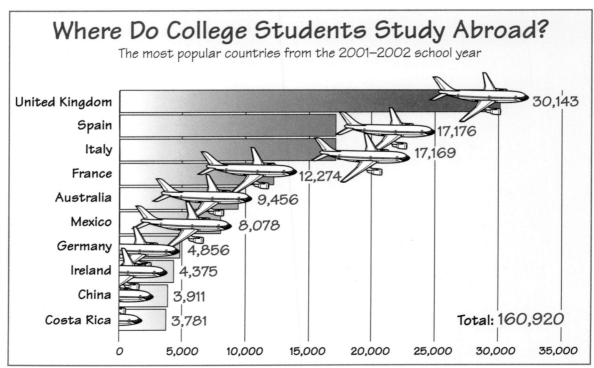

Where Do College Students Study Abroad?

The most popular countries from the 2001–2002 school year

United Kingdom	30,143
Spain	17,176
Italy	17,169
France	12,274
Australia	9,456
Mexico	8,078
Germany	4,856
Ireland	4,375
China	3,911
Costa Rica	3,781

Total: 160,920

SOURCE: Institute of International Education, *Open Doors 2003 Report*

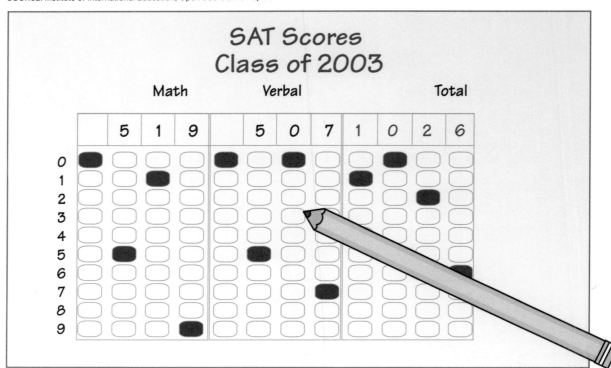

SAT Scores
Class of 2003

	Math			Verbal			Total			
	5	1	9	5	0	7	1	0	2	6

SOURCE: College Board

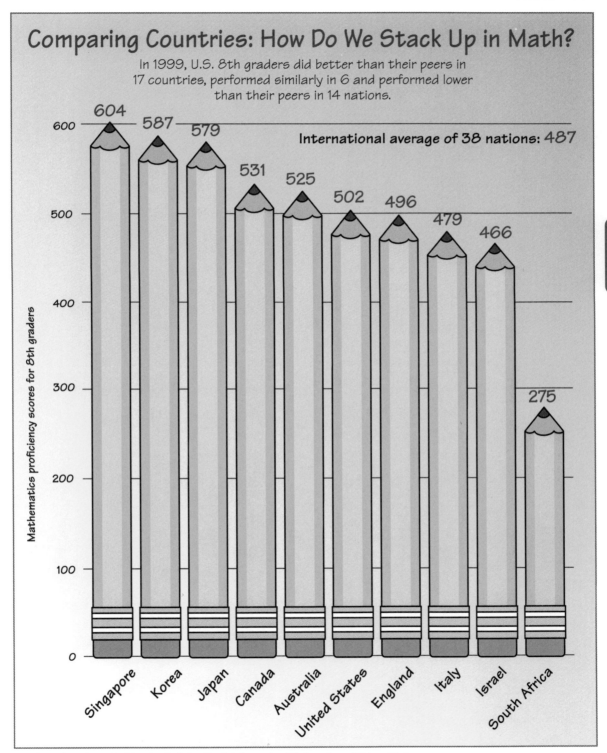

Comparing Countries: How Do We Stack Up in Math?

In 1999, U.S. 8th graders did better than their peers in 17 countries, performed similarly in 6 and performed lower than their peers in 14 nations.

International average of 38 nations: 487

Mathematics proficiency scores for 8th graders

Singapore	604
Korea	587
Japan	579
Canada	531
Australia	525
United States	502
England	496
Italy	479
Israel	466
South Africa	275

School

SOURCE: National Center for Education Statistics, *Trends in International Mathematics and Science Study*

School

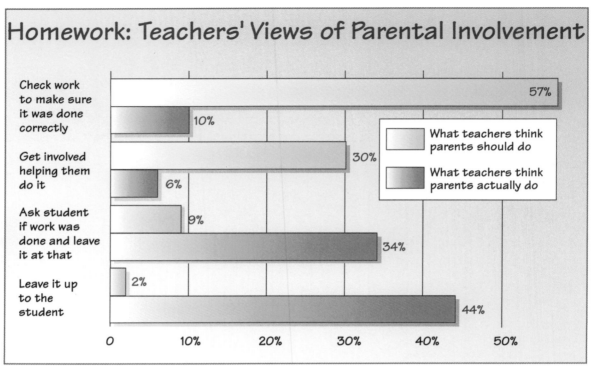

Homework: Teachers' Views of Parental Involvement

Check work to make sure it was done correctly — 57% / 10%

Get involved helping them do it — 30% / 6%

Ask student if work was done and leave it at that — 9% / 34%

Leave it up to the student — 2% / 44%

Legend:
- What teachers think parents should do
- What teachers think parents actually do

(Axis: 0, 10%, 20%, 30%, 40%, 50%)

SOURCE: Public Agenda

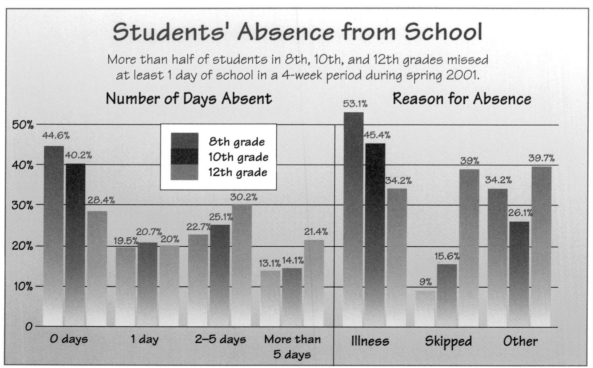

Students' Absence from School

More than half of students in 8th, 10th, and 12th grades missed at least 1 day of school in a 4-week period during spring 2001.

Number of Days Absent

Legend:
- 8th grade
- 10th grade
- 12th grade

0 days: 44.6%, 40.2%, 28.4%

1 day: 19.5%, 20.7%, 20%

2–5 days: 22.7%, 25.1%, 30.2%

More than 5 days: 13.1%, 14.1%, 21.4%

Reason for Absence

Illness: 53.1%, 45.4%, 34.2%

Skipped: 9%, 15.6%, 39%

Other: 34.2%, 26.1%, 39.7%

SOURCE: National Center for Education Statistics, *Student Effort and Educational Progress Report*

School Spending Spree

Consumers spent more than $14.1 billion before going back to school in 2003. Families with school-age children spent an average of $450.75 on back-to-school items.

How much was spent on each:

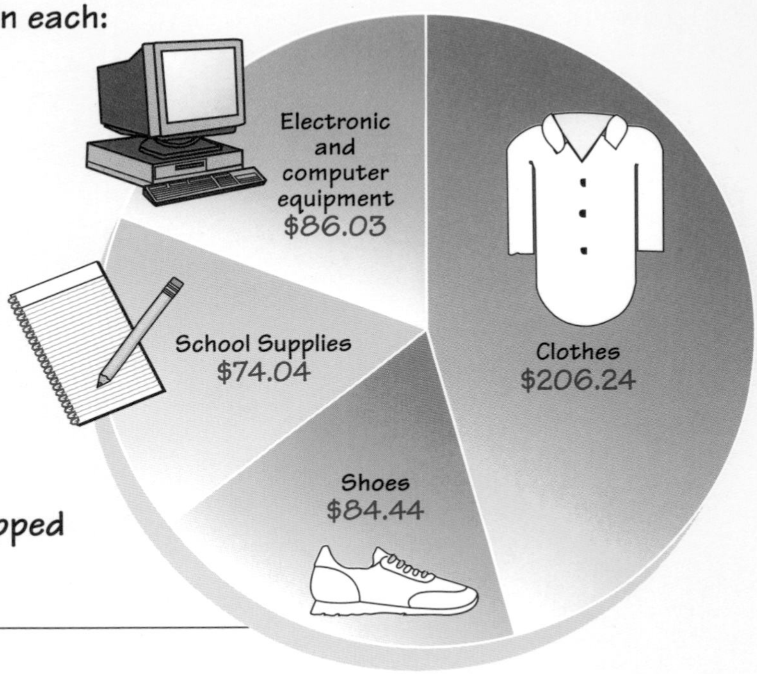

Electronic and computer equipment
$86.03

School Supplies
$74.04

Clothes
$206.24

Shoes
$84.44

School

Where consumers shopped

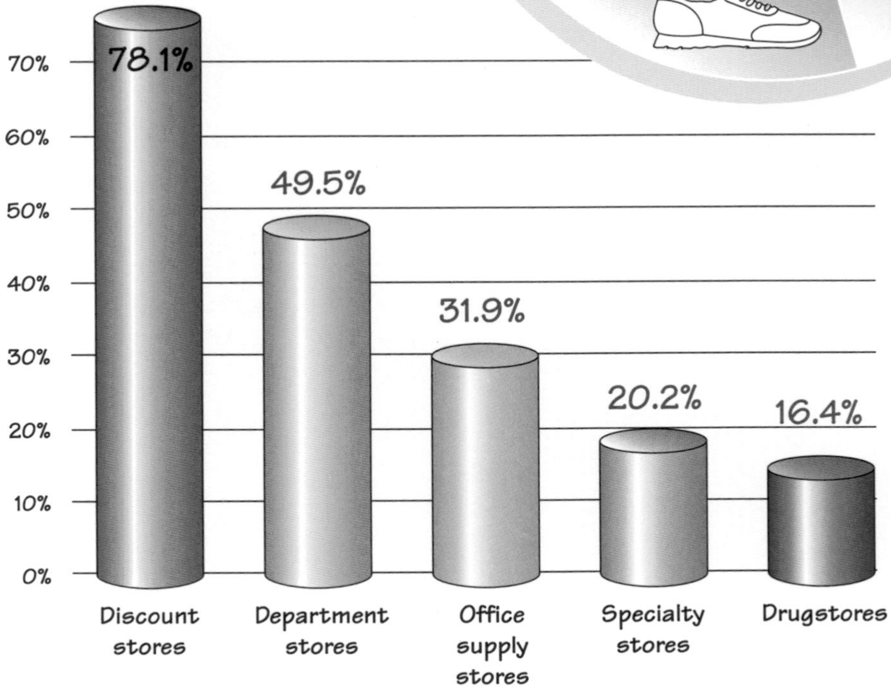

- 78.1% — Discount stores
- 49.5% — Department stores
- 31.9% — Office supply stores
- 20.2% — Specialty stores
- 16.4% — Drugstores

SOURCE: National Retail Federation, *NRF 2003 Back-to-School Consumer Intentions and Actions Survey*

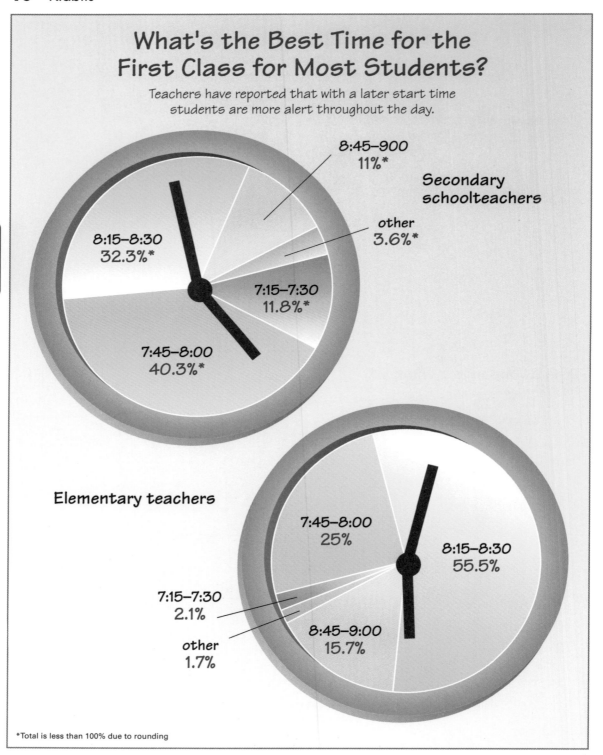

What's the Best Time for the First Class for Most Students?

Teachers have reported that with a later start time students are more alert throughout the day.

Secondary schoolteachers

8:45–900
11%*

other
3.6%*

8:15–8:30
32.3%*

7:15–7:30
11.8%*

7:45–8:00
40.3%*

Elementary teachers

7:45–8:00
25%

8:15–8:30
55.5%

7:15–7:30
2.1%

8:45–9:00
15.7%

other
1.7%

*Total is less than 100% due to rounding

SOURCE: Center for Applied Research and Educational Improvement, *School Start Time Survey*

School

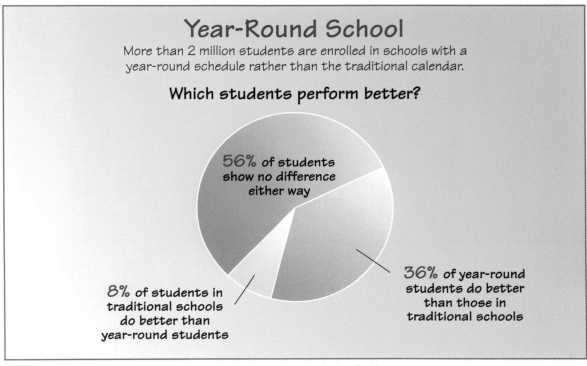

Year-Round School

More than 2 million students are enrolled in schools with a year-round schedule rather than the traditional calendar.

Which students perform better?

56% of students show no difference either way

8% of students in traditional schools do better than year-round students

36% of year-round students do better than those in traditional schools

School

SOURCE: Center for Applied Research and Educational Improvement, *Alternative Calendars: Final Report*

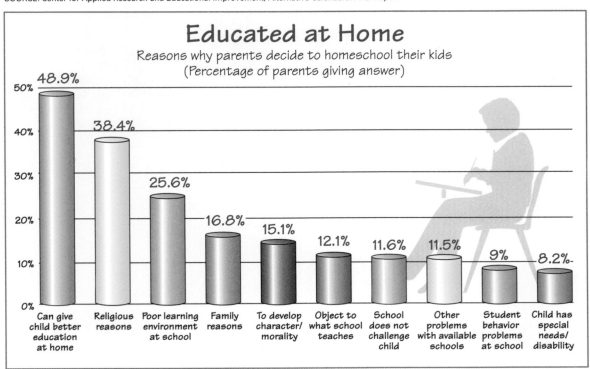

Educated at Home

Reasons why parents decide to homeschool their kids
(Percentage of parents giving answer)

- Can give child better education at home: 48.9%
- Religious reasons: 38.4%
- Poor learning environment at school: 25.6%
- Family reasons: 16.8%
- To develop character/morality: 15.1%
- Object to what school teaches: 12.1%
- School does not challenge child: 11.6%
- Other problems with available schools: 11.5%
- Student behavior problems at school: 9%
- Child has special needs/disability: 8.2%

SOURCE: National Center for Education Statistics, *Homeschooling in the United States 1999*

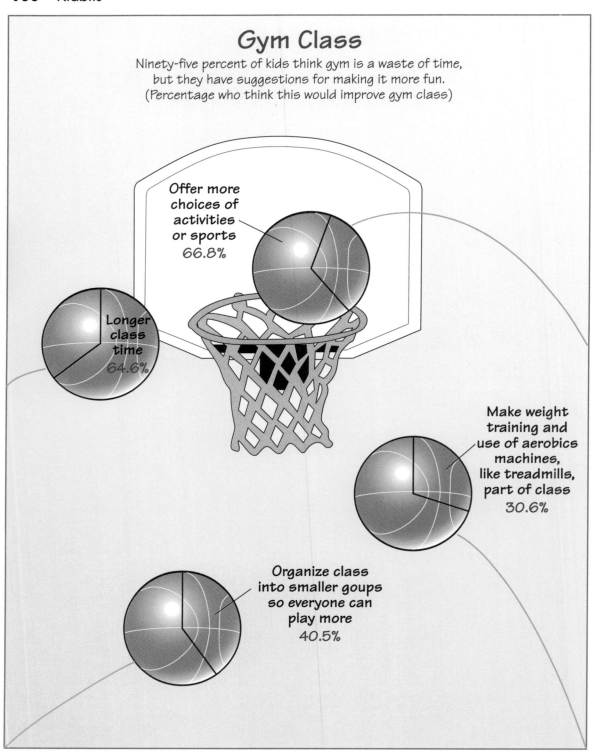

Gym Class

Ninety-five percent of kids think gym is a waste of time,
but they have suggestions for making it more fun.
(Percentage who think this would improve gym class)

Offer more
choices of
activities
or sports
66.8%

Longer
class
time
64.6%

Make weight
training and
use of aerobics
machines,
like treadmills,
part of class
30.6%

Organize class
into smaller goups
so everyone can
play more
40.5%

SOURCE: *Sports Illustrated for Kids,* "Omnibus Study"

School

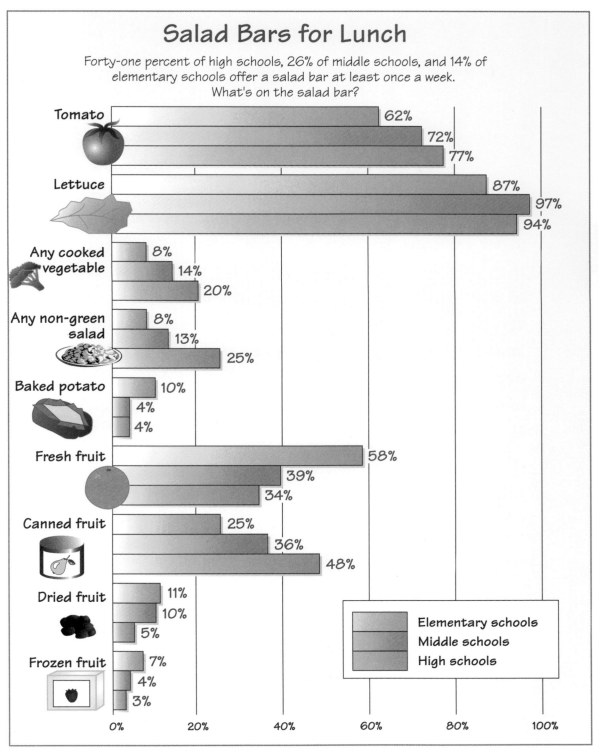

Salad Bars for Lunch

Forty-one percent of high schools, 26% of middle schools, and 14% of elementary schools offer a salad bar at least once a week. What's on the salad bar?

Tomato
- 62%
- 72%
- 77%

Lettuce
- 87%
- 97%
- 94%

Any cooked vegetable
- 8%
- 14%
- 20%

Any non-green salad
- 8%
- 13%
- 25%

Baked potato
- 10%
- 4%
- 4%

Fresh fruit
- 58%
- 39%
- 34%

Canned fruit
- 25%
- 36%
- 48%

Dried fruit
- 11%
- 10%
- 5%

Frozen fruit
- 7%
- 4%
- 3%

Legend:
- Elementary schools
- Middle schools
- High schools

0%   20%   40%   60%   80%   100%

School

SOURCE: U.S. Department of Agriculture Food and Nutrition Office, "School Lunch Salad Bars"

Health

To be healthy and physically fit, you need good health habits. These habits include eating properly, exercising regularly, getting enough sleep, and taking precautions to avoid accidents. For example, using safety belts reduces the risk of fatal injury to people riding in the front seat of a car by 45%. Receiving recommended childhood vaccines reduces the risk of contracting polio, hepatitis, and other diseases. Exercising reduces the risk of heart disease, cancer, and diabetes. Following good habits does more than lower your risk of getting sick or injured. It's also the key to living to a healthy old age.

One of the most serious U.S. health problems is the use of alcohol, tobacco, and illegal drugs. These substances are bad news—they ruin health and often cause death. Teachers, parents, and others try to make sure that kids know about the dangers of using drugs. But kids continue to use them. For example, each day more than 4,000 try smoking for the first time and half of them become regular, daily smokers.

Kidbits Tidbits

- Of the 33 largest cities in the United States, San Antonio has the highest percentage of obese adults. More than 31% of its residents are considered obese. Denver has the lowest—14.2%.
- At conception, you consisted of one cell. By the time you're an adult, your body will consist of 100 trillion cells.
- The largest organ in your body is your skin. An adult has about 20 square feet of skin.

Another serious problem is weight control. People of all ages are more likely to be overweight than they were 20 years ago. A full one-third of Americans are obese, or seriously over-weight. About 300,000 people die each year because their excess weight led to diabetes, heart disease, and other deadly illnesses. Many people try to fight the "battle of the bulge" by dieting. Billions of dollars are spent annually on special foods, diet clubs, and medicines—all in unsuccessful efforts to lose weight. Americans also spend billions of dollars yearly on vitamins and minerals, to try to make up for not eating enough of the proper foods.

Heart disease and cancer are the major causes of death in the United States. Accidents are the fifth-leading cause. Every ten minutes, two people are killed in accidents. Deadly infectious diseases also claim many lives each year. These are illnesses caused by viruses and other germs—they include AIDS, pneumonia, and the flu.

In comparison to many other countries, Americans are very healthy. Excellent medical care, safe food and water, and good sanitation means that Americans can expect to live an average of 77 years. In some countries, the average life expectancy is less than 50 years. In the United States, 6.75 infants 1 year old or less die per 1,000 live births. In more than a dozen countries where most people are very poor, over 100 infants die per 1,000 live births.

Kidbits Tidbits

- The United States spends more than $1 trillion a year on health care.
- In 2002, heart disease accounted for 28% of the total deaths in America.
- Unintentional injuries are the main cause of death for Americans between the ages of 1 and 24.
- Each year, more than 2,500 Americans under age 15 die in motor-vehicle accidents. About 11,000 people between the ages of 15 and 24 die in auto accidents.
- American kids consume 900 million packs of cig-arettes each year. More than 5 million children alive today will die from smoking-related illnesses.

Health

Do Teens Exercise Enough?

The recommended amount of physical activity for high school
students is at least 30 minutes of moderate activity
at least 5 days a week or vigorous activity 3 days.
(Percentage who achieved the recommended amount of physical activity)

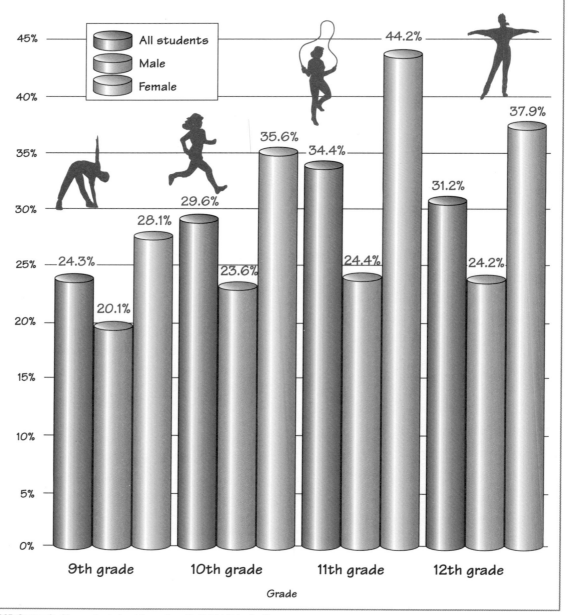

SOURCE: Centers for Disease Control and Prevention, *Youth Risk Behavior Survey*

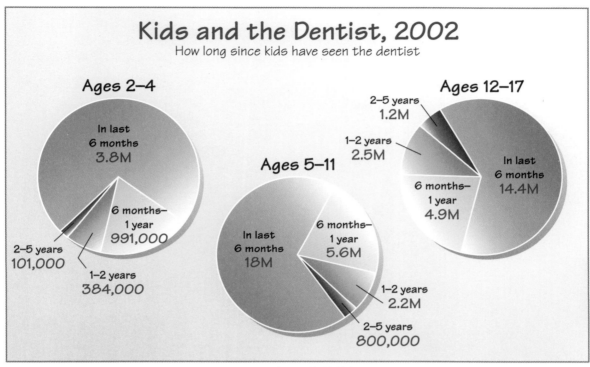

Kids and the Dentist, 2002
How long since kids have seen the dentist

Ages 2–4

In last 6 months 3.8M

6 months–1 year 991,000

2–5 years 101,000

1–2 years 384,000

Ages 5–11

In last 6 months 18M

6 months–1 year 5.6M

1–2 years 2.2M

2–5 years 800,000

Ages 12–17

2–5 years 1.2M

1–2 years 2.5M

In last 6 months 14.4M

6 months–1 year 4.9M

SOURCE: Centers for Disease Control and Prevention, "Monitoring the Nations Health 2002"

Health

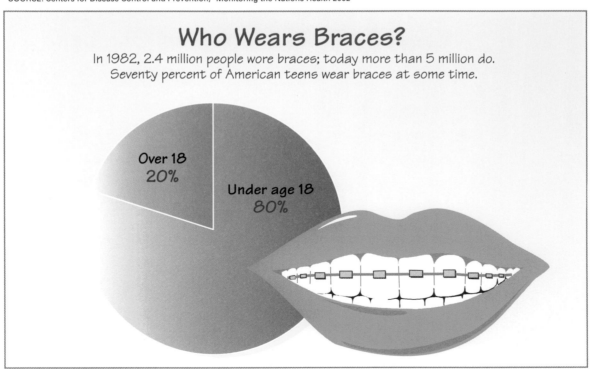

Who Wears Braces?
In 1982, 2.4 million people wore braces; today more than 5 million do.
Seventy percent of American teens wear braces at some time.

Over 18 20%

Under age 18 80%

SOURCE: American Association of Orthodontists

Health

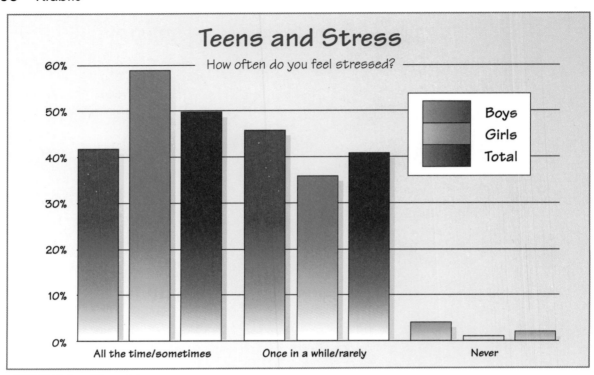

Teens and Stress

How often do you feel stressed?

Legend: Boys, Girls, Total

Categories: All the time/sometimes — Once in a while/rarely — Never

SOURCE: Mediamark Research, Inc.

Top 10 Reasons for Teens to Feel Stressed

	Boys	Girls	Total
1. Lot of school work	63%	72%	67%
2. Not enough sleep	42%	57%	49%
3. Not enough money	40%	48%	44%
4. Not enough time in day	35%	49%	42%
5. Relationships with friends	28%	50%	39%
6. Relationships with parents	30%	45%	37%
7. Relationships with siblings/other family	30%	42%	36%
8. Juggling too many responsibilities	30%	40%	35%
9. Weight/body image	19%	46%	32%
10. Relationship with boyfriend/girlfriend	24%	33%	29%

SOURCE: Mediamark Research, Inc.

Kids and Asthma, 2002

About 73 million U.S. kids have asthma.

Total number
who have
ever had
asthma
2 million
15.2%

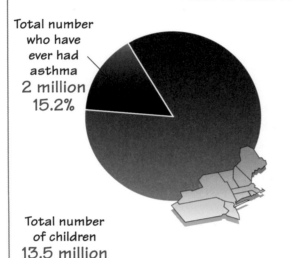

Total number
of children
13.5 million

Northeast

Total number
who have
ever had
asthma
2 million
11.6%

Total number
of children
17.4 million

Midwest

Total number who
have ever had
asthma
1.7 million
11.1%

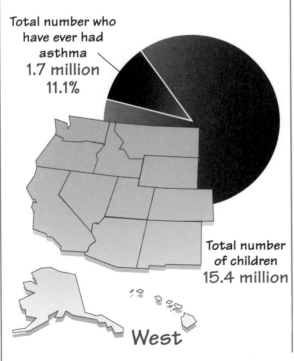

Total number
of children
15.4 million

West

Total number who
have ever had
asthma
3.2 million
11.9%

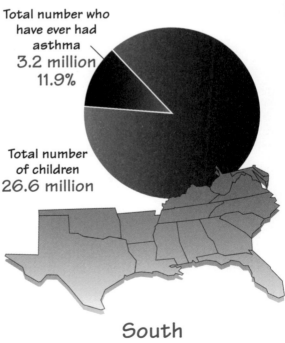

Total number
of children
26.6 million

South

SOURCE: Centers for Disease Control and Prevention, "Monitoring the Nation's Health 2002"

Health

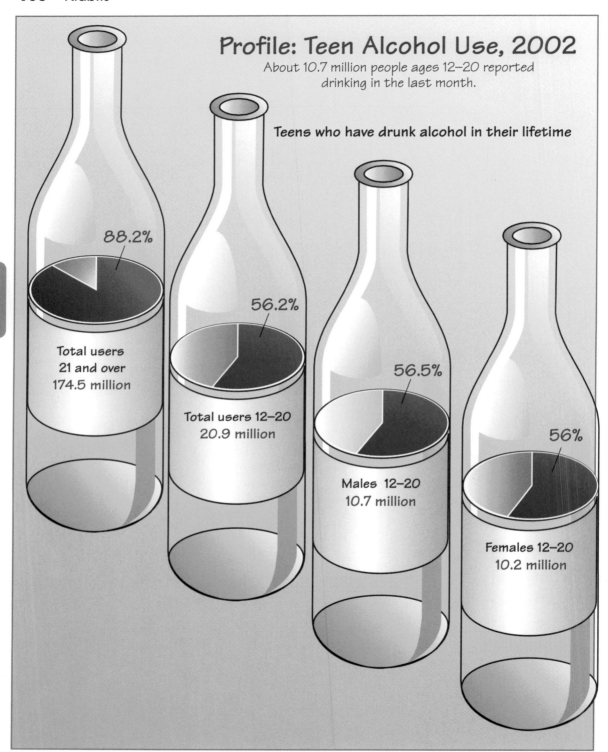

Profile: Teen Alcohol Use, 2002

About 10.7 million people ages 12–20 reported drinking in the last month.

Teens who have drunk alcohol in their lifetime

88.2%

Total users 21 and over 174.5 million

56.2%

Total users 12–20 20.9 million

56.5%

Males 12–20 10.7 million

56%

Females 12–20 10.2 million

Health

SOURCE: Deptartment of Health and Human Services, *2002 National Survey on Drug Use and Health*

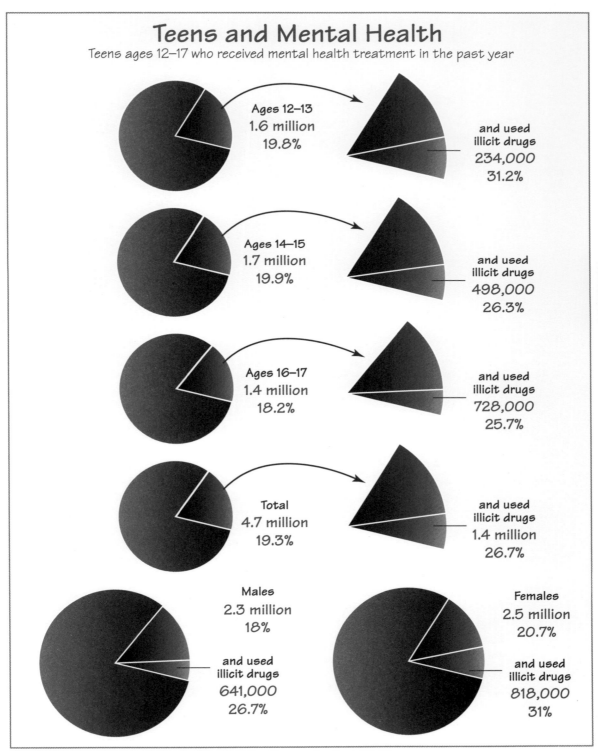

Teens and Mental Health

Teens ages 12–17 who received mental health treatment in the past year

Ages 12–13
1.6 million
19.8%

and used
illicit drugs
234,000
31.2%

Ages 14–15
1.7 million
19.9%

and used
illicit drugs
498,000
26.3%

Ages 16–17
1.4 million
18.2%

and used
illicit drugs
728,000
25.7%

Total
4.7 million
19.3%

and used
illicit drugs
1.4 million
26.7%

Males
2.3 million
18%

and used
illicit drugs
641,000
26.7%

Females
2.5 million
20.7%

and used
illicit drugs
818,000
31%

Health

SOURCE: Department of Health and Human Services, *2002 National Survey on Drug Use and Health*

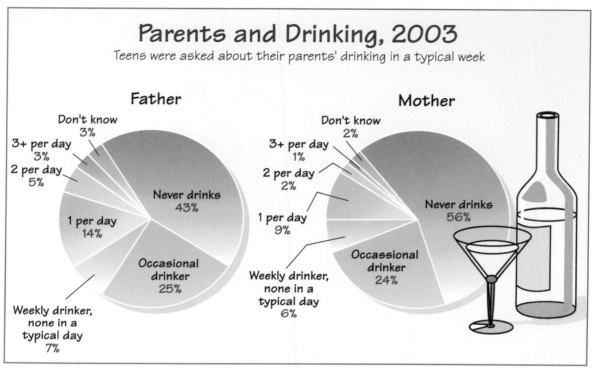

Parents and Drinking, 2003

Teens were asked about their parents' drinking in a typical week

Father

Don't know 3%
3+ per day 3%
2 per day 5%
1 per day 14%
Never drinks 43%
Occasional drinker 25%
Weekly drinker, none in a typical day 7%

Mother

Don't know 2%
3+ per day 1%
2 per day 2%
1 per day 9%
Never drinks 56%
Occasional drinker 24%
Weekly drinker, none in a typical day 6%

SOURCE: National Center on Addiction and Substance Abuse, *National Survey of American Attitudes on Substance Abuse VIII: Teen and Parents*

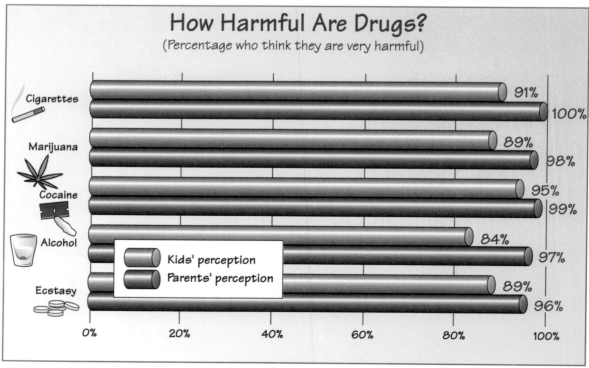

How Harmful Are Drugs?

(Percentage who think they are very harmful)

- Cigarettes — 91% / 100%
- Marijuana — 89% / 98%
- Cocaine — 95% / 99%
- Alcohol — 84% / 97%
- Ecstasy — 89% / 96%

Kids' perception
Parents' perception

0% 20% 40% 60% 80% 100%

SOURCE: National Center on Addiction and Substance Abuse, *National Survey of American Attitudes on Substance Abuse VIII: Teen and Parents*

Health

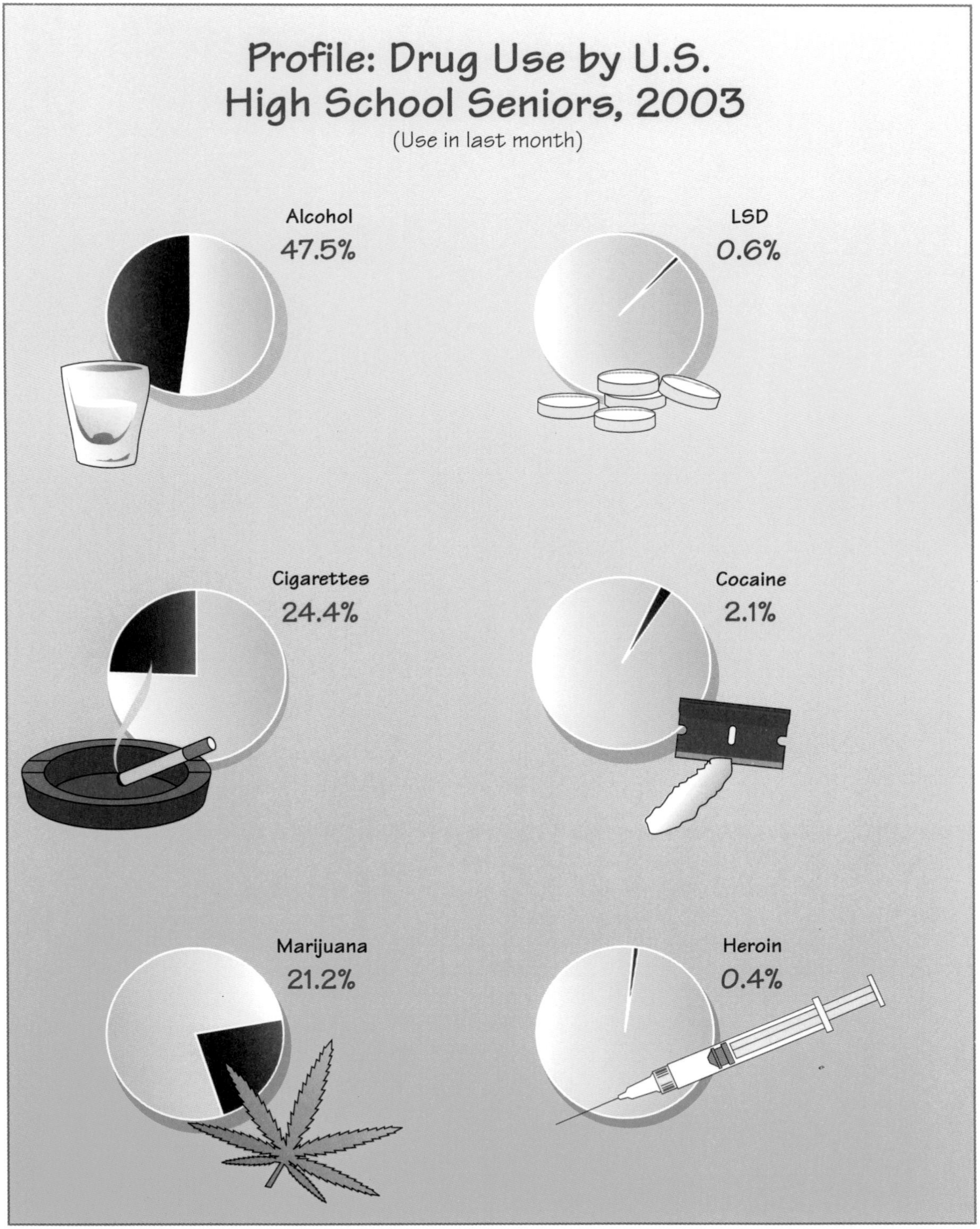
Profile: Drug Use by U.S. High School Seniors, 2003
(Use in last month)
Alcohol
47.5%
LSD
0.6%
Cigarettes
24.4%
Cocaine
2.1%
Marijuana
21.2%
Heroin
0.4%

SOURCE: National Institute on Drug Abuse, *Monitoring the Future 2003*

Health

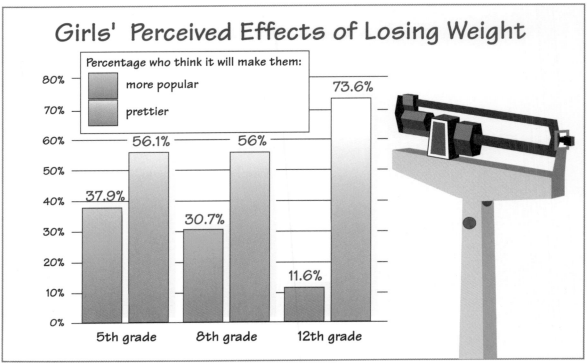

Girls' Perceived Effects of Losing Weight

Percentage who think it will make them:
- more popular
- prettier

5th grade: 37.9%, 56.1%
8th grade: 30.7%, 56%
12th grade: 11.6%, 73.6%

SOURCE: National Center on Addiction and Substance Abuse, *The Formative Years: Pathways to Substance Abuse Among Girls and Young Women Ages 8–22, 2003*

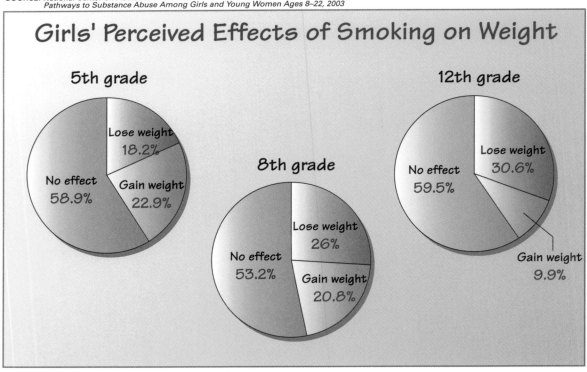

Girls' Perceived Effects of Smoking on Weight

5th grade: No effect 58.9%, Lose weight 18.2%, Gain weight 22.9%

8th grade: No effect 53.2%, Lose weight 26%, Gain weight 20.8%

12th grade: No effect 59.5%, Lose weight 30.6%, Gain weight 9.9%

SOURCE: National Center on Addiction and Substance Abuse, *The Formative Years: Pathways to Substance Abuse Among Girls and Young Women Ages 8–22, 2003*

Profile: Teenage Tobacco Users, 2003

Among teens, kids in the Midwest smoke more than any other kids.
(Percentage used in last month)

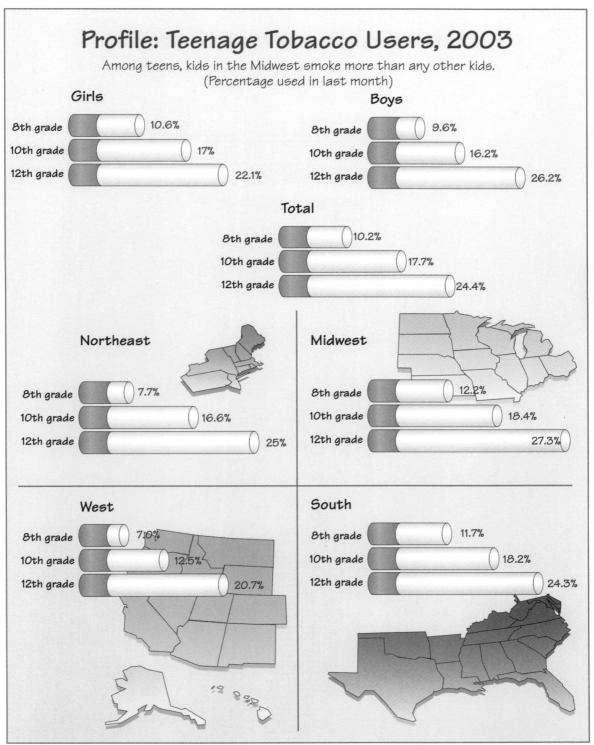

Girls

8th grade	10.6%
10th grade	17%
12th grade	22.1%

Boys

8th grade	9.6%
10th grade	16.2%
12th grade	26.2%

Total

8th grade	10.2%
10th grade	17.7%
12th grade	24.4%

Northeast

8th grade	7.7%
10th grade	16.6%
12th grade	25%

Midwest

8th grade	12.2%
10th grade	18.4%
12th grade	27.3%

West

8th grade	7.0%
10th grade	12.5%
12th grade	20.7%

South

8th grade	11.7%
10th grade	18.2%
12th grade	24.3%

Health

SOURCE: National Institute on Drug Abuse, *Monitoring the Future 2003*

Kids Are Getting Heavier

Since 1980, the proportion of overweight children ages 6–11 has doubled and the rate for teens has tripled. Being overweight is the most common childhood medical condition. (Percentage overweight in each age group)

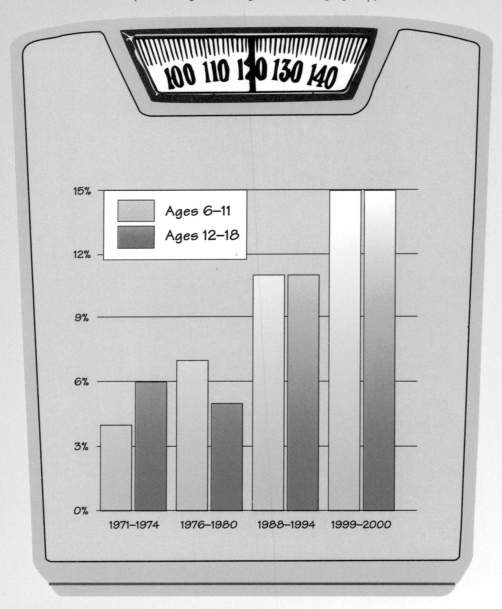

Ages 6–11
Ages 12–18

1971–1974   1976–1980   1988–1994   1999–2000

SOURCE: U.S. National Center for Health Statistics, Prevalence of Overweight Among Children and Adolescents

Quality of Kids' Diets as Measured by the Healthy Eating Index, 1999–2000

Percentage of kids whose diet

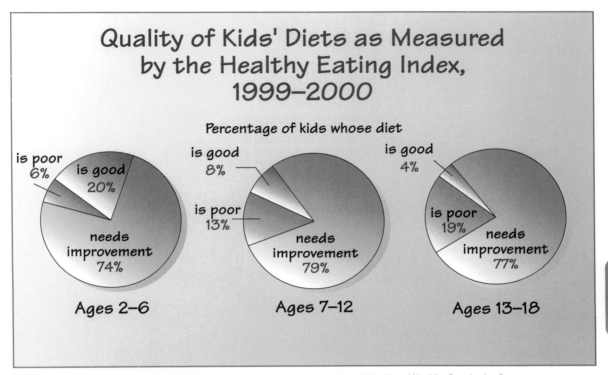

Ages 2–6 · Ages 7–12 · Ages 13–18

SOURCE: U.S. Department of Agriculture, Center for Nutrition Policy and Promotion, National Health and Nutrition Examination Survey

What Kids Eat, 2000

Percentage of kids meeting the dietary recommendations

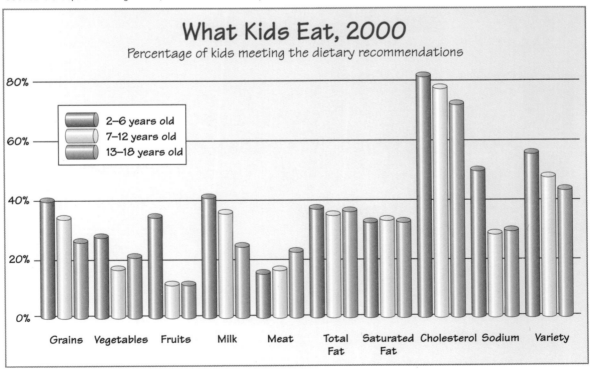

SOURCE: U.S. Department of Agriculture Center for Nutrition Policy and Promotion, National Health and Nutritional Examination Survey

Health

Health

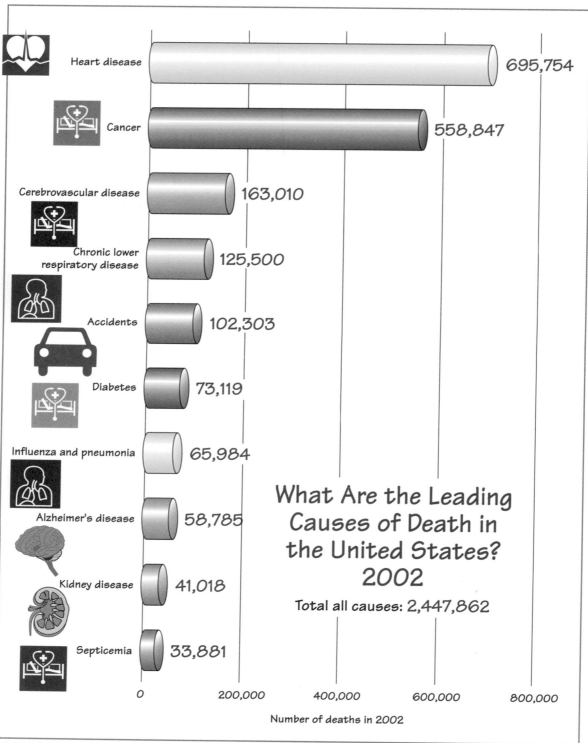

Heart disease — 695,754

Cancer — 558,847

Cerebrovascular disease — 163,010

Chronic lower respiratory disease — 125,500

Accidents — 102,303

Diabetes — 73,119

Influenza and pneumonia — 65,984

Alzheimer's disease — 58,785

Kidney disease — 41,018

Septicemia — 33,881

What Are the Leading Causes of Death in the United States? 2002

Total all causes: 2,447,862

0   200,000   400,000   600,000   800,000

Number of deaths in 2002

SOURCE: Centers for Disease Control and Prevention, *National Vital Statistics Report: Deaths Preliminary Data for 2002*

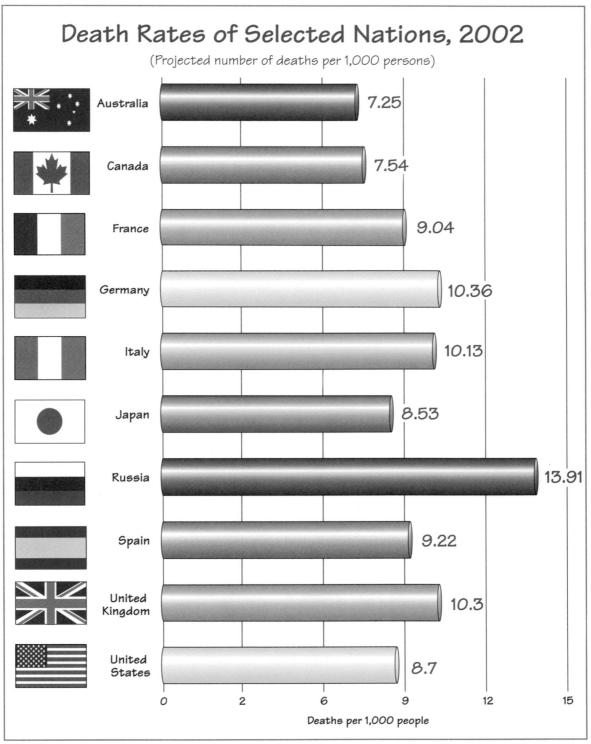

Death Rates of Selected Nations, 2002

(Projected number of deaths per 1,000 persons)

Nation	Deaths per 1,000
Australia	7.25
Canada	7.54
France	9.04
Germany	10.36
Italy	10.13
Japan	8.53
Russia	13.91
Spain	9.22
United Kingdom	10.3
United States	8.7

Deaths per 1,000 people

0   2   6   9   12   15

Health

SOURCE: *CIA World Factbook 2002*

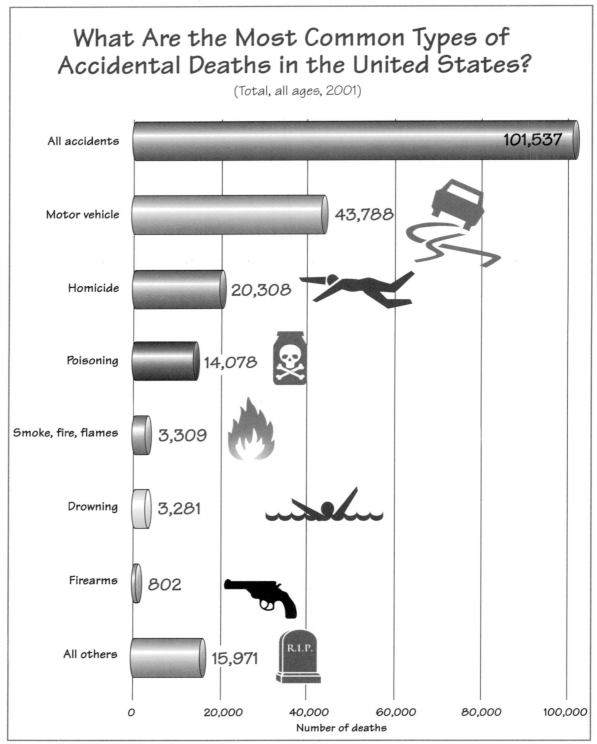

What Are the Most Common Types of Accidental Deaths in the United States?

(Total, all ages, 2001)

Type	Number of deaths
All accidents	101,537
Motor vehicle	43,788
Homicide	20,308
Poisoning	14,078
Smoke, fire, flames	3,309
Drowning	3,281
Firearms	802
All others	15,971

Number of deaths

SOURCE: U.S. National Center for Health Statistics, *Vital Statistics of the United States*

What Are the Most Common Causes Teenage Deaths in the United States?

(Ages 15–24, 2002)

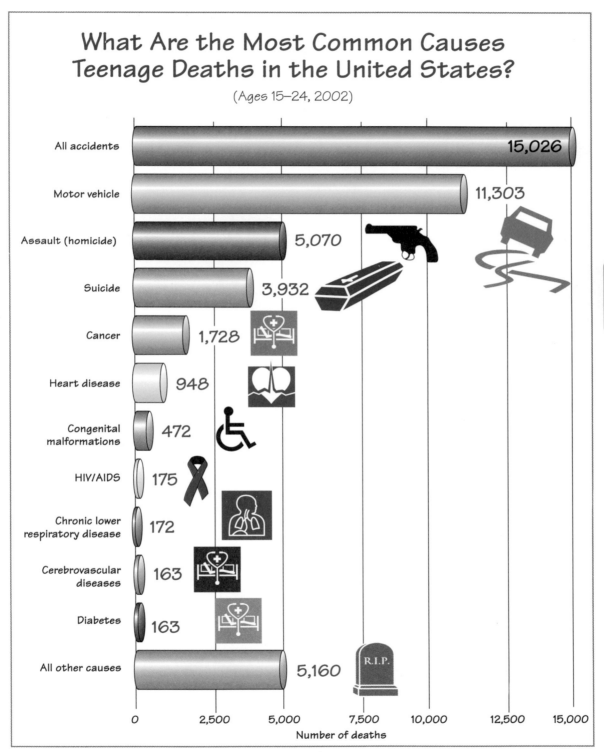

Cause	Number of deaths
All accidents	15,026
Motor vehicle	11,303
Assault (homicide)	5,070
Suicide	3,932
Cancer	1,728
Heart disease	948
Congenital malformations	472
HIV/AIDS	175
Chronic lower respiratory disease	172
Cerebrovascular diseases	163
Diabetes	163
All other causes	5,160

Number of deaths

Health

SOURCE: U.S. National Center for Health Statistics, *Vital Statistics of the United States*

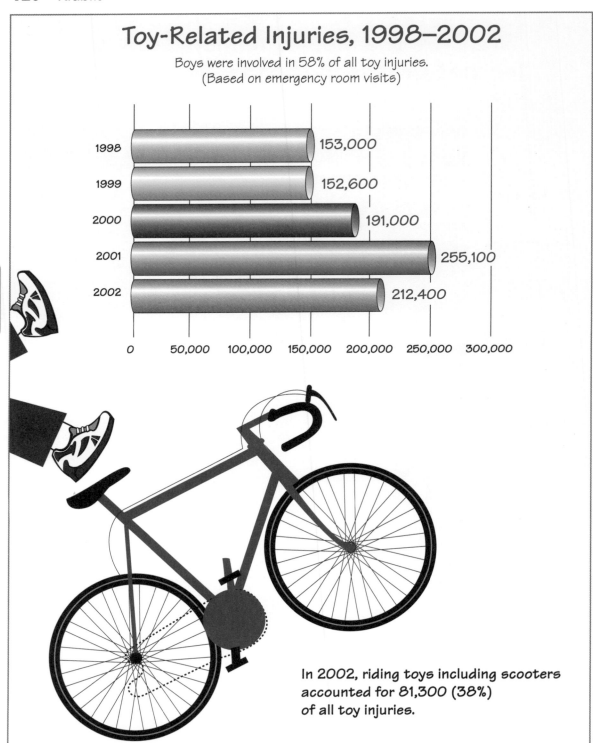

Toy-Related Injuries, 1998–2002

Boys were involved in 58% of all toy injuries.
(Based on emergency room visits)

Year	Injuries
1998	153,000
1999	152,600
2000	191,000
2001	255,100
2002	212,400

0   50,000   100,000   150,000   200,000   250,000   300,000

In 2002, riding toys including scooters accounted for 81,300 (38%) of all toy injuries.

SOURCE: U.S. Consumer Product Safety Commission National Electronic Injury Surveillance System

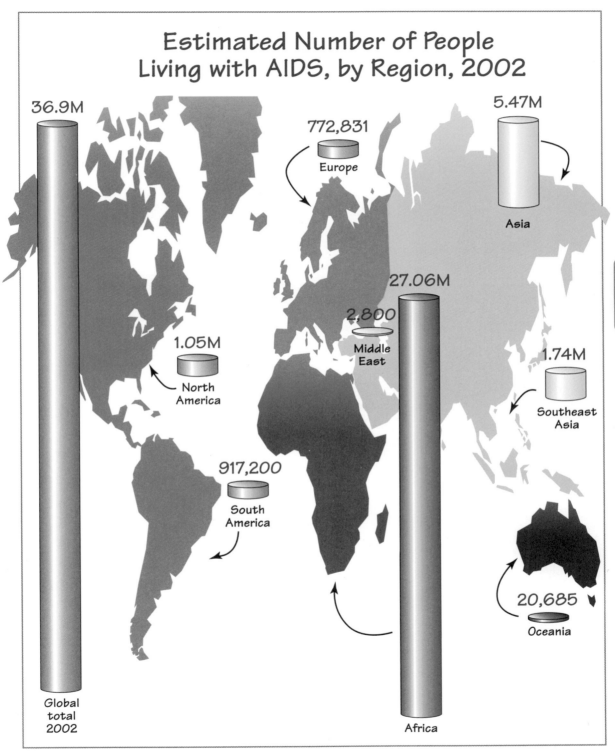

Estimated Number of People Living with AIDS, by Region, 2002

36.9M
Global total 2002

772,831
Europe

5.47M
Asia

27.06M
Africa

2,800
Middle East

1.05M
North America

1.74M
Southeast Asia

917,200
South America

20,685
Oceania

Health

SOURCE: *CIA World Factbook 2002*

How Many Kids Have AIDS?

(United States patients under 13 years old, as of the end of 2002, with probable cause)

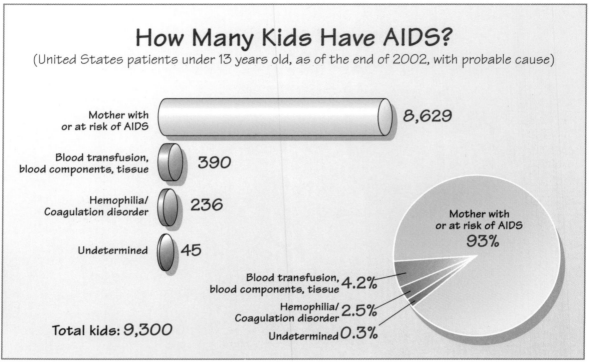

Mother with
or at risk of AIDS — 8,629

Blood transfusion,
blood components, tissue — 390

Hemophilia/
Coagulation disorder — 236

Undetermined — 45

Total kids: 9,300

Mother with
or at risk of AIDS
93%

Blood transfusion,
blood components, tissue 4.2%

Hemophilia/
Coagulation disorder 2.5%

Undetermined 0.3%

SOURCE: Centers for Disease Control and Prevention, *HIV/AIDS Surveillance Report*

Which States Have the Highest AIDS Populations?

(Cumulative number of AIDS cases as of December 2002)

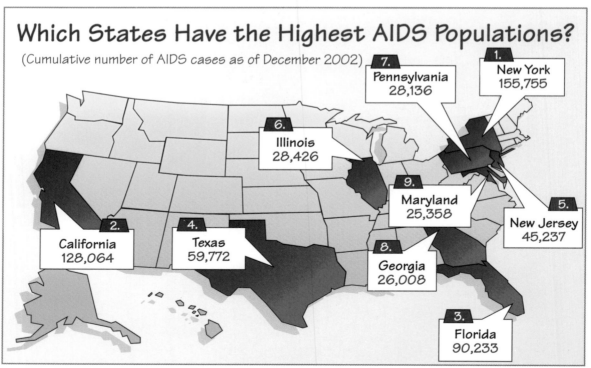

7. Pennsylvania
28,136

1. New York
155,755

6. Illinois
28,426

9. Maryland
25,358

5. New Jersey
45,237

2. California
128,064

4. Texas
59,772

8. Georgia
26,008

3. Florida
90,233

SOURCE: Centers for Disease Control and Prevention, *HIV/AIDS Surveillance Report*

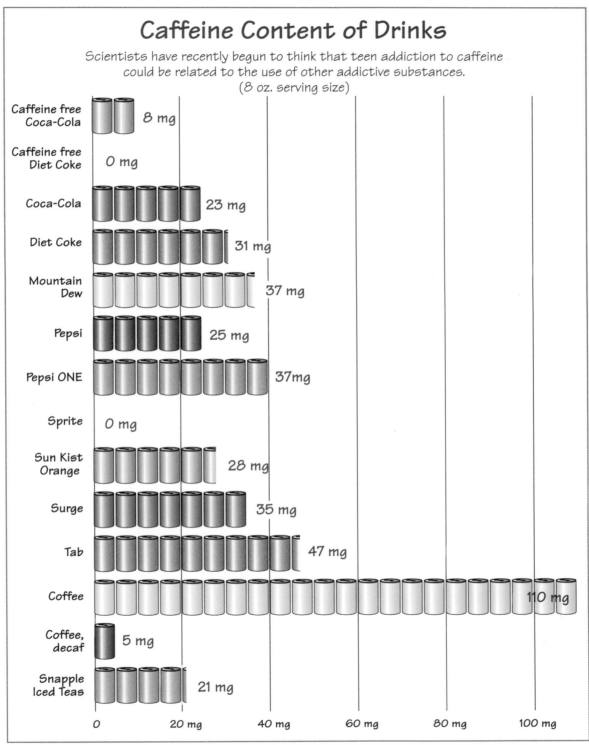

Caffeine Content of Drinks

Scientists have recently begun to think that teen addiction to caffeine could be related to the use of other addictive substances.
(8 oz. serving size)

Drink	Caffeine
Caffeine free Coca-Cola	8 mg
Caffeine free Diet Coke	0 mg
Coca-Cola	23 mg
Diet Coke	31 mg
Mountain Dew	37 mg
Pepsi	25 mg
Pepsi ONE	37mg
Sprite	0 mg
Sun Kist Orange	28 mg
Surge	35 mg
Tab	47 mg
Coffee	110 mg
Coffee, decaf	5 mg
Snapple Iced Teas	21 mg

0   20 mg   40 mg   60 mg   80 mg   100 mg

Health

SOURCE: National Sleep Foundation

Recreation

Kids have lots of free time—and lots of cool and exciting ways to fill it! Sports, games, dancing, amusement parks, movies and TV, hanging out with friends, talking on the phone—these are just a few of the things that kids do to relax and have fun.

Some recreational activities are more fun when done as part of a group, and kids are super joiners. About 2.9 million boys belong to the Boy Scouts of America. Almost 2.9 million girls are members of Girl Scouts of the USA. Sports teams, school bands, 4-H clubs, and religious groups are other organizations that attract millions of young people each year.

Taking trips with the family are also popular recreations. In fact, vacations are the best-loved activities of 52% of kids ages 7 to 12! Some vacations include long-distance trips to see famous places such as national parks, historic monuments, and Disney World. Other vacations are highlighted by shorter family activities, such as outings to local beaches or afternoons spent learning how to fish.

Kidbits Tidbits
- A survey of teens in 26 countries found that 93% enjoyed watching TV but only 76% enjoyed playing sports.
- Bowling is among the most popular recreational activities. About 91 million Americans age 5 and older bowl each year.
- Americans spend more than $25 billion a year on boating.
- More than 14 million people visited the Magic Kingdom at Walt Disney World in 2002.

Some activities are more popular with girls than boys, and vice versa. Boys and girls participate in swimming, bowling, and tennis in about equal numbers. But fishing and billiards are much more popular with boys. Horseback riding and volleyball, however, are more popular with girls. Age and finances also play roles in determining people's recreational favorites. More kids than adults play soccer—but more adults than kids can pay the fees required to ski and play golf.

People of all ages can have fun—and get a lot of satisfaction—while helping others. More than half of the kids in grades 6 through 12 are involved in some kind of volunteer service. For example, a Florida boy organized a program to deliver unused school cafeteria food to poor people. A Boy Scout troop grew vegetables for a homeless shelter. Many teens carry out conservation projects, teach younger kids to read, or assist the elderly and people with disabilities. Teens say that one of the main reasons they lend a helping hand to others is because they feel compassion for people in need.

Of course, not all recreation is for a noble cause. Some of the most popular pastimes in America include going to the movies and watching TV and videos. In fact, about 75% of the United States population says they exercise and go to the movies with much of their free time. For kids ages 7–12, movies and TV are ranked behind vacations, outdoor play, and listening to music as favorites.

Kidbits Tidbits
- Musical performances draw over 30 million attendees a year.
- Almost 50% of kids in grades 6 through 12 are involved in some kind of volunteer service.
- Teens who are asked to volunteer are much more likely to do so than teens who aren't asked.
- Each year, Americans donate about 15 hours a month to help each other and their communities.

Recreation

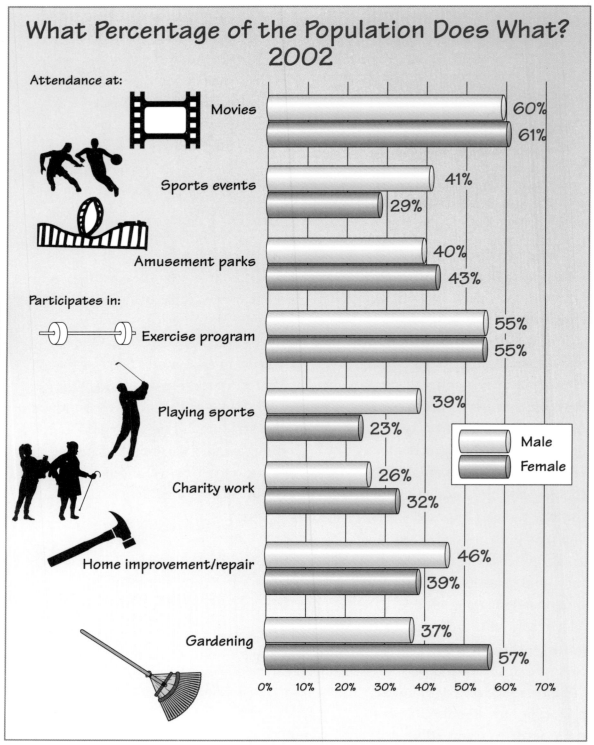

What Percentage of the Population Does What? 2002

Attendance at:

Movies — 60% (Male), 61% (Female)

Sports events — 41% (Male), 29% (Female)

Amusement parks — 40% (Male), 43% (Female)

Participates in:

Exercise program — 55% (Male), 55% (Female)

Playing sports — 39% (Male), 23% (Female)

Charity work — 26% (Male), 32% (Female)

Home improvement/repair — 46% (Male), 39% (Female)

Gardening — 37% (Male), 57% (Female)

Male
Female

0% 10% 20% 30% 40% 50% 60% 70%

SOURCE: U.S. National Endowment for the Arts, *Survey of Public Participation in the Arts, 2002*

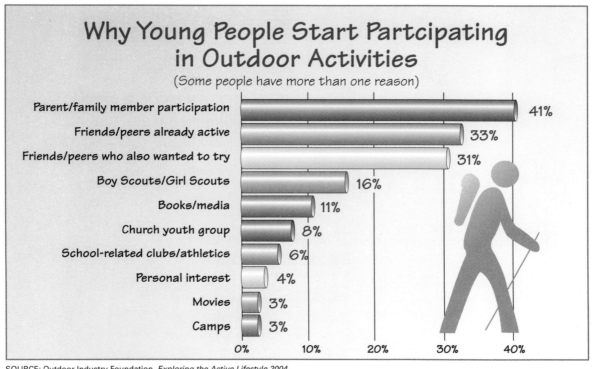

Why Young People Start Partcipating in Outdoor Activities

(Some people have more than one reason)

Reason	Percent
Parent/family member participation	41%
Friends/peers already active	33%
Friends/peers who also wanted to try	31%
Boy Scouts/Girl Scouts	16%
Books/media	11%
Church youth group	8%
School-related clubs/athletics	6%
Personal interest	4%
Movies	3%
Camps	3%

SOURCE: Outdoor Industry Foundation, *Exploring the Active Lifestyle 2004*

Why People Stop Partcipating in Outdoor Activities

Reason	Percent
Too busy	21%
Location not convenient	12%
Job got in the way	10%
Injuries/health reasons	10%
School commitments	8%
Lost interest/desire	7%
Pregnancy/birth of a child	6%
Family commitments	6%
Don't have equipment	5%
Got married	4%
Got driver's license/car	4%
Felt too old	1%

SOURCE: Outdoor Industry Foundation, *Exploring the Active Lifestyle 2004*

Recreation

Recreation

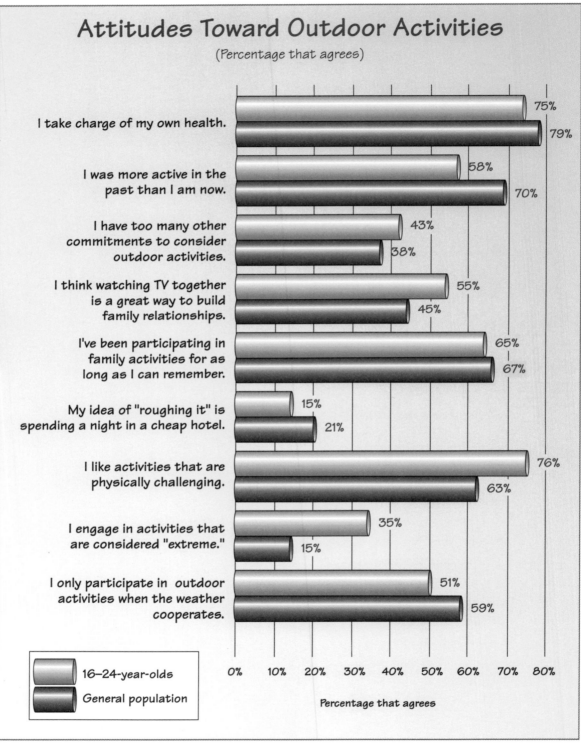

Attitudes Toward Outdoor Activities
(Percentage that agrees)

I take charge of my own health. — 75% / 79%

I was more active in the past than I am now. — 58% / 70%

I have too many other commitments to consider outdoor activities. — 43% / 38%

I think watching TV together is a great way to build family relationships. — 55% / 45%

I've been participating in family activities for as long as I can remember. — 65% / 67%

My idea of "roughing it" is spending a night in a cheap hotel. — 15% / 21%

I like activities that are physically challenging. — 76% / 63%

I engage in activities that are considered "extreme." — 35% / 15%

I only participate in outdoor activities when the weather cooperates. — 51% / 59%

16–24-year-olds
General population

Percentage that agrees

SOURCE: Outdoor Industry Foundation, *Exploring the Active Lifestyle 2004*

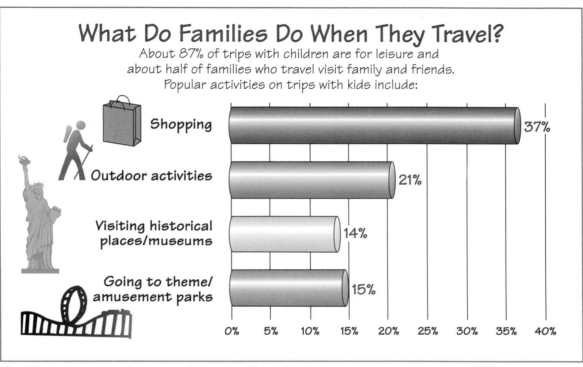

What Do Families Do When They Travel?

About 87% of trips with children are for leisure and
about half of families who travel visit family and friends.
Popular activities on trips with kids include:

- Shopping — 37%
- Outdoor activities — 21%
- Visiting historical places/museums — 14%
- Going to theme/amusement parks — 15%

SOURCE: Travel Industry Association of America, *Domestic Travel Report, 2003*

Recreation

Membership in the Boy Scouts and Girl Scouts

(In millions)

Members in millions

- Boy Scouts — 2.9M
- Girl Scouts — 2.9M

SOURCE: Boy Scouts of America; Girl Scouts of the USA

Best Roller Coasters in America, 2003

Wood		Year built
Raven	Holiday World, Santa Claus, IN	1995
Shivering Timbers	Michigan's Adventure, Muskegon, MI	1998
Boulder Dash	Lake Compounce, Bristol, CT	2000
Steel		
Superman Ride of Steel	Six Flags New England, Agawan, MA	2000
Millennium Force	Cedar Point, Sandusky, OH	2000
Magnum XL-200	Cedar Point, Sandusky, OH	1989

SOURCES: *Amusement Today*

Sports Participation over Time

As people get older, they often drop activites they did when they were younger, usually because they have no time for them.

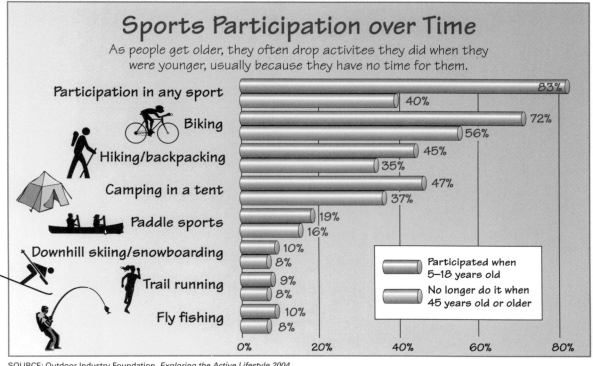

- Participation in any sport — 83% / 40%
- Biking — 72% / 56%
- Hiking/backpacking — 45% / 35%
- Camping in a tent — 47% / 37%
- Paddle sports — 19% / 16%
- Downhill skiing/snowboarding — 10% / 8%
- Trail running — 9% / 8%
- Fly fishing — 10% / 8%

Legend:
- Participated when 5–18 years old
- No longer do it when 45 years old or older

Recreation

SOURCE: Outdoor Industry Foundation, *Exploring the Active Lifestyle 2004*

Top 5 Amusement/Theme Parks in America, 2002

(Ranked by attendance)

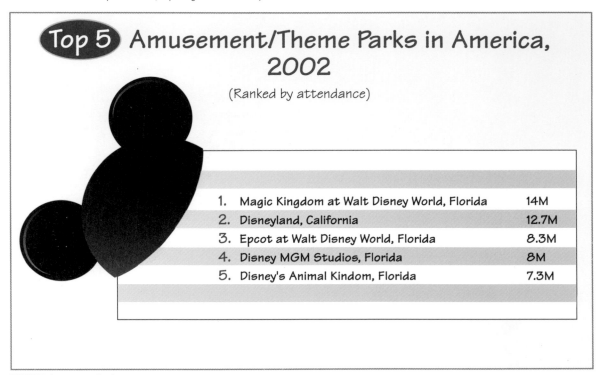

1.	Magic Kingdom at Walt Disney World, Florida	14M
2.	Disneyland, California	12.7M
3.	Epcot at Walt Disney World, Florida	8.3M
4.	Disney MGM Studios, Florida	8M
5.	Disney's Animal Kindom, Florida	7.3M

SOURCE: *Amusement Business*

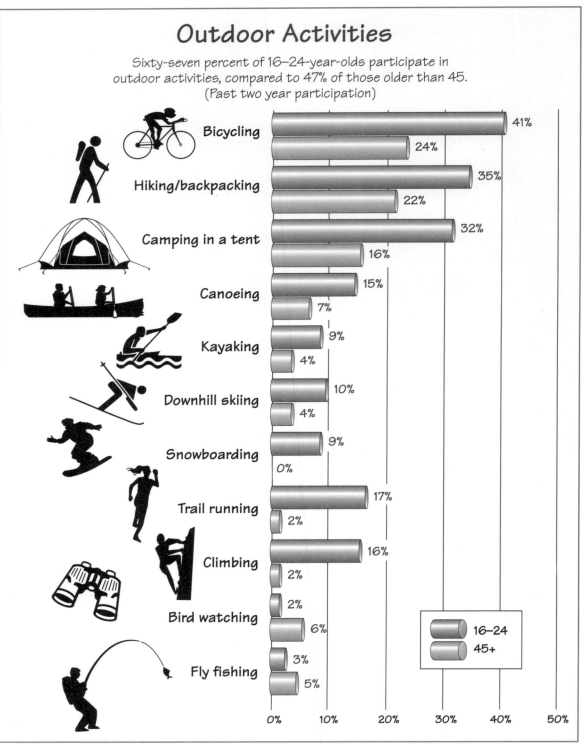

Outdoor Activities

Sixty-seven percent of 16–24-year-olds participate in outdoor activities, compared to 47% of those older than 45. (Past two year participation)

Activity	16–24	45+
Bicycling	41%	24%
Hiking/backpacking	35%	22%
Camping in a tent	32%	16%
Canoeing	15%	7%
Kayaking	9%	4%
Downhill skiing	10%	4%
Snowboarding	9%	0%
Trail running	17%	2%
Climbing	16%	2%
Bird watching	2%	6%
Fly fishing	3%	5%

0% 10% 20% 30% 40% 50%

SOURCE: Outdoor Industry Foundation, *Exploring the Active Lifestyle 2004*

Recreation

Favorite Outdoor Activites for Families

(Survey of parents with children ages 4–14)
Seventy-five percent of parents believe that participating
in outdoor activities strengthens family relationships.

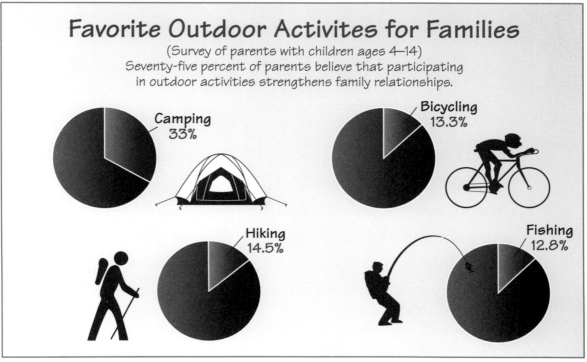

Camping
33%

Bicycling
13.3%

Hiking
14.5%

Fishing
12.8%

Recreation

SOURCE: REI Survey by Leisure Trends 2002

Where People Stay When Traveling

When Americans travel, about half of them go for three or more nights. The average
traveler spends three nights a year in a hotel, motel, or bed-and-breakfast.

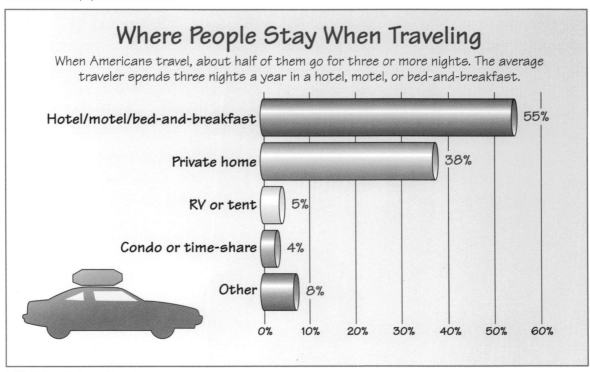

Hotel/motel/bed-and-breakfast — 55%

Private home — 38%

RV or tent — 5%

Condo or time-share — 4%

Other — 8%

0%   10%   20%   30%   40%   50%   60%

SOURCE: Travel Industry of America

Music

Music lovers today have lots of cool opportunities to hear their favorite groups on CDs, videos, television, and radio; in concert halls; and at live music festivals—even on the Internet! These days, it's not unusual for a CD to sell millions of copies in a matter of weeks, or for a concert to attract upwards of 100,000 fans!

Rock is by far the most popular type of music among young people, but many other kinds of music also enjoy wide appeal. Country, rap, pop, hip-hop, rhythm-and-blues, folk, gospel, jazz, and even classical all have solid followings. Some of American kids' favorite musicians include pop sensation Britney Spears, blues singer Jonny Lang, and the heart-throb Justin Timberlake.

Americans spent a whopping $12.6 billion on recorded music in 2002. Out of that, American teens are the biggest customers: people ages 15 to 19 accounted for about 14% of total sales; kids age 10 to 14 added another 8.7%. CDs are the most popular recorded music format, with 90.5% of 2002 sales. Cassettes were second with 2.4%.

Kidbits Tidbits

- In 2002, kids 15–19 accounted for 14% of all recorded music sales; kids 10–14 added another 8.7%.
- In 2002, rock was the most popular type of music sold, accounting for 24.7% of all sales. Rap/hip-hop was next, with 13.8%.
- In the 1960s, about 45 new albums were released each week. By 2003, an average of 25 music videos were released weekly.
- In 2000, the RIAA announced that Garth Brooks was the fastest-selling solo artist in music history. He sold 105 million albums from 1990 through 2003.

Young people's favorites constantly change. What's "hot" with kids today won't be "cool" with kids tomorrow. But, while some musicians are one-hit wonders, others keep going for years and years. For example, Elvis Presley records are still selling strong more than 25 years after his death. As of the end of 2003, the best-selling albums of all time in the United States were *Their Greatest Hits* from the Eagles (28 million) and Michael Jackson's *Thriller* (26 million copies). And, though the Rolling Stones have been around for over 30 years, they managed to gross $87.9 million on the American concert tour in 2002.

There are radios in 99% of American homes. Each weekday, 95% of Americans over age 12 listen to radio for an average of 3 hours. There are over 13,000 radio stations, with country music stations the most common (2,100).

Enjoying music isn't always a couch potato activity. Millions of kids sing and play instruments. And when music has a good beat, everyone wants to jump up and dance. Dance crazes come and go. The 1970s was disco. The 1980's was slam-dancing. The mid-1990s was macarena time. Any guesses which dances kids will be doing 10 years from now and what kind of music will be #1 on the charts?

Kidbits Tidbits

- About one third of all music recordings are bought in record stores; about half are bought in discount stores such as Wal-Mart and K-Mart.
- Elvis Presley's records have sold more than 117.5 million copies, making him the most successful solo recording artist ever.
- The best-selling single of all time is Elton John's *Candle in the Wind*, re-released when Princess Diana died in 1997.
- There were 13,304 commercial radio stations in 2003. Some 16% played country music, while 13% were news/talk stations.
- Radios are everywhere: Nearly every car in America has one and 99% of American homes own at least one, with the average American home having five.

Music

Music Piracy

It is estimated that one in three music discs sold in 2002 was pirated. More than 50 of the most popular songs of 2002 were pirated before they were even released.

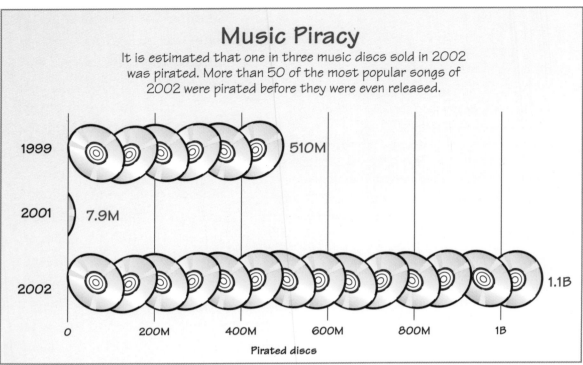

SOURCE: IFPI, "Commercial Piracy Report 2003"

What Is Being Pirated? 2002

More than 50 million pirated music discs, worth $4.6 billion were seized in 2002.

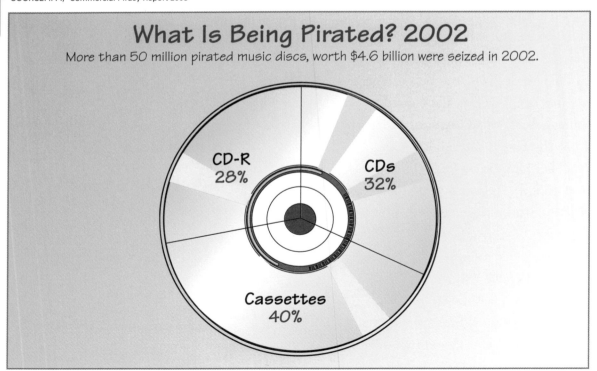

SOURCE: IFPI, "Commercial Piracy Report 2003"

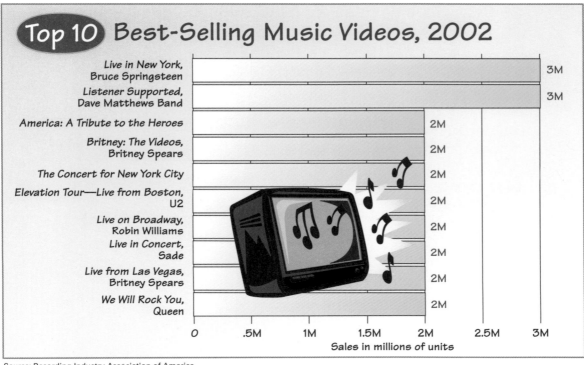

Top 10 Best-Selling Music Videos, 2002

Live in New York, Bruce Springsteen	3M
Listener Supported, Dave Matthews Band	3M
America: A Tribute to the Heroes	2M
Britney: The Videos, Britney Spears	2M
The Concert for New York City	2M
Elevation Tour—Live from Boston, U2	2M
Live on Broadway, Robin Williams	2M
Live in Concert, Sade	2M
Live from Las Vegas, Britney Spears	2M
We Will Rock You, Queen	2M

Sales in millions of units

Source: Recording Industry Association of America

Music

Top 5 Solo Artists with Most Album Sales in History
(Through November 2003)

1. Elvis Presley — 117.5M
2. Garth Brooks — 105M
3. Billy Joel — 78.5M
4. Barbra Streisand — 71.5M
5. Elton John — 67.5M

SOURCE: Recording Industry Association of America

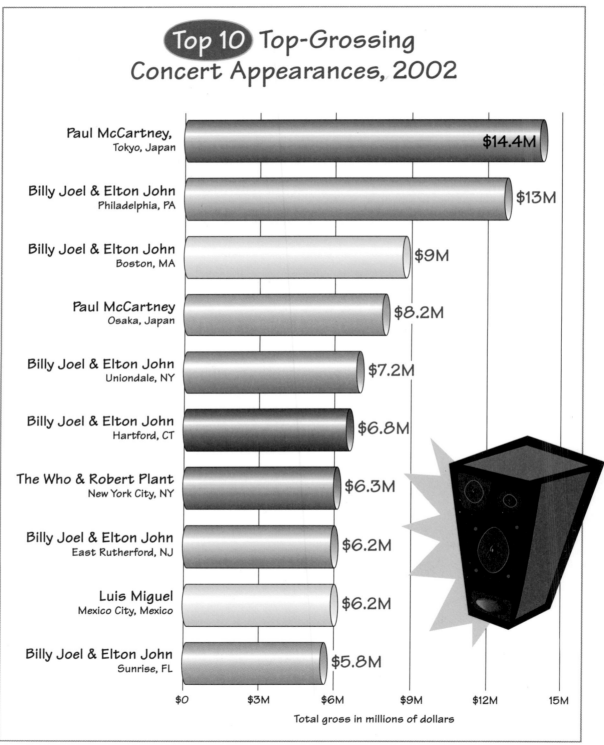

Top 10 Top-Grossing Concert Appearances, 2002

Artist	Location	Gross
Paul McCartney	Tokyo, Japan	$14.4M
Billy Joel & Elton John	Philadelphia, PA	$13M
Billy Joel & Elton John	Boston, MA	$9M
Paul McCartney	Osaka, Japan	$8.2M
Billy Joel & Elton John	Uniondale, NY	$7.2M
Billy Joel & Elton John	Hartford, CT	$6.8M
The Who & Robert Plant	New York City, NY	$6.3M
Billy Joel & Elton John	East Rutherford, NJ	$6.2M
Luis Miguel	Mexico City, Mexico	$6.2M
Billy Joel & Elton John	Sunrise, FL	$5.8M

Total gross in millions of dollars

Music

SOURCE: Billboard

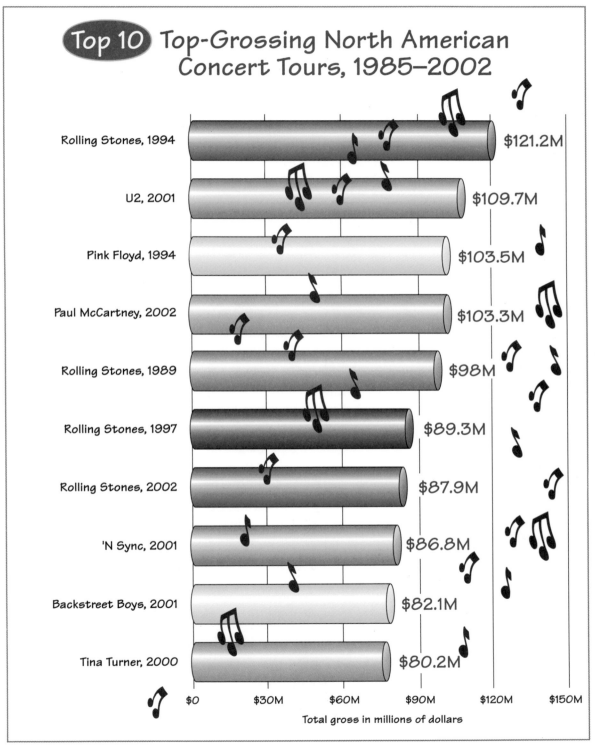

Top 10 Top-Grossing North American Concert Tours, 1985–2002

Tour	Total gross
Rolling Stones, 1994	$121.2M
U2, 2001	$109.7M
Pink Floyd, 1994	$103.5M
Paul McCartney, 2002	$103.3M
Rolling Stones, 1989	$98M
Rolling Stones, 1997	$89.3M
Rolling Stones, 2002	$87.9M
'N Sync, 2001	$86.8M
Backstreet Boys, 2001	$82.1M
Tina Turner, 2000	$80.2M

Total gross in millions of dollars

$0 $30M $60M $90M $120M $150M

Music

SOURCE: Pollstar

Music

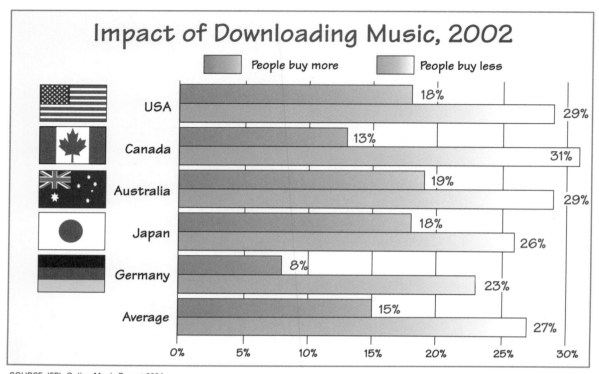

Impact of Downloading Music, 2002

People buy more | People buy less

Country	People buy more	People buy less
USA	18%	29%
Canada	13%	31%
Australia	19%	29%
Japan	18%	26%
Germany	8%	23%
Average	15%	27%

SOURCE: IFPI, *Online Music Report 2004*

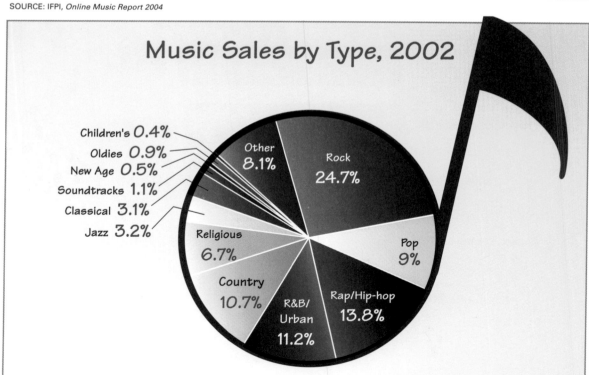

Music Sales by Type, 2002

Children's 0.4%
Oldies 0.9%
New Age 0.5%
Soundtracks 1.1%
Classical 3.1%
Jazz 3.2%
Other 8.1%
Rock 24.7%
Religious 6.7%
Pop 9%
Country 10.7%
R&B/Urban 11.2%
Rap/Hip-hop 13.8%

SOURCE: Recording Industry Association of America

Music Sales by Format, 2002

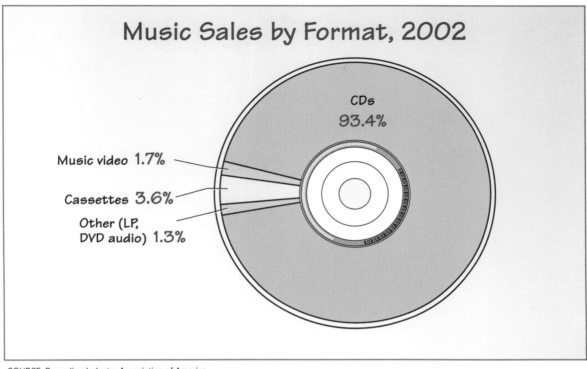

CDs
93.4%

Music video 1.7%

Cassettes 3.6%

Other (LP, DVD audio) 1.3%

SOURCE: Recording Industry Association of America

Music

How Much Music Do Kids Buy?

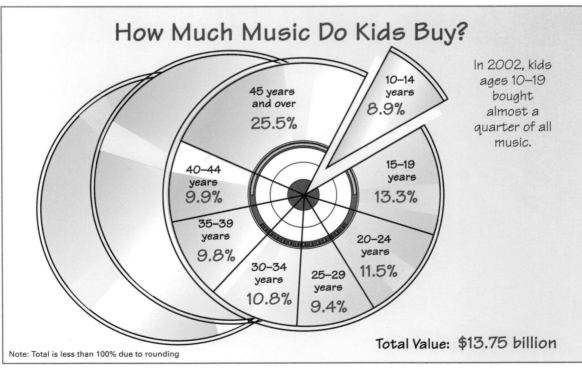

45 years and over
25.5%

10–14 years
8.9%

In 2002, kids ages 10–19 bought almost a quarter of all music.

40–44 years
9.9%

15–19 years
13.3%

35–39 years
9.8%

20–24 years
11.5%

30–34 years
10.8%

25–29 years
9.4%

Note: Total is less than 100% due to rounding

Total Value: $13.75 billion

SOURCE: Recording Industry Association of America

Music

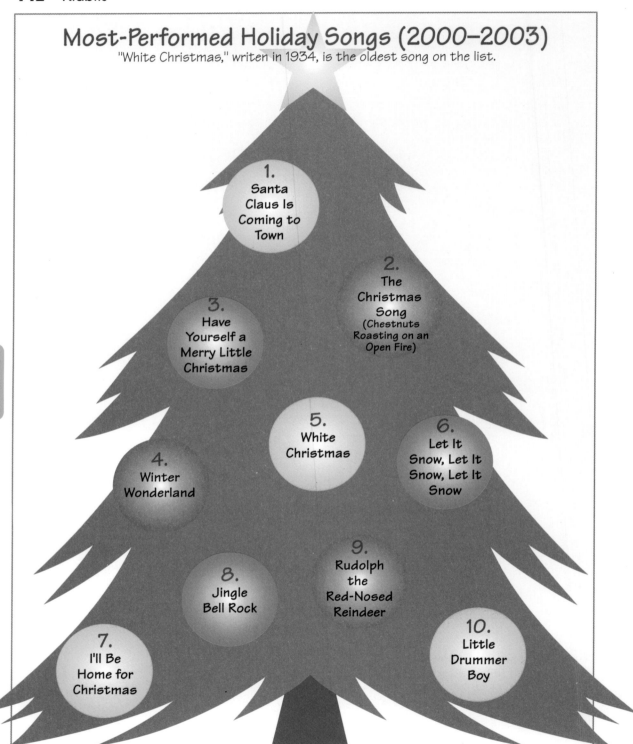

Most-Performed Holiday Songs (2000–2003)
"White Christmas," written in 1934, is the oldest song on the list.

1. Santa Claus Is Coming to Town

2. The Christmas Song (Chestnuts Roasting on an Open Fire)

3. Have Yourself a Merry Little Christmas

5. White Christmas

6. Let It Snow, Let It Snow, Let It Snow

4. Winter Wonderland

9. Rudolph the Red-Nosed Reindeer

8. Jingle Bell Rock

10. Little Drummer Boy

7. I'll Be Home for Christmas

SOURCE: American Society of Composers, Authors and Publishers (ASCAP)

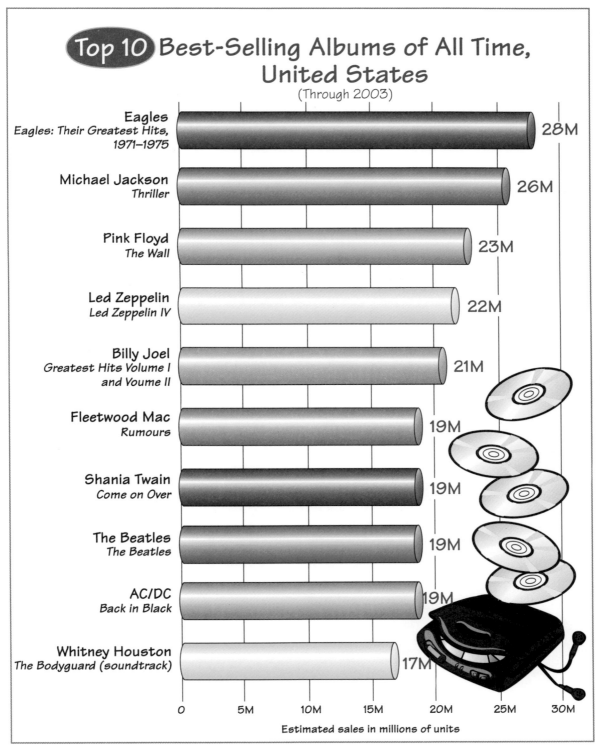

Top 10 Best-Selling Albums of All Time, United States
(Through 2003)

Eagles
Eagles: Their Greatest Hits, 1971–1975 — 28M

Michael Jackson
Thriller — 26M

Pink Floyd
The Wall — 23M

Led Zeppelin
Led Zeppelin IV — 22M

Billy Joel
Greatest Hits Volume I and Voume II — 21M

Fleetwood Mac
Rumours — 19M

Shania Twain
Come on Over — 19M

The Beatles
The Beatles — 19M

AC/DC
Back in Black — 19M

Whitney Houston
The Bodyguard (soundtrack) — 17M

Estimated sales in millions of units
(0, 5M, 10M, 15M, 20M, 25M, 30M)

Music

SOURCE: Recording Industry Association of America

Top 5 Music Videos, 2002

Major record companies released more than 1,300 individual titles in 2002.

	Artist	Title
1.	Dave Matthews Band	*Live at Folson Field* (BMG)
2.	Paul McCartney	*Back in the U.S.* (EMI)
3.	Pink Floyd	*The Wall* (Sony)
4.	Linkin Park	*Frat Party at the Pancake Festival* (Warner)
5.	U2	*The Best of 1990–2000* (Universal)

Source: IFPI, *The Recording Industry in Numbers (RIN) 2003*

Top 5 Most Popular Kinds of U.S. Radio Stations, 2003

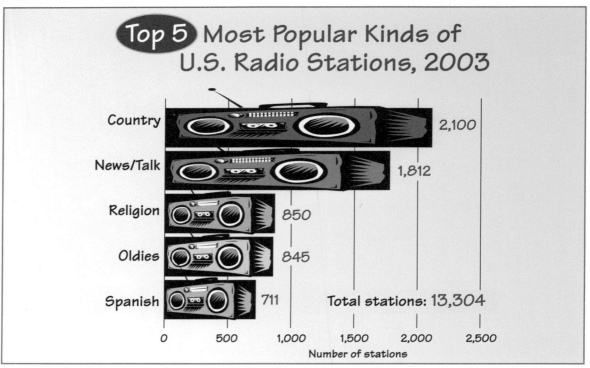

Country: 2,100
News/Talk: 1,812
Religion: 850
Oldies: 845
Spanish: 711

Total stations: 13,304

Number of stations

SOURCE: M Street Corporation

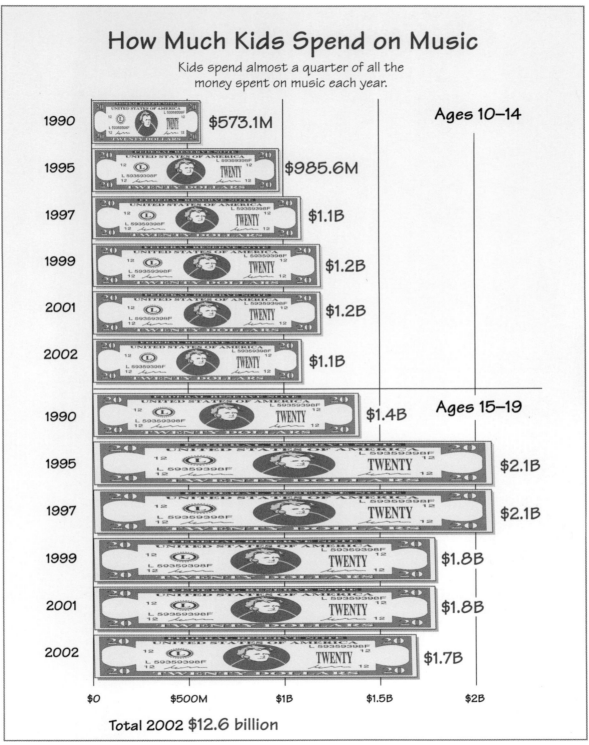

How Much Kids Spend on Music

Kids spend almost a quarter of all the
money spent on music each year.

Ages 10–14

1990	$573.1M
1995	$985.6M
1997	$1.1B
1999	$1.2B
2001	$1.2B
2002	$1.1B

Ages 15–19

1990	$1.4B
1995	$2.1B
1997	$2.1B
1999	$1.8B
2001	$1.8B
2002	$1.7B

$0 $500M $1B $1.5B $2B

Total 2002 $12.6 billion

Music

SOURCE: Recording Industry Association of America

Music

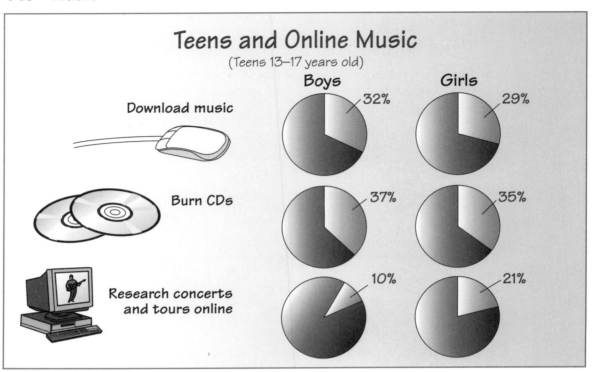

Teens and Online Music
(Teens 13–17 years old)

Boys   Girls

Download music — 32%   29%

Burn CDs — 37%   35%

Research concerts and tours online — 10%   21%

SOURCE: Jupiter Research, "Consmer Survey Report: Teen Music, 2003"

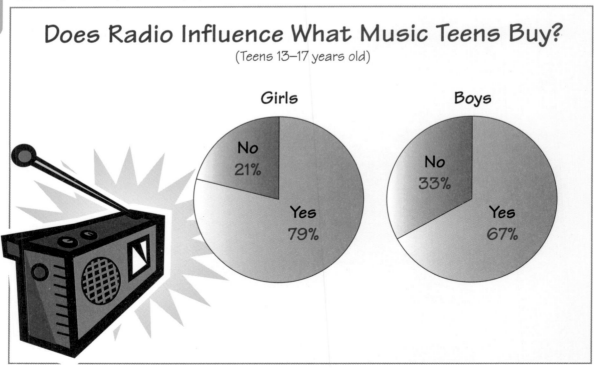

Does Radio Influence What Music Teens Buy?
(Teens 13–17 years old)

Girls   Boys

No 21% / Yes 79%   No 33% / Yes 67%

SOURCE: Jupiter Research, "Consumer Survey Report: Teen Music, 2003"

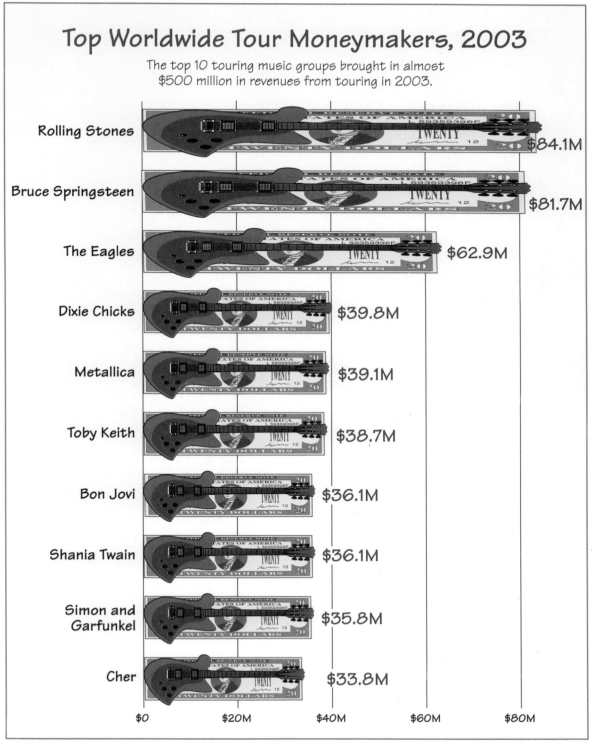

Top Worldwide Tour Moneymakers, 2003

The top 10 touring music groups brought in almost
$500 million in revenues from touring in 2003.

Rolling Stones — $84.1M

Bruce Springsteen — $81.7M

The Eagles — $62.9M

Dixie Chicks — $39.8M

Metallica — $39.1M

Toby Keith — $38.7M

Bon Jovi — $36.1M

Shania Twain — $36.1M

Simon and Garfunkel — $35.8M

Cher — $33.8M

$0 $20M $40M $60M $80M

Music

SOURCE: *Rolling Stone*

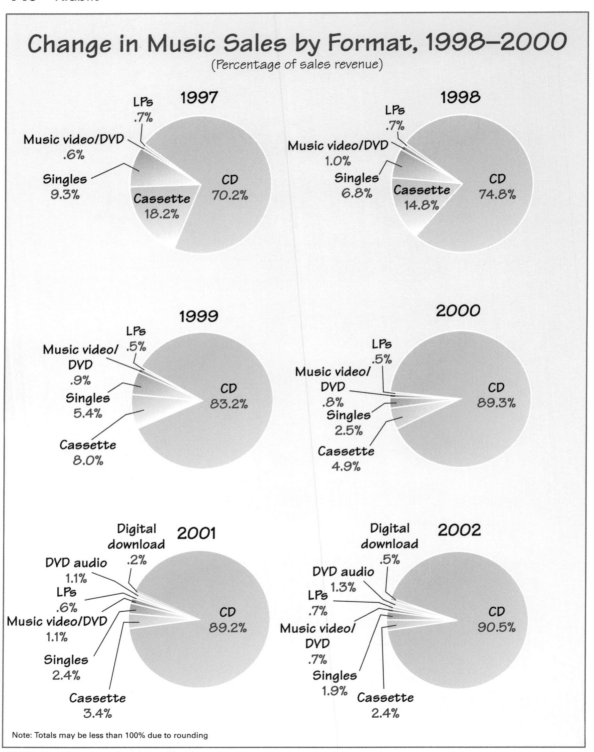

Change in Music Sales by Format, 1998–2000
(Percentage of sales revenue)

1997
- LPs .7%
- Music video/DVD .6%
- Singles 9.3%
- Cassette 18.2%
- CD 70.2%

1998
- LPs .7%
- Music video/DVD 1.0%
- Singles 6.8%
- Cassette 14.8%
- CD 74.8%

1999
- LPs .5%
- Music video/DVD .9%
- Singles 5.4%
- Cassette 8.0%
- CD 83.2%

2000
- LPs .5%
- Music video/DVD .8%
- Singles 2.5%
- Cassette 4.9%
- CD 89.3%

2001
- Digital download .2%
- DVD audio 1.1%
- LPs .6%
- Music video/DVD 1.1%
- Singles 2.4%
- Cassette 3.4%
- CD 89.2%

2002
- Digital download .5%
- DVD audio 1.3%
- LPs .7%
- Music video/DVD .7%
- Singles 1.9%
- Cassette 2.4%
- CD 90.5%

Note: Totals may be less than 100% due to rounding

SOURCE: Recording Industry Association of America

Music

Top-Selling Albums, 2003

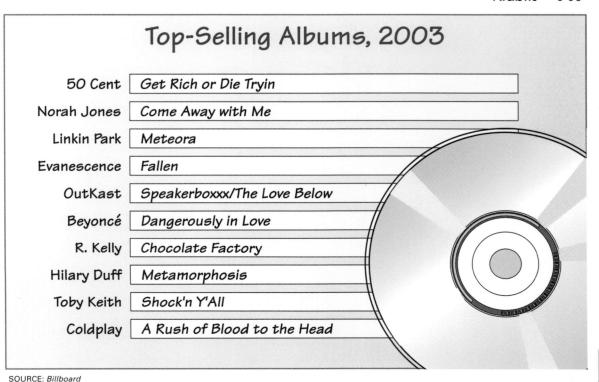

50 Cent	*Get Rich or Die Tryin*
Norah Jones	*Come Away with Me*
Linkin Park	*Meteora*
Evanescence	*Fallen*
OutKast	*Speakerboxxx/The Love Below*
Beyoncé	*Dangerously in Love*
R. Kelly	*Chocolate Factory*
Hilary Duff	*Metamorphosis*
Toby Keith	*Shock'n Y'All*
Coldplay	*A Rush of Blood to the Head*

SOURCE: *Billboard*

Where Music Is Bought

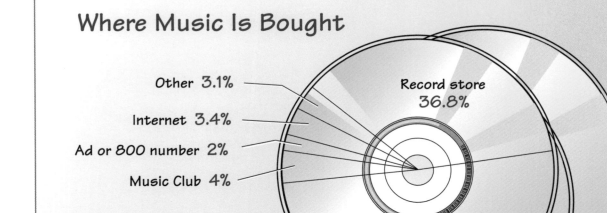

Other 3.1%

Internet 3.4%

Ad or 800 number 2%

Music Club 4%

Record store 36.8%

Other store 50.7%

SOURCE: Recording Industry Association of America

Music

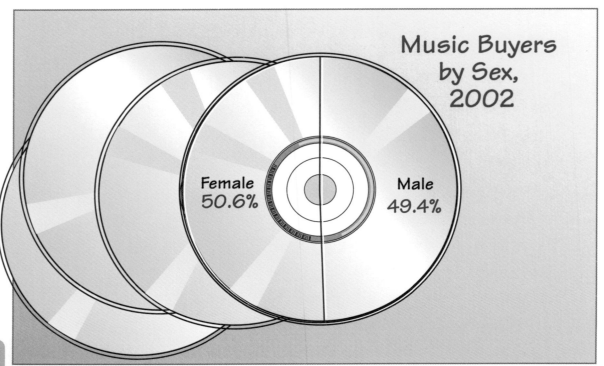

Music Buyers by Sex, 2002

Female 50.6%

Male 49.4%

SOURCE: Recording Industry Association of America

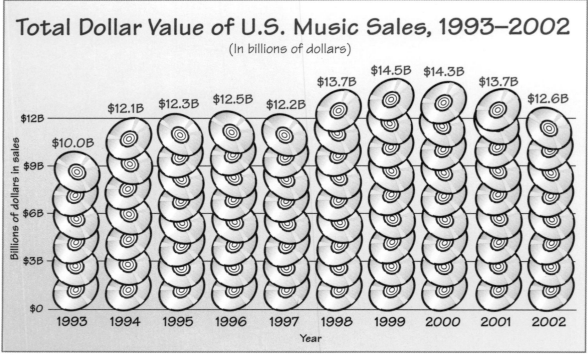

Total Dollar Value of U.S. Music Sales, 1993–2002
(In billions of dollars)

$10.0B $12.1B $12.3B $12.5B $12.2B $13.7B $14.5B $14.3B $13.7B $12.6B

Billions of dollars in sales

$12B

$9B

$6B

$3B

$0

1993   1994   1995   1996   1997   1998   1999   2000   2001   2002

Year

SOURCE: Recording Industry Association of America

MTV Video Music Awards, 1993–2003
Best Video

Year	Artist	Video
2003	Missy "Misdemeanor" Elliott	Work It
2002	Eminem	Without Me
2001	Christina Aguilera, Lil' Kim, Mya & Pink	Lady Marmalade
2000	Eminem	The Real Slim Shady
1999	Lauryn Hill	Doo-Wop (That Thing)
1998	Madonna	Ray of Light
1997	Jamiroquai	Virtual Insanity
1996	Smashing Pumpkins	Tonight, Tonight
1995	TLC	Waterfalls
1994	Aerosmith	Cryin'
1993	Pearl Jam	Jeremy

SOURCE: MTV

Music

MTV Video Music Awards, 1993–2003
Best Male Video

Year	Artist	Video
2003	Justin Timberlake	Cry Me A River
2002	Eminem	Without Me
2001	Moby, featuring Gwen Stefani	South Side
2000	Eminem	The Real Slim Shady
1999	Will Smith	Miami
1998	Will Smith	Just the Two of Us
1997	Beck	Devil's Haircut
1996	Beck	Where It's At
1995	Tom Petty and the Heartbreakers	You Don't Know How it Feels
1994	Tom Petty and the Heartbreakers	Mary Jane's Last Dance
1993	Lenny Kravitz	Are You Gonna Go My Way

SOURCE: MTV

MTV Video Music Awards, 1993–2003
Best Female Video

Year	Artist	Video
2003	Beyoncé Knowles	Crazy in Love
2002	Pink	Get the Party Started
2001	Eve, featuring Gwen Stefani	Let Me Blow Ya Mind
2000	Aaliyah	Try Again
1999	Lauryn Hill	Doo-Wop (That Thing)
1998	Madonna	Ray of Light
1997	Jewel	You Were Meant for Me
1996	Alanis Morissette	Ironic
1995	Madonna	Take a Bow
1994	Janet Jackson	If
1993	k.d. lang	Constant Craving

SOURCE: MTV

MTV Video Music Awards, 1993–2003
Best Group Video

Year	Artist	Video
2003	Coldplay	The Scientist
2002	No Doubt, featuring Bounty Killer	Hey Baby
2001	'N Sync	Pop
2000	Blink-182	All the Small Things
1999	TLC	No Secrets
1998	Backstreet Boys	Everybody
1997	No Doubt	Don't Speak
1996	Foo Fighters	Big Me
1995	TLC	Waterfalls
1994	Aerosmith	Cryin'
1993	Pearl Jam	Jeremy

SOURCE: MTV

Music

MTV Video Music Awards, 1993–2003
Best New Artist in a Video

Year	Artist	Video
2003	50 Cent	In Da Club
2002	Avril Lavigne	Complicated
2001	Alicia Keys	Fallin'
2000	Macy Gray	I Try
1999	Eminem	My Name Is
1998	Natalie Imbruglia	Torn
1997	Fiona Apple	Sleep to Dream
1996	Alanis Morissette	Ironic
1995	Hootie & the Blowfish	Hold My Hand
1994	Counting Crows	Mr. Jones
1993	Stone Temple Pilots	Plush

SOURCE: MTV

Grammy Winners, 1993–2003
Record of the Year

Year	Artist	Record
2003	Coldplay	Clocks
2002	Norah Jones	Don't Know Why
2001	U2	Walk On
2000	U2	Beautiful Day
1999	Santana	Smooth
1998	Celine Dion	My Heart Will Go On
1997	Shawn Colvin	Sunny Came Home
1996	Eric Clapton	Change the World
1995	Seal	Kiss from a Rose
1994	Sheryl Crow	All I Wanna Do
1993	Whitney Houston	I Will Always Love You

SOURCE: National Academy of Recording Arts and Sciences

Grammy Winners, 1993–2003
Album of the Year

Year	Artist	Album
2003	OutKast	Speakerboxxx/ The Love Below
2002	Norah Jones	Come Away with Me
2001	Various artists	O Brother, Where Art Thou
2000	Steely Dan	Two Against Nature
1999	Santana	Supernatural
1998	Lauryn Hill	The Miseducation of Lauryn Hill
1997	Bob Dylan	Time Out of Mind
1996	Celine Dion	Falling into You
1995	Alanis Morissette	Jagged Little Pill
1994	Tony Bennett	MTV Unplugged
1993	Whitney Houston	The Bodyguard

SOURCE: National Academy of Recording Arts and Sciences

Music

Grammy Winners, 1993–2003
Song of the Year

Year	Artist	Song
2003	Richard Marx & Luther Vandross	Dance with My Father
2002	Norah Jones	Don't Know Why
2001	Alicia Keys	Fallin'
2000	U2	Beautiful Day
1999	Itaal Shur & Rob Thomas	Smooth
1998	Will Jennings	My Heart Will Go On
1997	Shawn Colvin	Sunny Came Home
1996	Wayne Kirkpatrick & Tommy Sims	Change the World
1995	Seal	Kiss from a Rose
1994	Bruce Springsteen	Streets of Philadelphia
1993	Alan Menken & Tim Rice	A Whole New World (Aladdin's Theme)

SOURCE: National Academy of Recording Arts and Sciences

Grammy Winners, 1993–2003
Best Male Vocal Performance

Year	Artist	Performance
2003	Justin Timberlake	Cry Me a River
2002	John Mayer	Your Body Is a Wonderland
2001	James Taylor	Don't Let Me Be Lonely Tonight
2000	Sting	She Walks This Earth (Soberana Rosa)
1999	Sting	Brand New Day
1998	Eric Clapton	My Father's Eyes
1997	Elton John	Candle in the Wind 1997
1996	Eric Clapton	Change the World
1995	Seal	Kiss from a Rose
1994	Elton John	Can You Feel the Love Tonight
1993	Sting	If I Ever Lose My Faith in You

SOURCE: National Academy of Recording Arts and Sciences

Grammy Winners, 1993–2003
Best Female Vocal Performance

Year	Artist	Performance
2003	Christina Aguilera	Beautiful
2002	Norah Jones	Don't Know Why
2001	Nelly Furtado	I'm Like a Bird
2000	Macy Gray	I Try
1999	Sarah McLachlan	I Will Remember You
1998	Celine Dion	My Heart Will Go On
1997	Sarah McLachlan	Building a Mystery
1996	Toni Braxton	Unbreak My Heart
1995	Annie Lennox	No More "I Love Yous"
1994	Sheryl Crow	All I Wanna Do
1993	Whitney Houston	I Will Always Love You

SOURCE: National Academy of Recording Arts and Sciences

Television

Almost every U.S. home has at least one color television set. Most have two or more sets. And these sets are busy! On average, a home has at least one TV on for more than 7 hours every day. The typical American watches about 4 hours of television daily. On average, adults watch more TV than children do.

Most viewing time is spent watching shows on the major networks, such as ABC, CBS, FOX, and NBC. Cable networks, such as ESPN and CNN, haven't been around as long, but they have been growing in popularity. By 2002, a total of 69% of U.S. homes with television sets subscribed to basic cable services. Of those, the top pay channel—by far—is HBO. The next big thing in television is high-definition television, or HDTV. This technology brings wide-screen, super-sharp pictures into the average home, complete with six-channel "surround sound."

Kids enjoy all kinds of programs, including comedies, cartoons, movies, and animal shows. Sports—from football games to ice-skating competitions—are among the most popular shows. If a show includes young people, so much the better. Disney Channel's

Kidbits Tidbits

- Ninety-eight percent of U.S. homes have at least one color TV set.
- In 2003, about 92% of U.S. homes had at least one VCR.
- Children ages 2 to 11 watch about 3 hours of television a day. Those ages 12 to 17 watch almost as much.
- Children spend more time watching TV than in any other activity except sleep. Boys are more likely to watch sports and cartoons while girls are more likely to watch talk shows.

Lizzie McGuire became a hit because Hilary Duff as Lizzie was a teen navigating the middle-school years. *Joan of Arcadia* drew lots of young viewers who watch the main character struggle through high school as she tries to follow the directions God gives her.

Television use is monitored by the A.C. Nielsen Company. If a show has a Nielsen rating of 12, it was watched by 12% of all television owners. During the 2002–2003 season, America's top-rated show was *CSI*. It had a rating of 16.1. It was followed by *Friends* at 15.1 and *ER* at 13.9.

Most TV programs are paid for by companies that buy advertising time. The bigger the audience a program gets, the more companies are willing to pay to advertise their products during its commercial breaks. For example, it cost an average of $2.3 million for a 30-second ad during the 2004 Super Bowl, an event that drew as many as 90 million viewers. Why do companies pay so much? Can you think of another way to get the attention of 90 million people all at once for 30 seconds?

In addition to TVs, the great majority of U.S. homes have at least one VCR. But the popularity of DVDs has caught on. About 20 million DVD players were sold in 2003 and it's estimated that 90% of American homes will have a DVD player by 2008.

Kidbits Tidbits

- Basic cable systems had more than 69 million subscribers in 2002.
- Thanks to the hit show *The Sopranos* HBO had 38 million subscribers in 2003.
- In 1980, the average monthly basic cable bill was $7.69. In 2002, it was $40.11.
- HDTV uses digital signals, just like a computer. Conventional TVs use analog waves for broadcasting.
- About 56% of children ages 8–16 have a television in their bedroom. Boys, on average, watch TV for 43 hours more than girls each year.

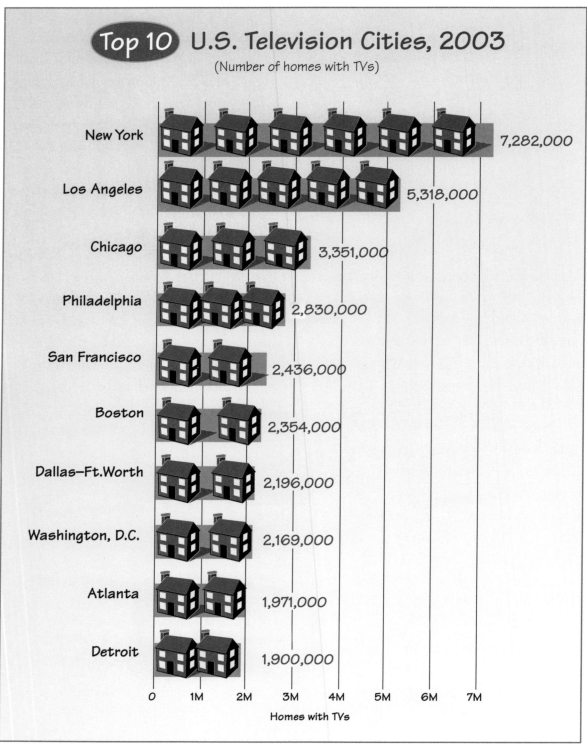

Top 10 U.S. Television Cities, 2003

(Number of homes with TVs)

City	Homes with TVs
New York	7,282,000
Los Angeles	5,318,000
Chicago	3,351,000
Philadelphia	2,830,000
San Francisco	2,436,000
Boston	2,354,000
Dallas–Ft.Worth	2,196,000
Washington, D.C.	2,169,000
Atlanta	1,971,000
Detroit	1,900,000

Homes with TVs: 0 1M 2M 3M 4M 5M 6M 7M

SOURCE: Nielsen Media Research

Television

Top 10 TV Shows, 2003 (Prime time)

(Based on Lycos searches)

1. American Idol

2. Buffy the Vampire Slayer

3. The Simpsons

4. Survivor

5. Charmed

6. Joe Millionaire

7. Big Brother

8. The Bachelor

9. Friends

10. Smallville

Television

SOURCE: Lycos

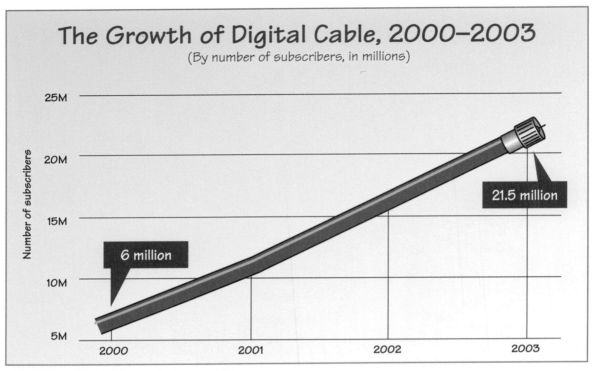

The Growth of Digital Cable, 2000–2003
(By number of subscribers, in millions)

6 million

21.5 million

SOURCE: National Cable & Telecommunications Association

Television

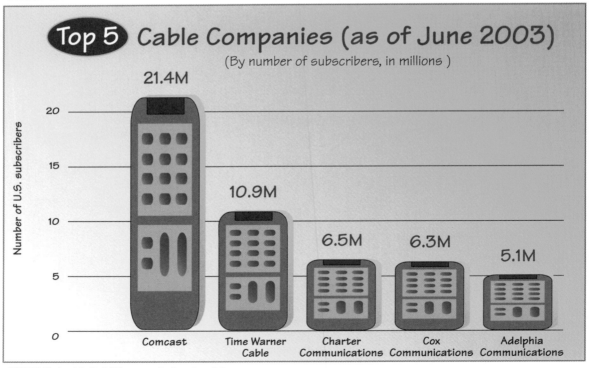

Top 5 Cable Companies (as of June 2003)
(By number of subscribers, in millions)

21.4M — Comcast

10.9M — Time Warner Cable

6.5M — Charter Communications

6.3M — Cox Communications

5.1M — Adelphia Communications

SOURCE: National Cable & Telecommunications Association

Top 10 Cable TV Networks, 2004

Network	Number of subscribers (In millions)
1. TBS Superstation	87.7
2. ESPN	86.7
3. C-SPAN	86.6
4. Discovery Channel	86.5
5. USA Network	86.3
6. CNN	86.2
7. TNT	86.2
8. Lifetime Television	86.0
9. Nickelodeon	86.0
10. A&E Network	85.9

SOURCE: National Cable & Telecommunications Association

Average Kids and Teens TV Viewing Time, 2002
(Per week)

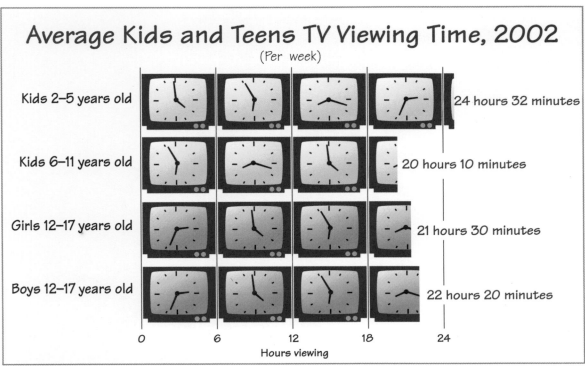

Kids 2–5 years old — 24 hours 32 minutes
Kids 6–11 years old — 20 hours 10 minutes
Girls 12–17 years old — 21 hours 30 minutes
Boys 12–17 years old — 22 hours 20 minutes

Hours viewing: 0 6 12 18 24

Television

SOURCE: *Time Almanac 2004* with data from Nielsen Media Research

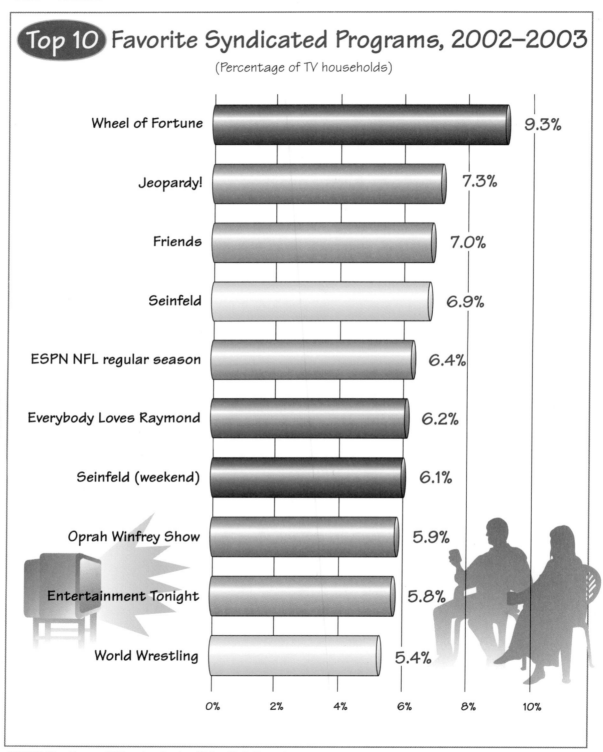

Top 10 Favorite Syndicated Programs, 2002–2003

(Percentage of TV households)

Program	Percentage
Wheel of Fortune	9.3%
Jeopardy!	7.3%
Friends	7.0%
Seinfeld	6.9%
ESPN NFL regular season	6.4%
Everybody Loves Raymond	6.2%
Seinfeld (weekend)	6.1%
Oprah Winfrey Show	5.9%
Entertainment Tonight	5.8%
World Wrestling	5.4%

Television

SOURCE: *Time Almanac 2004* based on data from Nielsen Media Research

Getting Wired: U.S. Households with Cable TV

(Percentage of homes with TVs getting cable 1980–2002)

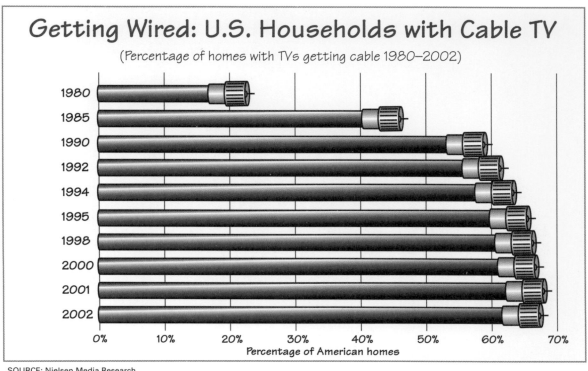

Percentage of American homes

SOURCE: Nielsen Media Research

Television

How Parents Feel About TV Ratings

About 56% of parents use the TV ratings system to make decisions about what their child is allowed to watch.

Of those parents:

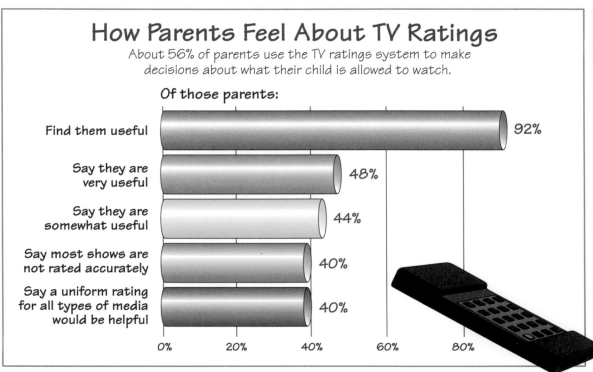

SOURCE: Kaiser Family Foundation

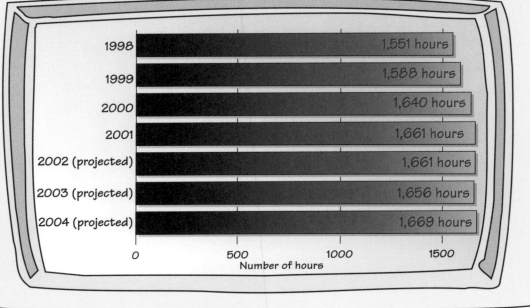

Average Number of Hours a Year a Person Watches TV

Year	Number of hours
1998	1,551 hours
1999	1,588 hours
2000	1,640 hours
2001	1,661 hours
2002 (projected)	1,661 hours
2003 (projected)	1,656 hours
2004 (projected)	1,669 hours

Number of hours

SOURCE: U.S. Census Bureau, *Statistical Abstract of the United States, 2003*

America Adores American Idol

Beginning as the TV show *Pop Idol* in Britain, *American Idol* came to the United States in summer 2002 and was an overnight success.

	1st Season (2002)	2nd Season (2003)
Premiere show (Number of viewers)	5 million	26 million
Average (Number of viewers)	12 million	21 million
Finale (Number of viewers)	23 million	38 million
Winner	Kelly Clarkson	Ruben Stoddard

SOURCE: idolonfox.com

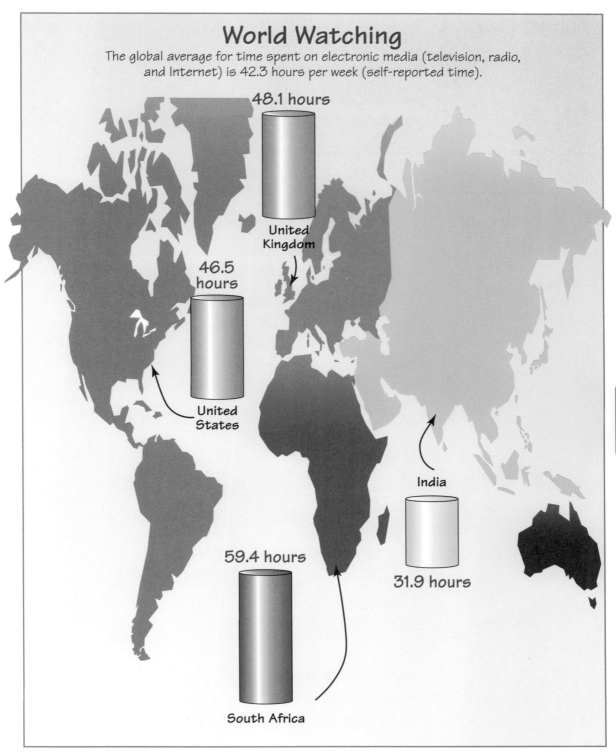

World Watching

The global average for time spent on electronic media (television, radio, and Internet) is 42.3 hours per week (self-reported time).

48.1 hours
United Kingdom

46.5 hours
United States

59.4 hours
South Africa

India
31.9 hours

Television

SOURCE: Roper ASW, "2002 Worldwide Time Study"

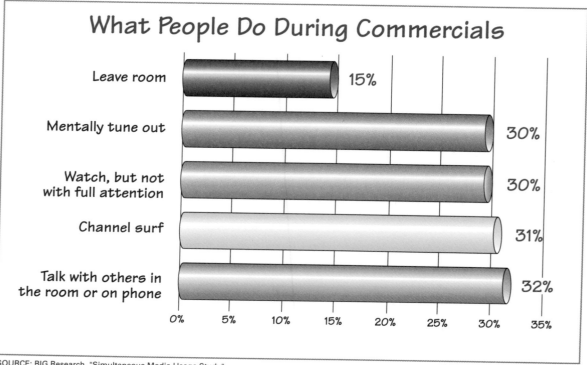

What People Do During Commercials

Leave room	15%
Mentally tune out	30%
Watch, but not with full attention	30%
Channel surf	31%
Talk with others in the room or on phone	32%

0%   5%   10%   15%   20%   25%   30%   35%

SOURCE: BIG Research, "Simultaneous Media Usage Study"

Top Rated TV Shows, 1993–2003

Year	Program	Rating
2003	CSI	16.1
2002	Friends	15.3
2001	Survivor II	17.4
2000	Who Wants to Be a Millionaire	18.6
1999	ER	17.8
1998	Seinfeld	22.0
1997	ER	21.2
1996	ER	22.0
1995	Seinfeld	20.5
1994	Home Improvement	21.9
1993	60 Minutes	21.6

SOURCE: *World Almanac and Book of Facts 2004* with data from Nielsen Media Research

Favorite Programs for Younger Viewers, 2003

Rank	Ages 6–11	Ages 12–17
1	American Idol	American Idol
2	The Simpsons	The Simpsons
3	Wonderful World of Disney	Joe Millionaire
4	Malcolm in the Middle	Malcolm in the Middle
5	Survivor: Thailand	Oliver Beene

SOURCE: Nielsen Media Research

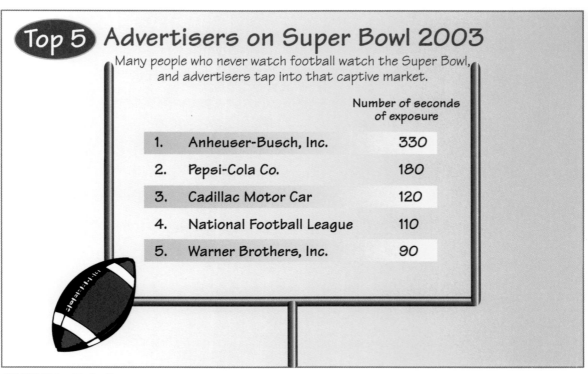

Top 5 Advertisers on Super Bowl 2003

Many people who never watch football watch the Super Bowl, and advertisers tap into that captive market.

		Number of seconds of exposure
1.	Anheuser-Busch, Inc.	330
2.	Pepsi-Cola Co.	180
3.	Cadillac Motor Car	120
4.	National Football League	110
5.	Warner Brothers, Inc.	90

SOURCE: Nielson Monitor-Plus

Television

TV Tidbits

Average number of hours per week that American one-year-old children watch television: 6

Percentage of children ages 8–16 who have a TV in their bedroom: 56

Percent of total television time that children older than 7 spend without their parents: 95

Percentage of children ages 8 and up who have no rules about watching TV: 61

Percentage of children who say they have felt scared or upset by violence on television: 91

Children can develop brand loyalty by age 2.

During 4 hours of Saturday morning cartoons, there are more than 200 ads for junk food.

About a third of local TV news broadcasting time is devoted to advertising.

More than half of kids age 4–6 would rather watch TV than spend time with their dads.

The average American youth spends more than 1,000 hours a year watching TV and 900 hours in school.

Television

SOURCE: TV-Turnoff Network

Who Spends More Time in Front of the Tube? 2002
(Per week)

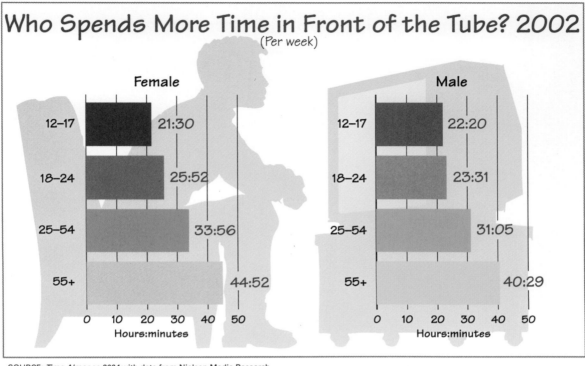

Female

12–17	21:30
18–24	25:52
25–54	33:56
55+	44:52

0 10 20 30 40 50
Hours:minutes

Male

12–17	22:20
18–24	23:31
25–54	31:05
55+	40:29

0 10 20 30 40 50
Hours:minutes

SOURCE: *Time Almanac 2004* with data from Nielsen Media Research

Television

Who Watches Public Television?

Ninety-nine percent of all U.S. homes with a TV can receive a public TV station and about 70% watch it, tuning in for about 2 hours a week.

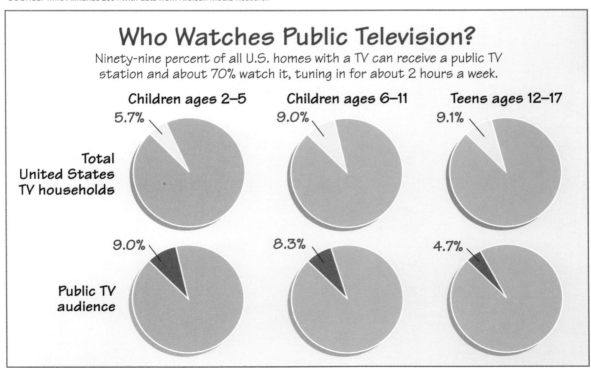

Children ages 2–5   Children ages 6–11   Teens ages 12–17

5.7%   9.0%   9.1%

Total United States TV households

9.0%   8.3%   4.7%

Public TV audience

SOURCE: PBS.com

Television

Younger Teens and Commercials

Teens are among the most active commercial "zappers."

Networks most likely to hold the attention of 11–14-year-olds:

1.   Disney Channel

2.   Nickelodeon

3.   Animal Planet

4.   Cartoon Network

5.   Toon

6.   Discovery Kids

7.   MTV

8.   TLC

9.   ABC Family

10.   Nick-at-Nite

SOURCE: *Jack Myers Teen Media Brand Tracker Report, 2003*

Older Teens and Commercials

Teens are least likely to pay attention to commercials on ABC, CBS, NBC, and UPN. Animal Planet commercials are the ones they're most likely to watch overall.

Networks most likely to hold the attention of 15–17-year-olds:

1. Fuse
2. MTV
3. Discovery Kids
4. Animal Planet
5. ESPN
6. BET
7. TLC
8. Nickelodeon
9. Disney Channel
10. Cartoon Network

Television

SOURCE: *Jack Myers Teen Media Brand Tracker Report, 2003*

U.S. Television Ownership, 2003

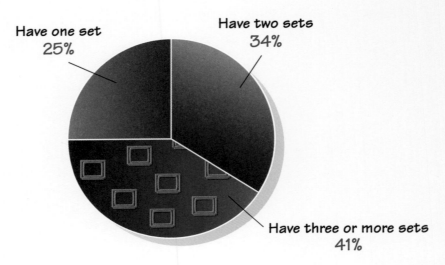

Have one set
25%

Have two sets
34%

Have three or more sets
41%

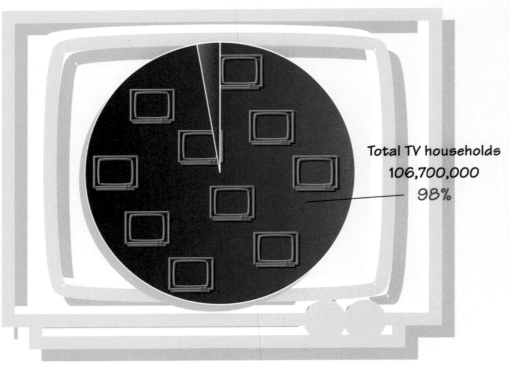

Total TV households
106,700,000
98%

SOURCE: Nielsen Media Research

Television

Top 10 Best Shows for Families on Prime Time Broadcast TV, 2003

1.	Touched by an Angel
2.	Doc
3.	Sue Thomas F.B. Eye
4.	7th Heaven
5.	Life with Bonnie
6.	Smallville
7.	Reba
8.	Star Search
9.	George Lopez
10.	8 Simple Rules for Dating My Teenage Daughter

SOURCE: Children's Television Council

Violence on TV

After years of growing alarm about the amount of violence on TV, it seems that producers are starting to listen. Between 1999 and 2001, the amount of serious violence on TV during prime time fell by 17%

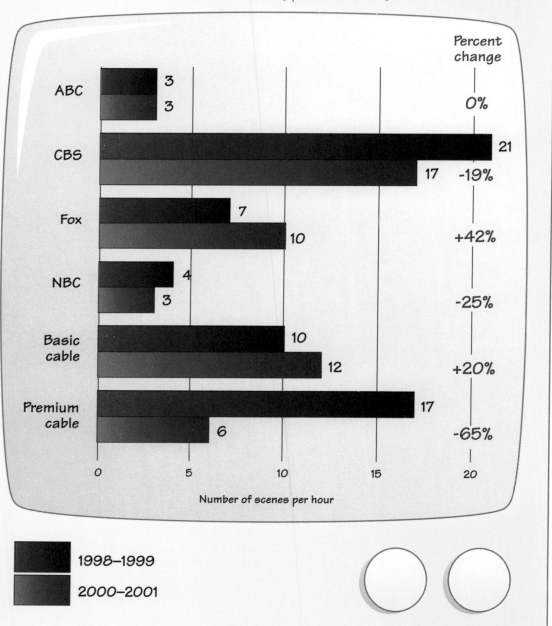

Number of scenes per hour

1998–1999
2000–2001

Television

SOURCE: Center for Media and Public Affairs, "Hollywood Cleans Up Its Act"

Best of the Soaps
2002–2003 Daytime Emmy Awards

Outstanding Drama Series		As the World Turns (CBS)
Lead Actor	Maurice Benard	General Hospital (ABC)
Lead Actress	Susan Flannery	The Bold and the Beautiful (CBS)
Supporting Actor	Benjamin Hendrickson	As the World Turns (CBS)
Supporting Actress	Vanessa Marcil	General Hospital (ABC)

SOURCE: Academy of Teievision Arts and Sciences

Emmy Winners, 1993–2003
Best TV Miniseries

Year	Miniseries	Network
2003	Steven Spielberg Presents Taken	Sci Fi
2002	Band of Brothers	HBO
2001	Anne Frank	ABC
2000	The Corner	HBO
1999	Horatio Hornblower: The Even Chance	HBO
1998	From the Earth to the Moon	HBO
1997	Prime Suspect 5: Errors of Judgement	PBS
1996	Gulliver's Travels	NBC
1995	Joseph	TNT
1994	Prime Suspect 3	PBS
1993	Prime Suspect 2	PBS

SOURCE: Academy of Television Arts and Sciences

Television

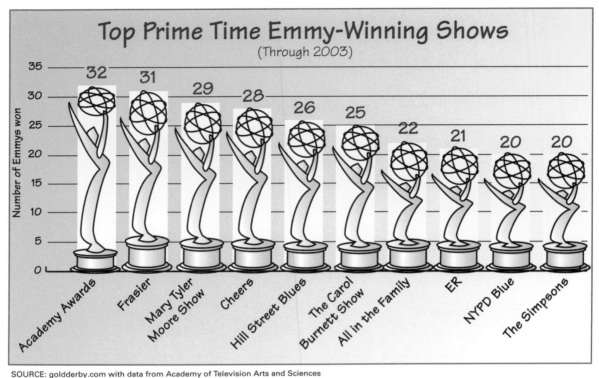

Top Prime Time Emmy-Winning Shows
(Through 2003)

SOURCE: goldderby.com with data from Academy of Television Arts and Sciences

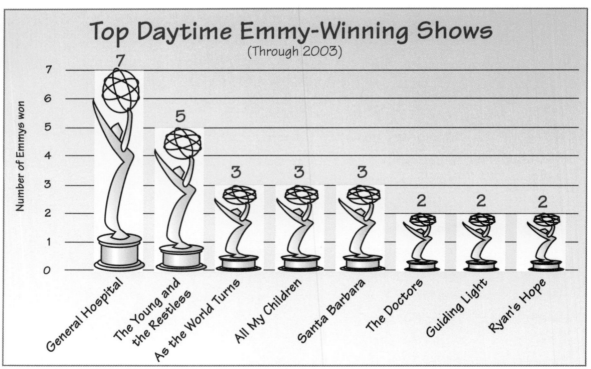

Top Daytime Emmy-Winning Shows
(Through 2003)

SOURCE: goldderby.com with data from Academy of Television Arts and Sciences

Most Emmy Nominations for a Series in a Season
(Through 2003)

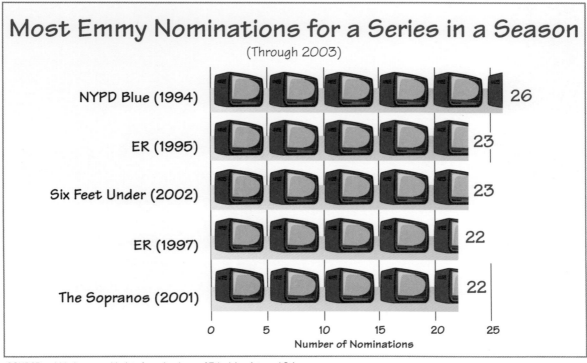

NYPD Blue (1994) — 26
ER (1995) — 23
Six Feet Under (2002) — 23
ER (1997) — 22
The Sopranos (2001) — 22

Number of Nominations

SOURCE: goldderby.com with data from Academy of Television Arts and Sciences

Most Emmys Won By a Series in a Season
(Through 2003)

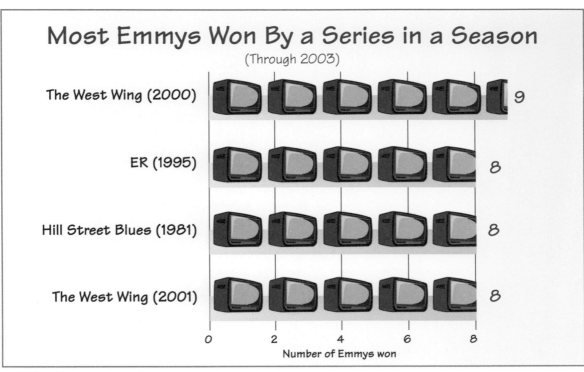

The West Wing (2000) — 9
ER (1995) — 8
Hill Street Blues (1981) — 8
The West Wing (2001) — 8

Number of Emmys won

SOURCE: goldderby.com with data from Academy of Television Arts and Sciences

Television

Emmy Winners, 1993–2003
Lead Actress in a Comedy Series

Year	Actress	Character	Program
2003	Debra Messing	Grace Adler	Will & Grace
2002	Jennifer Aniston	Rachel Green	Friends
2001	Patricia Heaton	Debra Barone	Everybody Loves Raymond
2000	Patricia Heaton	Debra Barone	Everybody Loves Raymond
1999	Helen Hunt	Jamie Buchman	Mad About You
1998	Helen Hunt	Jamie Buchman	Mad About You
1997	Helen Hunt	Jamie Buchman	Mad About You
1996	Helen Hunt	Jamie Buchman	Mad About You
1995	Candice Bergen	Murphy Brown	Murphy Brown
1994	Candice Bergen	Murphy Brown	Murphy Brown
1993	Roseanne	Roseanne Arnold	Roseanne

SOURCE: Academy of Television Arts and Sciences

Emmy Winners, 1993–2003
Lead Actor in a Comedy Series

Year	Actor	Character	Program
2003	Tony Shalhoub	Adrian Monk	Monk
2002	Ray Romano	Ray Barone	Everybody Loves Raymond
2001	Eric McCormack	Will Truman	Will & Grace
2000	Michael J. Fox	Mike Flaherty	Spin City
1999	John Lithgow	Dick Solomon	3rd Rock from the Sun
1998	Kelsey Grammer	Dr. Frasier Crane	Frasier
1997	John Lithgow	Dick Solomon	3rd Rock from the Sun
1996	John Lithgow	Dick Solomon	3rd Rock from the Sun
1995	Kelsey Grammer	Dr. Frasier Crane	Frasier
1994	Kelsey Grammer	Dr. Frasier Crane	Frasier
1993	Ted Danson	Sam Malone	Cheers

SOURCE: Academy of Television Arts and Sciences

Television

Emmy Winners, 1993–2003
Lead Actress in a Drama Series

Year	Actress	Character	Program
2003	Edie Falco	Carmela Soprano	The Sopranos
2002	Allison Janney	CJ Cregs	The West Wing
2001	Edie Falco	Carmela Soprano	The Sopranos
2000	Sela Ward	Lily Manning	Once and Again
1999	Edie Falco	Carmella Soprano	The Sopranos
1998	Christine Lahti	Dr. Kathryn Austin	Chicago Hope
1997	Gillian Anderson	Agent Dana Scully	The X-Files
1996	Kathy Baker	Jill Brock	Picket Fences
1995	Kathy Baker	Jill Brock	Picket Fences
1994	Sela Ward	Teddy Reed	Sisters
1993	Kathy Baker	Jill Brock	Picket Fences

SOURCE: Academy of Television Arts and Sciences

Emmy Winners, 1993–2003
Lead Actor in a Drama Series

Year	Actor	Character	Program
2003	James Gandolfini	Tony Soprano	The Sopranos
2002	Michael Chiklis	Vic Mackey	The Shield
2001	James Gandolfini	Tony Soprano	The Sopranos
2000	James Gandolfini	Tony Soprano	The Sopranos
1999	Dennis Franz	Detective Andy Sipowicz	NYPD Blue
1998	Andre Braugher	Detective Frank Pembleton	Homicide
1997	Dennis Franz	Detective Andy Sipowicz	NYPD Blue
1996	Dennis Franz	Detective Andy Sipowicz	NYPD Blue
1995	Mandy Patinkin	Dr. Jeffrey Geiger	Chicago Hope
1994	Dennis Franz	Detective Andy Sipowicz	NYPD Blue
1993	Tom Skerritt	Jimmy Brock	Picket Fences

SOURCE: Academy of Television Arts and Sciences

Television

Television

Emmy Winners, 1993–2003
Best Comedy Series

Year	Program
2003	Everybody Loves Raymond
2002	Friends
2001	Sex and the City
2000	Will & Grace
1999	Ally McBeal
1998	Frasier
1997	Frasier
1996	Frasier
1995	Frasier
1994	Frasier
1993	Seinfeld

SOURCE: Academy of Television Arts and Sciences

Emmy Winners, 1993–2003
Best Drama Series

Year	Program
2003	The West Wing
2002	The West Wing
2001	The West Wing
2000	The West Wing
1999	The Practice
1998	The Practice
1997	Law & Order
1996	ER
1995	NYPD Blue
1994	Picket Fences
1993	Picket Fences

SOURCE: Academy of Television Arts and Sciences

Emmy Winners, 1993–2003
Supporting Actor in a Comedy Series

Year	Actor	Character	Program
2003	Brad Garrett	Robert Barone	Everybody Loves Raymond
2002	Brad Garrett	Robert Barone	Everybody Loves Raymond
2001	Peter MacNicol	John Cage	Ally McBeal
2000	Sean Hayes	Jack McFarland	Will & Grace
1999	David Hyde Pierce	Dr. Niles Crane	Frasier
1998	David Hyde Pierce	Dr. Niles Crane	Frasier
1997	Michael Richards	Kramer	Seinfeld
1996	Rip Torn	Arthur	The Larry Sanders Show
1995	David Hyde Pierce	Dr. Niles Crane	Frasier
1994	Michael Richards	Kramer	Seinfeld
1993	Michael Richards	Kramer	Seinfeld

SOURCE: Academy of Television Arts and Sciences

Emmy Winners, 1993–2003
Supporting Actress in a Comedy Series

Year	Actress	Character	Program
2003	Doris Roberts	Marie Barone	Everybody Loves Raymond
2002	Doris Roberts	Marie Barone	Everybody Loves Raymond
2001	Doris Roberts	Marie Barone	Everybody Loves Raymond
2000	Megan Mullally	Karen Walker	Will & Grace
1999	Kristen Johnston	Sally Solomon	3rd Rock from the Sun
1998	Lisa Kudrow	Phoebe Buffay	Friends
1997	Kristen Johnston	Sally Solomon	3rd Rock from the Sun
1996	Julia Louis-Dreyfus	Elaine Benes	Seinfeld
1995	Christine Baranski	Maryann Thorpe	Cybill
1994	Laurie Metcalf	Jackie Harris	Roseanne
1993	Laurie Metcalf	Jackie Harris	Roseanne

SOURCE: Academy of Television Arts and Sciences

Television

Movies

About 450 new films are released in the United States each year. Some disappear quickly. Others remain popular for years and years—not only in cinemas and on DVD and video, but in the spin-offs and merchandise they create: toys and games, clothing, and recordings of their musical scores.

Americans spend about $9 billion a year on movie tickets, with an average admission charge of $5.81. As 2004 began, the film that held the U.S. record for making the most money at the box office was *Titanic*, a 1997 movie that had sold more than $600 million worth of tickets. Worldwide, it also held the record, having pulled in close to $2 billion. It also became the first movie to tie the all-time record for Oscar nominations, with 14 total. On Oscar night in March 1998, it also became the first movie to tie the all-time record for Oscar wins: The film tied the 1959 epic *Ben-Hur* with 11 awards. In 2004, *The Lord of the Rings: The Return of the King* tied both of those films with 11 Oscars also.

Kidbits Tidbits

- The American Film Institute has rated *Citizen Kane* the best movie of all time.
- In 1997, *Titanic* became the most expensive movie ever made. It cost $200 million.
- North America's top-grossing movie in 2003 was *The Lord of the Rings: The Return of the King,* with $371 million.
- *Ben-Hur,* a 1959 movie, held the Oscar record of 11 Academy Awards for 39 years, until *Titanic* tied in 1998.

Teenagers make up a hefty portion of the movie audience, in part because they have more leisure time than older people. In a recent study, 46% of 12- to 17-year-olds said they see a movie frequently, as compared with only 25% of people age 18 and older.

In addition to viewing movies in cinemas, kids watch lots of movies at home. More than 92% of U.S. homes have VCRs—a higher percentage than in any other country in the world. Most of these homes rent at least one movie a month. But DVD players have also caught on. It is estimated that by 2008, 90% of American homes will have a DVD player.

Of all the categories of movies being rented, action films and comedies are the favorites. For the first six months of 2003, rental income from *The Bourne Identity,* a 2002 action movie, was $85.4 million. *My Big Fat Greek Wedding* (2002) was the favorite comedy rental, taking in $65.8 million

Films are given a rating by the Motion Picture Association of America. The rating is a reflection of a movie's violence and sexual content. The majority of the films released each year receive an "R" rating, which means that people under age 17 can be admitted only if accompanied by a parent or adult guardian. Other ratings include G (general audience), PG (parental guidance advised), PG-13 (may not be suitable for preteens), and NC-17 (persons under age 17 not admitted).

Kidbits Tidbits

- In 2002, people rented 50.2 million video cassettes and 69.2 million DVDs.
- In 2002, the top-selling video of all time was *The Lion King.* The number 1 rental video of all time was *Pretty Woman.*
- Movies often reinforce misleading images of society. For example, one survey of top-grossing films of the 1990s found that 80% of the male leads smoked.

DVDs Are Replacing Videos

In 1997, there were 600 titles on DVD; by 2002, there were more than 20,000.

Number of DVD players sold

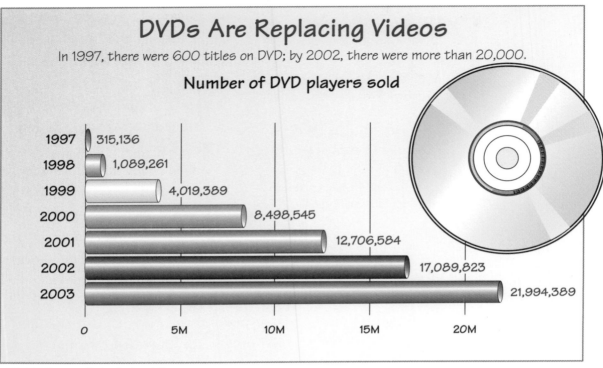

Year	Number
1997	315,136
1998	1,089,261
1999	4,019,389
2000	8,498,545
2001	12,706,584
2002	17,089,823
2003	21,994,389

0   5M   10M   15M   20M

SOURCE: Consumer Electronics Association

Top 10 Top-Selling Videos of All Time (VHS)
(As of 2002)

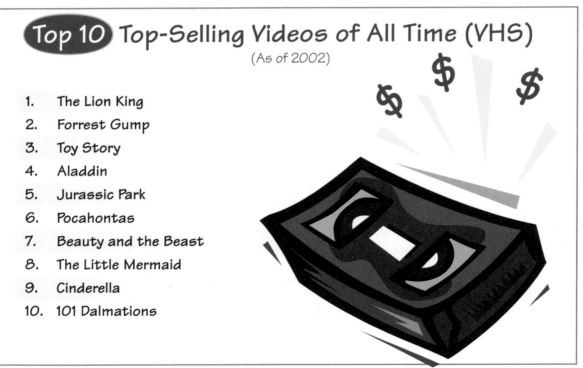

1. The Lion King
2. Forrest Gump
3. Toy Story
4. Aladdin
5. Jurassic Park
6. Pocahontas
7. Beauty and the Beast
8. The Little Mermaid
9. Cinderella
10. 101 Dalmations

Movies

SOURCE: Alexander & Associates

Top 10 Top-Renting Videos of All Time (VHS)
(As of 2002)

1. Pretty Woman
2. Top Gun
3. The Little Mermaid
4. Home Alone
5. Ghost
6. The Lion King
7. Beauty and the Beast
8. Terminator 2: Judgment Day
9. Forrest Gump
10. Aladdin

SOURCE: Alexander & Associates

U.S. Box Office Revenues, 1926–2003

Box office receipts (in billions)

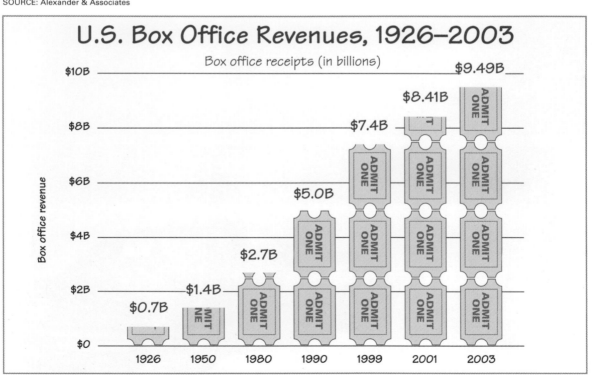

SOURCE: Motion Picture Association, "U.S. Entertainment Industry: 2003 MPA Market Statistics"

Movies

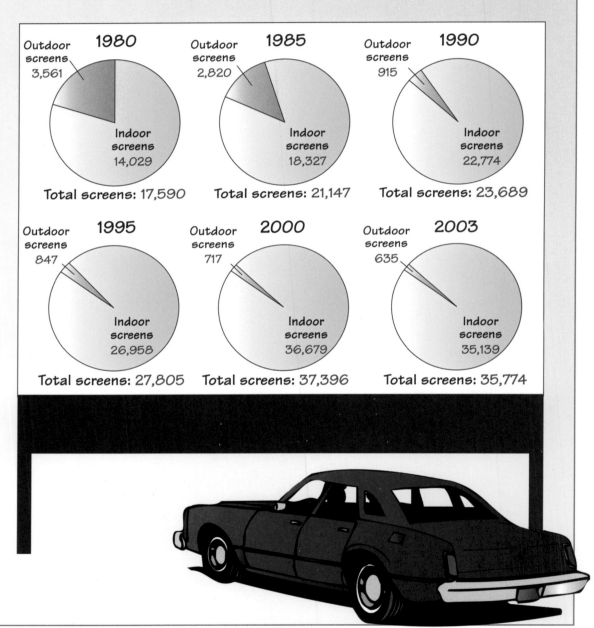

Disappearing Drive-Ins

While the number of movie screens in the United States has more than doubled since 1980, the number of outdoor screens has dropped from 20% to 2%.

1980
Outdoor screens
3,561
Indoor screens
14,029
Total screens: 17,590

1985
Outdoor screens
2,820
Indoor screens
18,327
Total screens: 21,147

1990
Outdoor screens
915
Indoor screens
22,774
Total screens: 23,689

1995
Outdoor screens
847
Indoor screens
26,958
Total screens: 27,805

2000
Outdoor screens
717
Indoor screens
36,679
Total screens: 37,396

2003
Outdoor screens
635
Indoor screens
35,139
Total screens: 35,774

Movies

SOURCE: Motion Picture Association, "U.S. Entertainment Industry: 2003 MPA Market Statistics"

Movie Theaters Are Supersizing

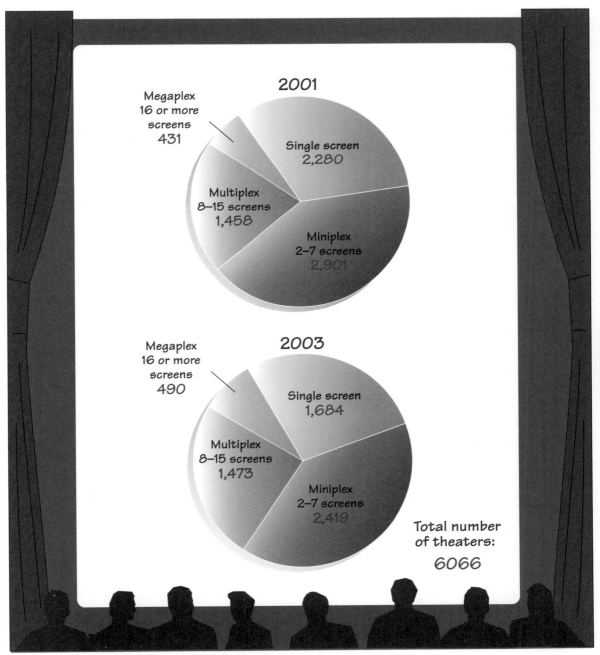

2001

Megaplex
16 or more
screens
431

Single screen
2,280

Multiplex
8–15 screens
1,458

Miniplex
2–7 screens
2,901

2003

Megaplex
16 or more
screens
490

Single screen
1,684

Multiplex
8–15 screens
1,473

Miniplex
2–7 screens
2,419

Total number
of theaters:
6066

Movies

SOURCE: Motion Picture Association, "U.S. Entertainment Industry: 2003 MPA Market Statistics"

Top 10 Highest-Grossing Movies in the United States
(Box office revenues as of August 3, 2003)

Movies

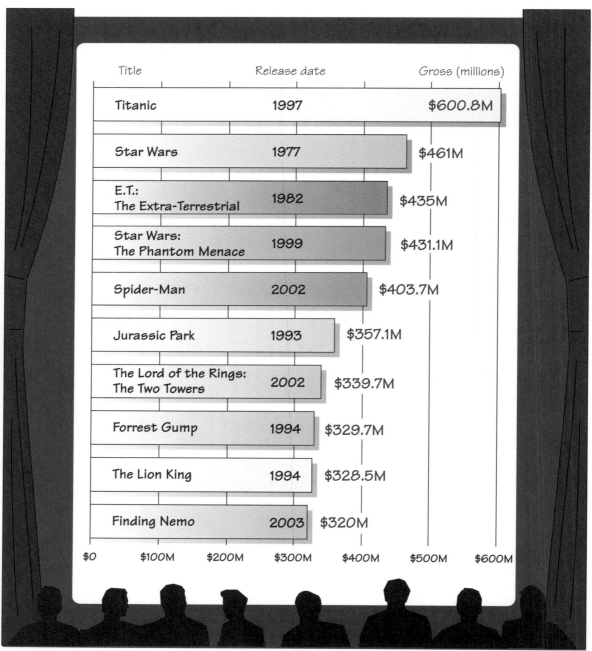

Title	Release date	Gross (millions)
Titanic	1997	$600.8M
Star Wars	1977	$461M
E.T.: The Extra-Terrestrial	1982	$435M
Star Wars: The Phantom Menace	1999	$431.1M
Spider-Man	2002	$403.7M
Jurassic Park	1993	$357.1M
The Lord of the Rings: The Two Towers	2002	$339.7M
Forrest Gump	1994	$329.7M
The Lion King	1994	$328.5M
Finding Nemo	2003	$320M

$0 $100M $200M $300M $400M $500M $600M

SOURCE: *Time Almanac 2004*

Top 10   Movies of All Time by Admissions

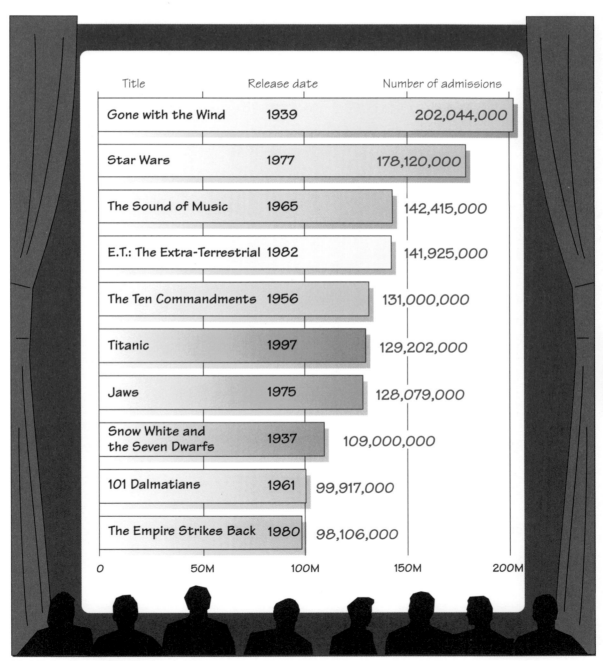

Title	Release date	Number of admissions
Gone with the Wind	1939	202,044,000
Star Wars	1977	178,120,000
The Sound of Music	1965	142,415,000
E.T.: The Extra-Terrestrial	1982	141,925,000
The Ten Commandments	1956	131,000,000
Titanic	1997	129,202,000
Jaws	1975	128,079,000
Snow White and the Seven Dwarfs	1937	109,000,000
101 Dalmatians	1961	99,917,000
The Empire Strikes Back	1980	98,106,000

0   50M   100M   150M   200M

Movies

SOURCE: *Encyclopaedia Britannica Almanac 2004*

Top Oscar Winners

Movie	Year	Awards
The Lord of the Rings: The Return of the King	2004	11
Titanic	1998	11
Ben-Hur	1959	11
West Side Story	1961	10
The English Patient	1996	9
The Last Emperor	1987	9
Gigi	1958	9
Amadeus	1984	8
Gandhi	1982	8
Cabaret	1972	8
My Fair Lady	1964	8
On the Waterfront	1954	8
From Here to Eternity	1953	8
Gone with the Wind	1939	8

SOURCE: Academy of Motion Picture Arts and Sciences

Movies

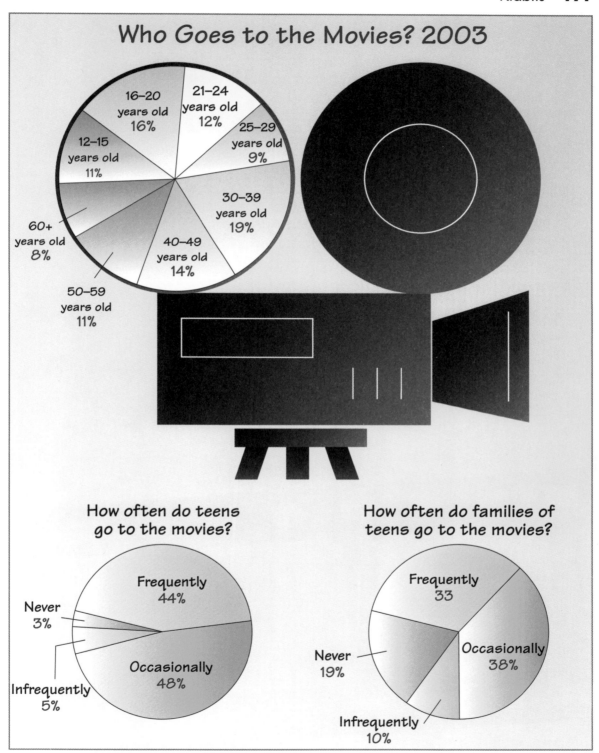

Who Goes to the Movies? 2003

16–20 years old 16%

21–24 years old 12%

25–29 years old 9%

12–15 years old 11%

30–39 years old 19%

60+ years old 8%

40–49 years old 14%

50–59 years old 11%

How often do teens go to the movies?

Frequently 44%

Never 3%

Occasionally 48%

Infrequently 5%

How often do families of teens go to the movies?

Frequently 33

Never 19%

Occasionally 38%

Infrequently 10%

SOURCE: Motion Picture Association, "U.S. Movie Attendance Study 2003"

Movies

Million Dollar Movie Weekends

(Through January 12, 2004)

Top opening weekends of all time based on gross receipts at the box office.

Film	Opening date	Gross	Number of theaters
1. Spider-Man	5-03-02	$114.8M	3,615
2. Lost World (4-day)	5-23-97	$92.7M	3,281
3. The Matrix, Reloaded	5-16-03	$91.8M	3,603
4. Harry Potter and the Sorcerer's Stone	11-16-01	$90.3M	3,672
5. Harry Potter and the Chamber of Secrets	11-16-02	$88.4M	3,682

SOURCE: einsiders.com

Movies

Kid-Friendly Movies

Seven of the top 20 highest-grossing movies in 2002 were rated G or PG. None of the top 20 were rated R.

R 0%
PG 30%
PG-13 65%
G 5%

SOURCE: Motion Picture Association, "U.S. Entertainment Industry: 2002 MPA Market Statistics"

Top 10 Highest-Grossing Movies of All-time
(Worldwide)
(Through March 16, 2004)

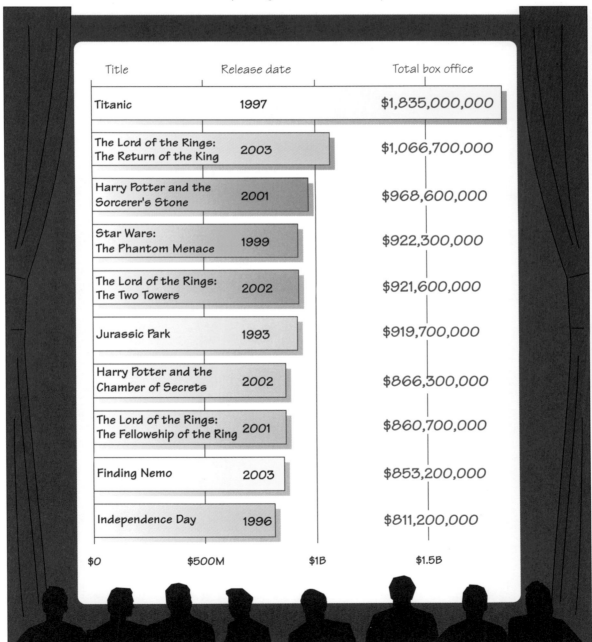

Title	Release date	Total box office
Titanic	1997	$1,835,000,000
The Lord of the Rings: The Return of the King	2003	$1,066,700,000
Harry Potter and the Sorcerer's Stone	2001	$968,600,000
Star Wars: The Phantom Menace	1999	$922,300,000
The Lord of the Rings: The Two Towers	2002	$921,600,000
Jurassic Park	1993	$919,700,000
Harry Potter and the Chamber of Secrets	2002	$866,300,000
The Lord of the Rings: The Fellowship of the Ring	2001	$860,700,000
Finding Nemo	2003	$853,200,000
Independence Day	1996	$811,200,000

$0 $500M $1B $1.5B

Movies

SOURCE: einsiders.com

Top 10 Best American Animation Movies of All Time

Film	Year
1. Finding Nemo	2003
2. Toy Story 2	1999
3. Shrek	2001
4. Monsters, Inc.	2001
5. Toy Story	1995
6. Fantasia	1940
7. Snow White and the Seven Dwarfs	1937
8. Beauty and the Beast	1991
9. Iron Giant	1999
10. Pinocchio	1940

SOURCE: The Internet Movie Database (IMDb)

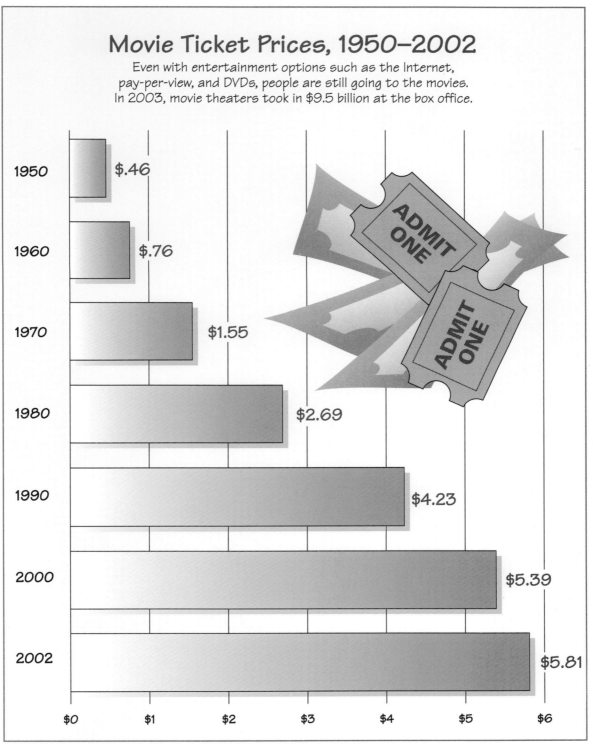

Movie Ticket Prices, 1950–2002

Even with entertainment options such as the Internet,
pay-per-view, and DVDs, people are still going to the movies.
In 2003, movie theaters took in $9.5 billion at the box office.

1950	$.46
1960	$.76
1970	$1.55
1980	$2.69
1990	$4.23
2000	$5.39
2002	$5.81

$0 $1 $2 $3 $4 $5 $6

Movies

SOURCE: Motion Picture Association of America, "2002 U.S. Theatrical Market"

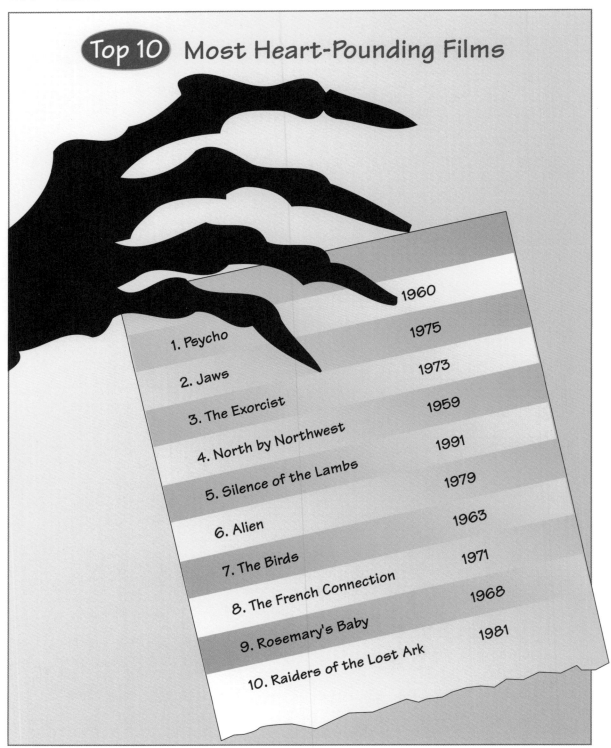

Top 10 Most Heart-Pounding Films

Film	Year
1. Psycho	1960
2. Jaws	1975
3. The Exorcist	1973
4. North by Northwest	1959
5. Silence of the Lambs	1991
6. Alien	1979
7. The Birds	1963
8. The French Connection	1971
9. Rosemary's Baby	1968
10. Raiders of the Lost Ark	1981

Movies

SOURCE: American Film Institute

Top 10 **American Films of the 20th Century**

1. Citizen Kane	1941
2. Casablanca	1942
3. The Godfather	1972
4. Gone with the Wind	1939
5. Lawrence of Arabia	1962
6. The Wizard of Oz	1939
7. The Graduate	1967
8. On the Waterfront	1954
9. Schindler's List	1993
10. Singin' in the Rain	1952

Movies

SOURCE: American Film Institute

Golden Globe Awards for "Best Performance by an Actor in a Motion Picture—Drama," 1994–2004

Year	Actor	Film
2004	Sean Penn	Mystic River
2003	Jack Nicholson	About Schmidt
2002	Russell Crowe	A Beautiful Mind
2001	Tom Hanks	Castaway
2000	Denzel Washington	The Hurricane
1999	Jim Carrey	The Truman Show
1998	Peter Fonda	Ulee's Gold
1997	Geoffrey Rush	Shine
1996	Nicolas Cage	Leaving Las Vegas
1995	Tom Hanks	Forrest Gump
1994	Tom Hanks	Philadelphia

SOURCE: Academy of Motion Picture Arts and Sciences

Golden Globe Awards for "Best Performance by an Actress in a Motion Picture—Drama," 1994–2004

Year	Actress	Film
2004	Charlize Theron	Monster
2003	Nicole Kidman	The Hours
2002	Sissy Spacek	In the Bedroom
2001	Julia Roberts	Erin Brockovich
2000	Hilary Swank	Boys Don't Cry
1999	Cate Blanchett	Elizabeth
1998	Judi Dench	Mrs. Brown
1997	Brenda Blethyn	Secrets and Lies
1996	Sharon Stone	Casino
1995	Jessica Lange	Blue Sky
1994	Holly Hunter	The Piano

SOURCE: Academy of Motion Picture Arts and Sciences

Movies

Golden Globe Awards for "Best Performance by an Actor in a Motion Picture—Musical or Comedy," 1994–2004

Year	Actor	Film
2004	Bill Murray	Lost in Translation
2003	Richard Gere	Chicago
2002	Gene Hackman	The Royal Tenenbaums
2001	George Clooney	O Brother, Where Art Thou?
2000	Jim Carrey	Man on the Moon
1999	Michael Caine	Little Voice
1998	Jack Nicholson	As Good As It Gets
1997	Tom Cruise	Jerry Maguire
1996	John Travolta	Get Shorty
1995	Hugh Grant	Four Weddings and a Funeral
1994	Robin Williams	Mrs. Doubtfire

SOURCE: Academy of Motion Picture Arts and Sciences

Golden Globe Awards for "Best Performance by an Actress in a Motion Picture—Musical or Comedy," 1994–2004

Year	Actress	Film
2004	Diane Keaton	Something's Gotta Give
2003	Renée Zellweger	Chicago
2002	Nicole Kidman	Moulin Rouge
2001	Renée Zellweger	Nurse Betty
2000	Janet McTeer	Tumbleweeds
1999	Gwyneth Paltrow	Shakespeare in Love
1998	Helen Hunt	As Good as It Gets
1997	Madonna	Evita
1996	Nicole Kidman	To Die For
1995	Jamie Lee Curtis	True Lies
1994	Angela Bassett	What's Love Got to Do with It?

SOURCE: Academy of Motion Picture Arts and Sciences

Movies

Golden Globe Awards for "Best Motion Picture— Musical or Comedy," 1994–2004

Year	Film
2004	Lost in Translation
2003	Chicago
2002	Moulin Rouge
2001	Almost Famous
2000	Toy Story 2
1999	Shakespeare in Love
1998	As Good as It Gets
1997	Evita
1996	Babe
1995	The Lion King
1994	Mrs. Doubtfire

SOURCE: Academy of Motion Picture Arts and Sciences

Movies

Top Oscar-Nominated Actors of All Time
(Through 2004)

		Number of nominations	Number of awards
1.	Meryl Streep	13	2
2.	Katharine Hepburn	12	4
3.	Jack Nicholson	12	3
4.	Bette Davis	10	2
5.	Laurence Olivier	10	1
6.	Paul Newman	9	1
7.	Spencer Tracy	9	2

SOURCE: Academy of Motion Picture Arts and Sciences

Best Picture Oscars: 1993–2003

Year	Film
2003	The Lord of the Rings: The Return of the King
2002	Chicago
2001	A Beautiful Mind
2000	Gladiator
1999	American Beauty
1998	Shakespeare in Love
1997	Titanic
1996	The English Patient
1995	Braveheart
1994	Forrest Gump
1993	Schindler's List

SOURCE: Motion Picture Association of America

Best Director Oscars: 1993–2003

Year	Director	Film
2003	Peter Jackson	The Lord of the Rings: The Return of the King
2002	Roman Polanski	The Pianist
2001	Ron Howard	A Beautiful Mind
2000	Steven Soderbergh	Traffic
1999	Sam Mendes	American Beauty
1998	Steven Spielberg	Saving Private Ryan
1997	James Cameron	Titanic
1996	Anthony Minghella	The English Patient
1995	Mel Gibson	Braveheart
1994	Robert Zemeckis	Forrest Gump
1993	Steven Spielberg	Schindler's List

SOURCE: Motion Picture Association of America

Movies

Best Actress Oscars: 1993–2003

Year	Actress
2003	Charlize Theron (*Monster*)
2002	Nicole Kidman (*The Hours*)
2001	Halle Berry (*Monster's Ball*)
2000	Julia Roberts (*Erin Brockovich*)
1999	Hilary Swank (*Boys Don't Cry*)
1998	Gwyneth Paltrow (*Shakespeare in Love*)
1997	Helen Hunt (*As Good as It Gets*)
1996	Frances McDormand (*Fargo*)
1995	Susan Sarandon (*Dead Man Walking*)
1994	Jessica Lange (*Blue Sky*)
1993	Holly Hunter (*The Piano*)

SOURCE: Motion Picture Association of America

Best Actor Oscars: 1993–2003

Year	Actor
2003	Sean Penn (*Mystic River*)
2002	Adrien Brody (*The Pianist*)
2001	Denzel Washington (*Training Day*)
2000	Russell Crowe (*Gladiator*)
1999	Kevin Spacey (*American Beauty*)
1998	Roberto Benigni (*Life Is Beautiful*)
1997	Jack Nicholson (*As Good as It Gets*)
1996	Geoffrey Rush (*Shine*)
1995	Nicolas Cage (*Leaving Las Vegas*)
1994	Tom Hanks (*Forrest Gump*)
1993	Tom Hanks (*Philadelphia*)

SOURCE: Motion Picture Association of America

Movies

Best Supporting Actress Oscars: 1993–2003

Year	Actress
2003	Renée Zellweger (*Cold Mountain*)
2002	Catherine Zeta-Jones (*Chicago*)
2001	Jennifer Connelly (*A Beautiful Mind*)
2000	Marcia Gay Harden (*Pollock*)
1999	Angelina Jolie (*Girl, Interrupted*)
1998	Judi Dench (*Shakespeare in Love*)
1997	Kim Basinger (*L.A. Confidential*)
1996	Juliette Binoche (*The English Patient*)
1995	Mira Sorvino (*Mighty Aphrodite*)
1994	Dianne Wiest (*Bullets over Broadway*)
1993	Anna Paquin (*The Piano*)

SOURCE: Motion Picture Association of America

Best Supporting Actor Oscars: 1993–2003

Year	Actor
2003	Tim Robbins (*Mystic River*)
2002	Chris Cooper (*Adaptation*)
2001	Jim Broadbent (*Iris*)
2000	Benicio Del Toro (*Traffic*)
1999	Michael Caine (*Cider House Rules*)
1998	James Coburn (*Affliction*)
1997	Robin Williams (*Good Will Hunting*)
1996	Cuba Gooding Jr. (*Jerry Maguire*)
1995	Kevin Spacey (*The Usual Suspects*)
1994	Martin Landau (*Ed Wood*)
1993	Tommy Lee Jones (*The Fugitive*)

SOURCE: Motion Picture Association of America

Movies

Pro Sports

Even very young children love to follow professional sports. By the time they enter middle school and high school, millions of kids are fanatics! They root for their favorite team, collect trading cards that picture their favorite players, and wear sweatshirts and caps with team logos. Many dream of the day when they, too, might become pro players. Of course, very few children realize these dreams. Very few develop the skills needed to compete at a professional level. But for those who are successful, the payoff can be enormous.

Top professionals earn millions of dollars each year, not only in salaries but also from their endorsements of clothing, video games, cereals, and other products. Professionals are paid for their endorsements because companies know that they'll sell more merchandise—especially to young people—if it carries Michael Jordan's picture or Tiger Wood's name.

This wasn't always true. Professional sports have changed tremendously over the years. In 1959, members of the

Kidbits Tidbits

- Spring training costs each baseball team about $1 million and about 60% of baseball revenues goes to players' salaries.
- The highest paid football player in 2002 was Michael Strahan, who received $20.6 million.
- Under the 2003–2004 NBA agreement, teams cannot pay players more than $14 million* each, and cannot spend more than $34 million on the team as a whole.

Professional Bowlers Association competed in three tournaments for prizes worth a total of $49,500; by 1997 they were competing in four seasonal tours for more than $8 million in prize money. When Babe Ruth played baseball, there were no night games, no domed ballparks, no coast-to-coast travel, no million-dollar salaries—and no black players in the major leagues. When Ray Harroun won the first Indianapolis 500 in 1911, he drove at an average speed of less than 75 mph; when Gil de Ferran won in 2003, his average speed was 156.291 mph.

Today, the media—particularly TV—spends big bucks on sports. These dollars help pay for salaries. In return, the media has a large part in deciding everything from the starting times of games to playing dates.

Another big change has been the growth of women's professional sports. For example, the 1990s saw the beginning of the Women's National Basketball Association and other pro leagues. Much of the credit for this change belongs to the passage of a federal law in 1972. The law—called Title IX—outlaws discrimination in school sports on the basis of gender. The law meant that girls could have equal opportunities to develop as athletes. As a result, many girls have grown up to be strong, skilled professional athletes. Women's winnings and salaries, however, still do not equal those of men. For example, the number one woman golfer in 2003 earned $1,914,506. The number one male golfer earned $7,573,907.

Kidbits Tidbits

- In 1997, at the ripe old age of 21, Tiger Woods became the youngest golfer ever to win the Masters.
- The most valuable NFL franchise in 2003 was the Washington Redskins ($952 million). The most valuable MLB franchise was the New York Yankees ($730 million).
- The final game in the 1999 Women's World Cup drew more than 90,000 spectators—the largest audience for any women's sporting event.

*There are exceptions to this agreement as demonstrated by the salaries on page 209.

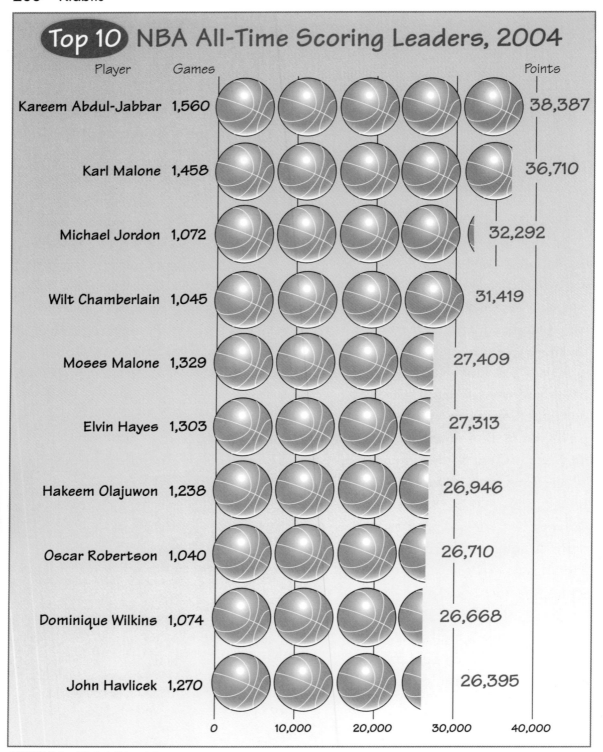

Top 10 NBA All-Time Scoring Leaders, 2004

Player	Games		Points
Kareem Abdul-Jabbar	1,560		38,387
Karl Malone	1,458		36,710
Michael Jordon	1,072		32,292
Wilt Chamberlain	1,045		31,419
Moses Malone	1,329		27,409
Elvin Hayes	1,303		27,313
Hakeem Olajuwon	1,238		26,946
Oscar Robertson	1,040		26,710
Dominique Wilkins	1,074		26,668
John Havlicek	1,270		26,395

0   10,000   20,000   30,000   40,000

SOURCE: National Basketball Association

Pro Sports

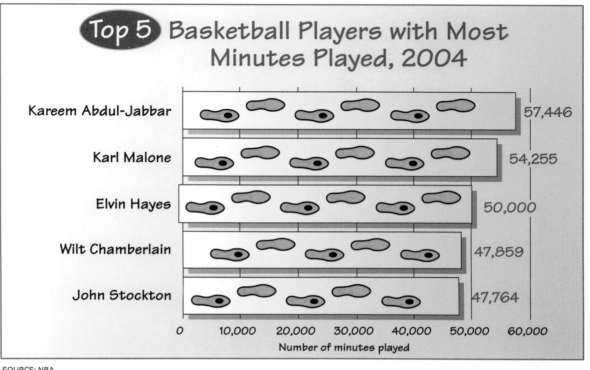

Top 5 Basketball Players with Most Minutes Played, 2004

Player	Number of minutes played
Kareem Abdul-Jabbar	57,446
Karl Malone	54,255
Elvin Hayes	50,000
Wilt Chamberlain	47,859
John Stockton	47,764

Number of minutes played

SOURCE: NBA

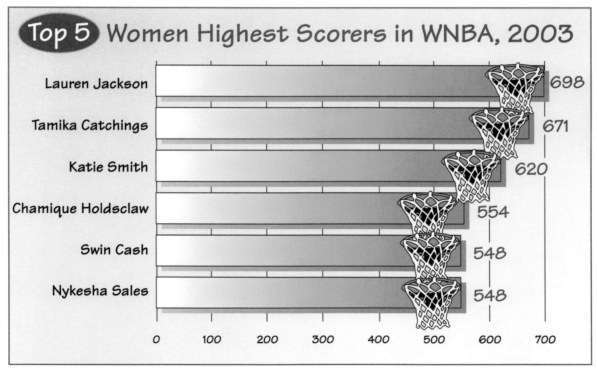

Top 5 Women Highest Scorers in WNBA, 2003

Player	Score
Lauren Jackson	698
Tamika Catchings	671
Katie Smith	620
Chamique Holdsclaw	554
Swin Cash	548
Nykesha Sales	548

Pro Sports

SOURCE: Women's National Basketball Association

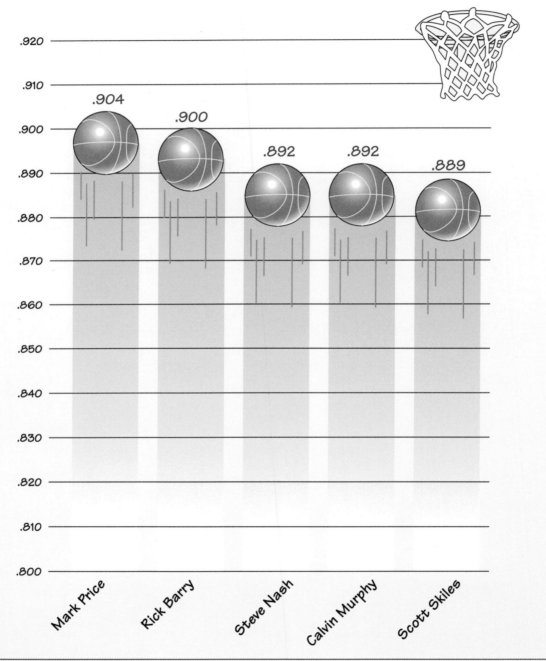

Top 5 Basketball Players, by Free Throw Percentages, 2004

- Mark Price — .904
- Rick Barry — .900
- Steve Nash — .892
- Calvin Murphy — .892
- Scott Skiles — .889

Pro Sports

SOURCE: National Basketball Association

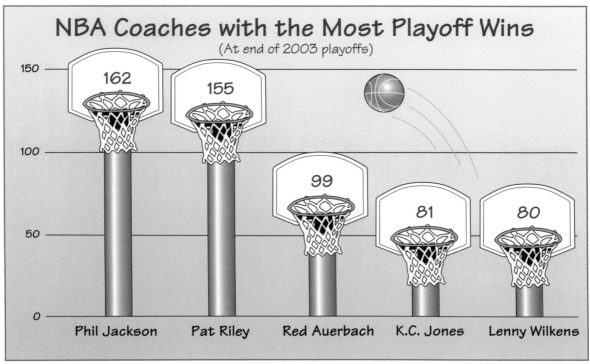

NBA Coaches with the Most Playoff Wins
(At end of 2003 playoffs)

Phil Jackson	Pat Riley	Red Auerbach	K.C. Jones	Lenny Wilkens
162	155	99	81	80

SOURCE: National Basketball Association

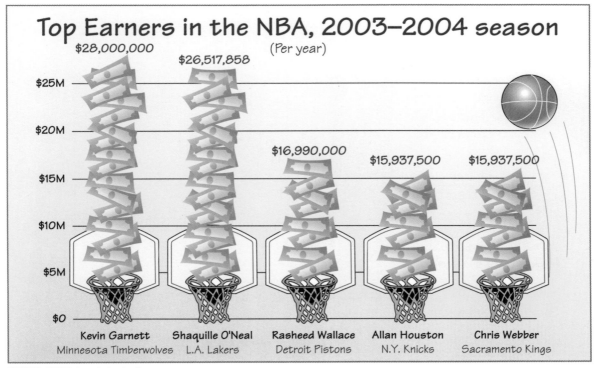

Top Earners in the NBA, 2003–2004 season
(Per year)

Kevin Garnett	Shaquille O'Neal	Rasheed Wallace	Allan Houston	Chris Webber
Minnesota Timberwolves	L.A. Lakers	Detroit Pistons	N.Y. Knicks	Sacramento Kings
$28,000,000	$26,517,858	$16,990,000	$15,937,500	$15,937,500

SOURCE: *USA Today* salaries database

Pro Sports

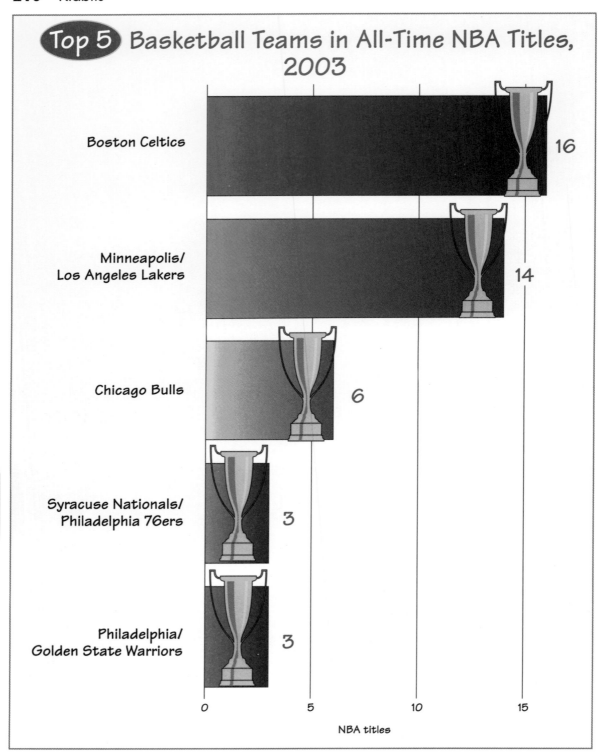

Top 5 Basketball Teams in All-Time NBA Titles, 2003

Boston Celtics — 16

Minneapolis/ Los Angeles Lakers — 14

Chicago Bulls — 6

Syracuse Nationals/ Philadelphia 76ers — 3

Philadelphia/ Golden State Warriors — 3

NBA titles

Pro Sports

SOURCE: National Basketball Association

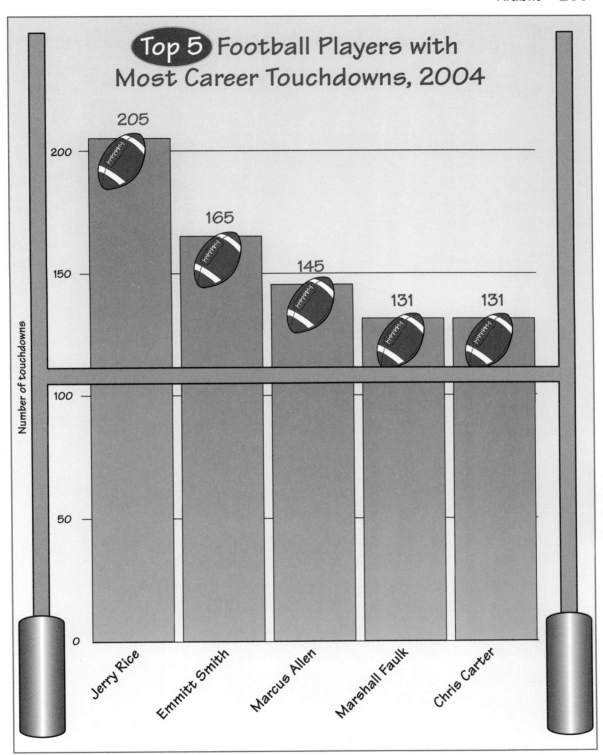

Top 5 Football Players with Most Career Touchdowns, 2004

SOURCE: ESPN

Top 5 NFL All-Time Points Leaders, 2004

Player	Points
Gary Anderson	2,348
Morten Andersen	2,257
George Blanda	2,002
Norm Johnson	1,736
Nick Lowery	1,711

SOURCE: ESPN

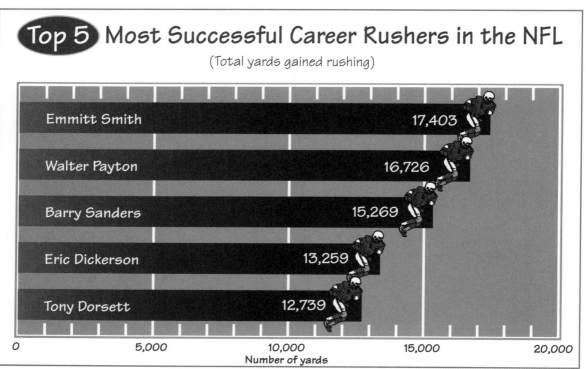

Top 5 Most Successful Career Rushers in the NFL

(Total yards gained rushing)

Player	Number of yards
Emmitt Smith	17,403
Walter Payton	16,726
Barry Sanders	15,269
Eric Dickerson	13,259
Tony Dorsett	12,739

SOURCE: ESPN

Pro Sports

Top All-Time Passing Records in the NFL, 2004

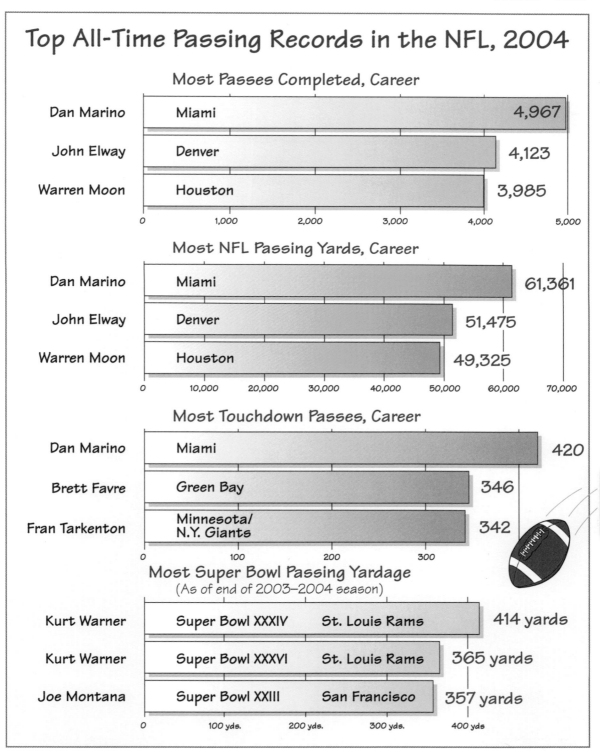

Most Passes Completed, Career

Dan Marino	Miami	4,967
John Elway	Denver	4,123
Warren Moon	Houston	3,985

0 · 1,000 · 2,000 · 3,000 · 4,000 · 5,000

Most NFL Passing Yards, Career

Dan Marino	Miami	61,361
John Elway	Denver	51,475
Warren Moon	Houston	49,325

0 · 10,000 · 20,000 · 30,000 · 40,000 · 50,000 · 60,000 · 70,000

Most Touchdown Passes, Career

Dan Marino	Miami	420
Brett Favre	Green Bay	346
Fran Tarkenton	Minnesota/ N.Y. Giants	342

0 · 100 · 200 · 300

Most Super Bowl Passing Yardage
(As of end of 2003–2004 season)

Kurt Warner	Super Bowl XXXIV	St. Louis Rams	414 yards
Kurt Warner	Super Bowl XXXVI	St. Louis Rams	365 yards
Joe Montana	Super Bowl XXIII	San Francisco	357 yards

0 · 100 yds. · 200 yds. · 300 yds. · 400 yds

Pro Sports

SOURCE: National Football League

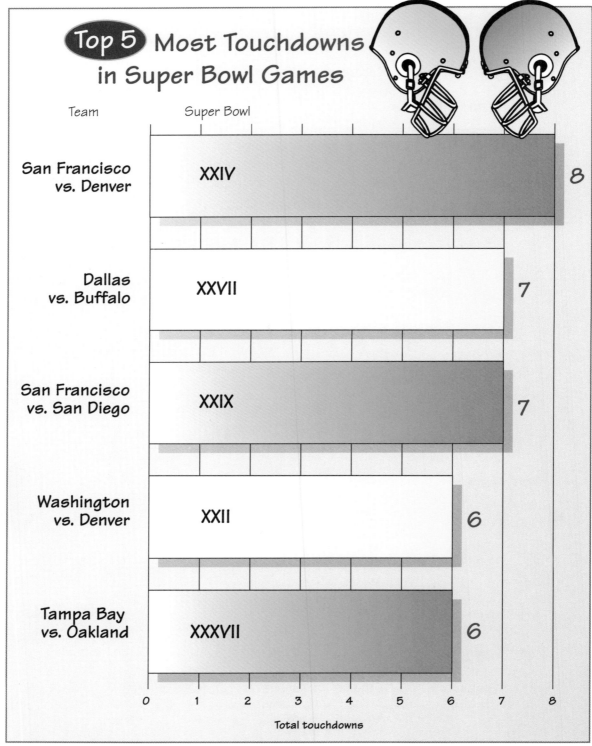

Top 5 Most Touchdowns in Super Bowl Games

Team	Super Bowl	Total touchdowns
San Francisco vs. Denver	XXIV	8
Dallas vs. Buffalo	XXVII	7
San Francisco vs. San Diego	XXIX	7
Washington vs. Denver	XXII	6
Tampa Bay vs. Oakland	XXXVII	6

Total touchdowns

0 1 2 3 4 5 6 7 8

Pro Sports

SOURCE: National Football League

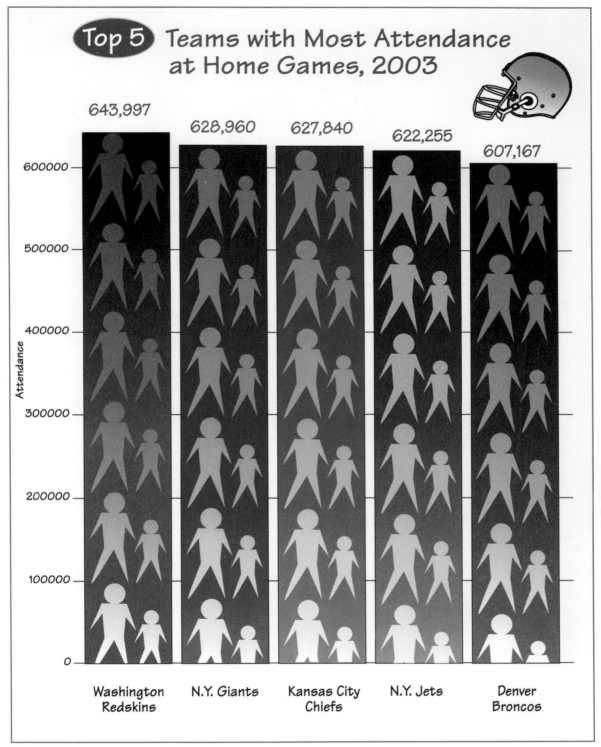

Top 5 Teams with Most Attendance at Home Games, 2003

643,997 — Washington Redskins
628,960 — N.Y. Giants
627,840 — Kansas City Chiefs
622,255 — N.Y. Jets
607,167 — Denver Broncos

Attendance

600000
500000
400000
300000
200000
100000
0

Pro Sports

SOURCE: ESPN

Pro Sports

Top 5 NFL Stadiums by Number of Seats, 2003

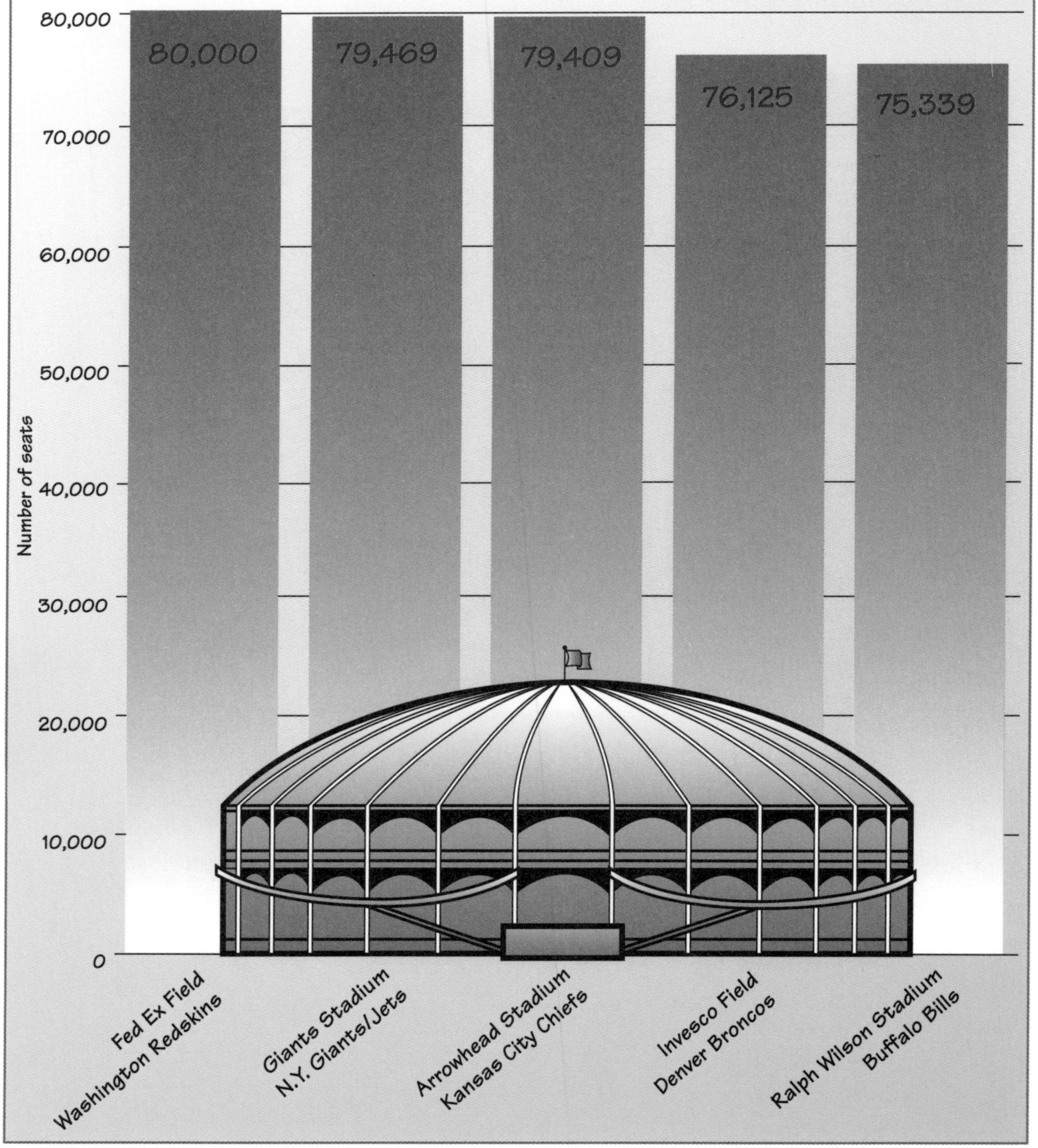

Number of seats

80,000	Fed Ex Field / Washington Redskins
79,469	Giants Stadium / N.Y. Giants/Jets
79,409	Arrowhead Stadium / Kansas City Chiefs
76,125	Invesco Field / Denver Broncos
75,339	Ralph Wilson Stadium / Buffalo Bills

SOURCE: stadiumsofnfl.com

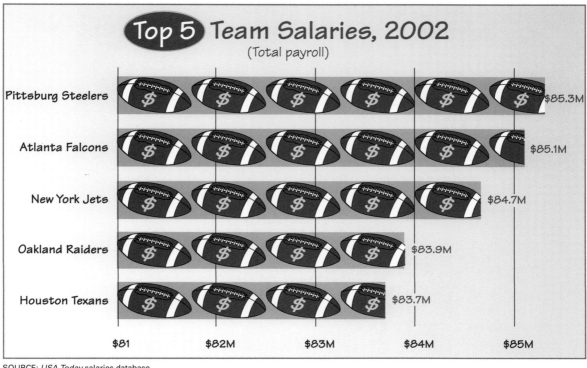

Top 5 Team Salaries, 2002
(Total payroll)

Pittsburg Steelers	$85.3M
Atlanta Falcons	$85.1M
New York Jets	$84.7M
Oakland Raiders	$83.9M
Houston Texans	$83.7M

$81 $82M $83M $84M $85M

SOURCE: *USA Today* salaries database

Top Earners in NFL, 2002

Michael Strahan	N.Y. Giants	$20,599,980
Donovan McNabb	Philadelphia Eagles	$14,736,284
Curtis Martin	N.Y. Jets	$13,503,600
Larry Allen	Dallas Cowboys	$13,022,520
David Carr	Houston Texans	$11,960,000

$20M $15M $10M $5M $0

SOURCE: *USA Today* salaries database

Pro Sports

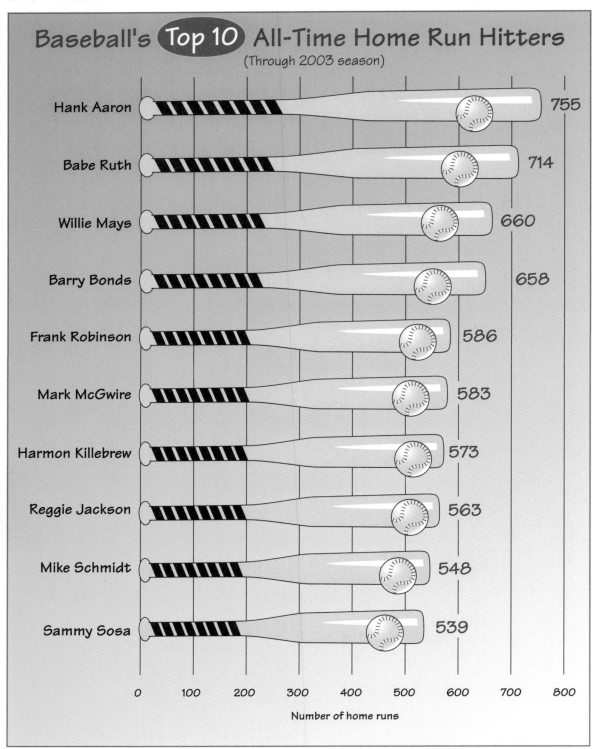

Baseball's Top 10 All-Time Home Run Hitters
(Through 2003 season)

Hank Aaron	755
Babe Ruth	714
Willie Mays	660
Barry Bonds	658
Frank Robinson	586
Mark McGwire	583
Harmon Killebrew	573
Reggie Jackson	563
Mike Schmidt	548
Sammy Sosa	539

0   100   200   300   400   500   600   700   800

Number of home runs

SOURCE: ESPN

Top Baseball Pitchers with Most Career Games
(Through 2003 season)

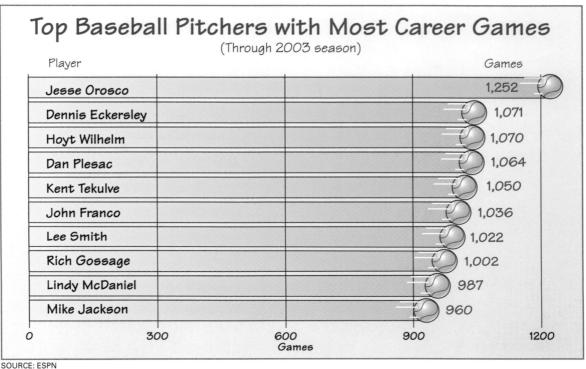

Player / Games

Player	Games
Jesse Orosco	1,252
Dennis Eckersley	1,071
Hoyt Wilhelm	1,070
Dan Plesac	1,064
Kent Tekulve	1,050
John Franco	1,036
Lee Smith	1,022
Rich Gossage	1,002
Lindy McDaniel	987
Mike Jackson	960

0   300   600   900   1200
Games

SOURCE: ESPN

Top 5 Baseball Players with Most Career Games
(Through 2003 season)

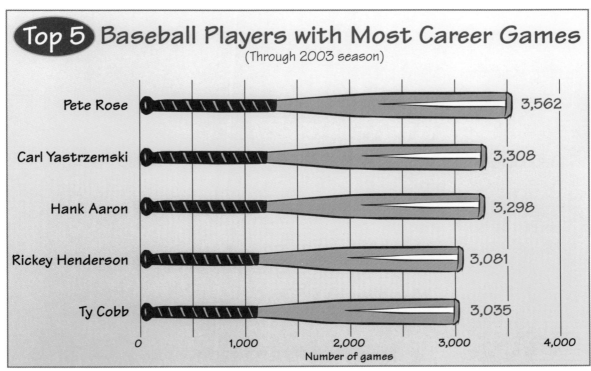

Player	Number of games
Pete Rose	3,562
Carl Yastrzemski	3,308
Hank Aaron	3,298
Rickey Henderson	3,081
Ty Cobb	3,035

0   1,000   2,000   3,000   4,000
Number of games

SOURCE: ESPN

Pro Sports

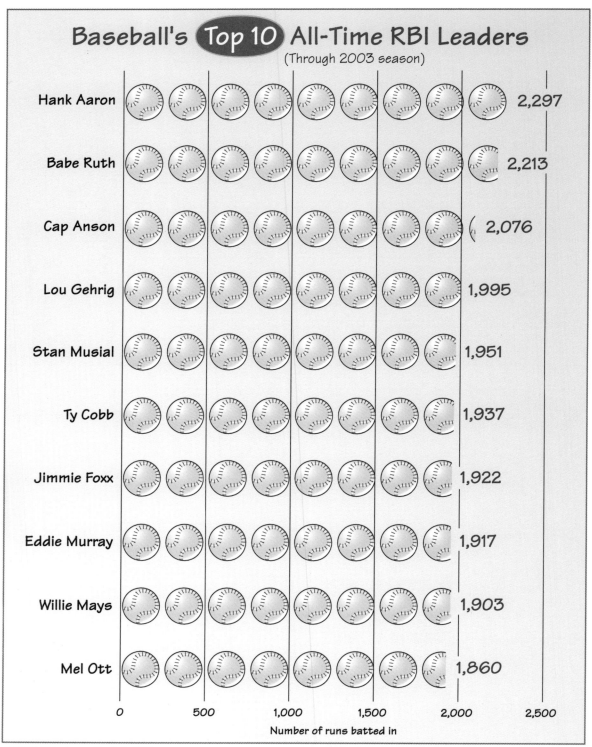

Baseball's Top 10 All-Time RBI Leaders

(Through 2003 season)

Player	RBI
Hank Aaron	2,297
Babe Ruth	2,213
Cap Anson	2,076
Lou Gehrig	1,995
Stan Musial	1,951
Ty Cobb	1,937
Jimmie Foxx	1,922
Eddie Murray	1,917
Willie Mays	1,903
Mel Ott	1,860

0   500   1,000   1,500   2,000   2,500

Number of runs batted in

Pro Sports

SOURCE: Major League Baseball, ESPN

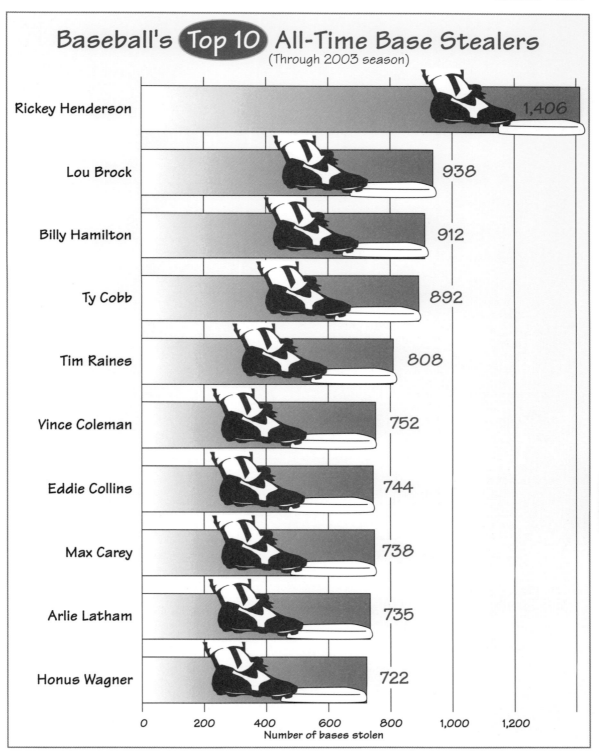

Baseball's Top 10 All-Time Base Stealers
(Through 2003 season)

Player	Number of bases stolen
Rickey Henderson	1,406
Lou Brock	938
Billy Hamilton	912
Ty Cobb	892
Tim Raines	808
Vince Coleman	752
Eddie Collins	744
Max Carey	738
Arlie Latham	735
Honus Wagner	722

Number of bases stolen

0   200   400   600   800   1,000   1,200

Pro Sports

SOURCE: Major League Baseball, ESPN

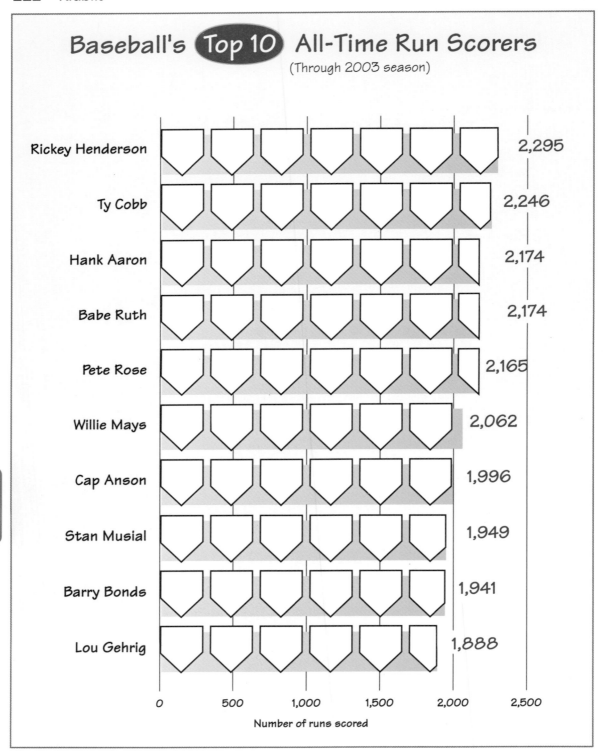

Baseball's Top 10 All-Time Run Scorers
(Through 2003 season)

Player	Runs
Rickey Henderson	2,295
Ty Cobb	2,246
Hank Aaron	2,174
Babe Ruth	2,174
Pete Rose	2,165
Willie Mays	2,062
Cap Anson	1,996
Stan Musial	1,949
Barry Bonds	1,941
Lou Gehrig	1,888

Number of runs scored

Pro Sports

SOURCE: Major League Baseball, ESPN

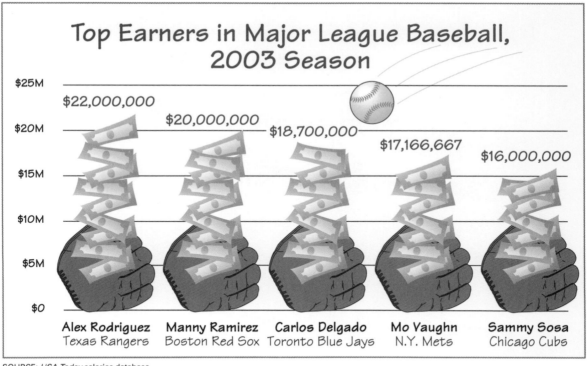

Top Earners in Major League Baseball, 2003 Season

$25M

$22,000,000

$20M

$20,000,000

$18,700,000

$17,166,667

$15M

$16,000,000

$10M

$5M

$0

| Alex Rodriguez | Manny Ramirez | Carlos Delgado | Mo Vaughn | Sammy Sosa |
| Texas Rangers | Boston Red Sox | Toronto Blue Jays | N.Y. Mets | Chicago Cubs |

SOURCE: *USA Today* salaries database

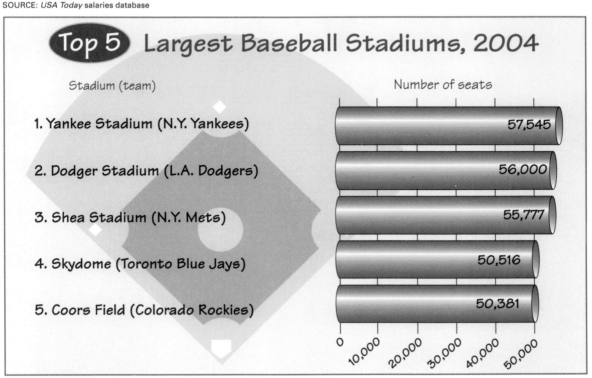

Top 5 Largest Baseball Stadiums, 2004

Stadium (team)   Number of seats

1. Yankee Stadium (N.Y. Yankees)   57,545

2. Dodger Stadium (L.A. Dodgers)   56,000

3. Shea Stadium (N.Y. Mets)   55,777

4. Skydome (Toronto Blue Jays)   50,516

5. Coors Field (Colorado Rockies)   50,381

0   10,000   20,000   30,000   40,000   50,000

SOURCE: *Baseball Almanac*

Pro Sports

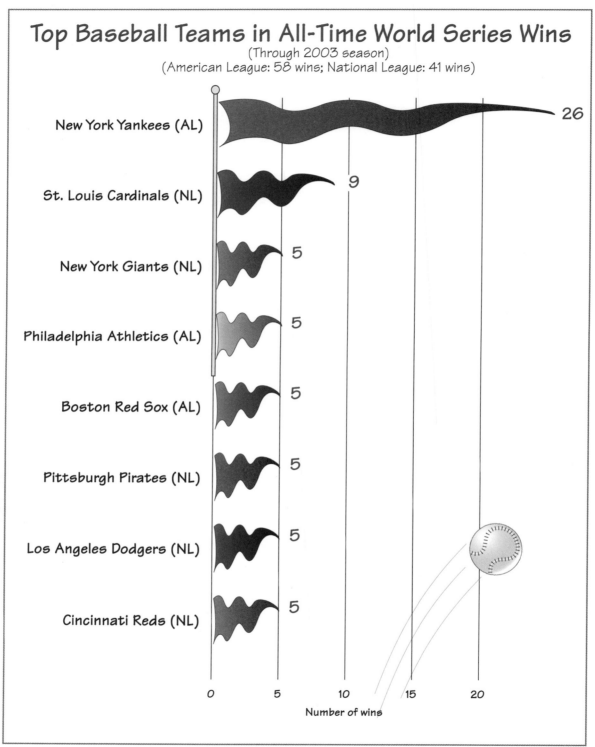

Top Baseball Teams in All-Time World Series Wins
(Through 2003 season)
(American League: 58 wins; National League: 41 wins)

New York Yankees (AL) — 26

St. Louis Cardinals (NL) — 9

New York Giants (NL) — 5

Philadelphia Athletics (AL) — 5

Boston Red Sox (AL) — 5

Pittsburgh Pirates (NL) — 5

Los Angeles Dodgers (NL) — 5

Cincinnati Reds (NL) — 5

0   5   10   15   20

Number of wins

Pro Sports

SOURCE: Major League Baseball

Hockey's Top 5 NHL Playoff Goal Scorers
(Through 2002–2003 season)

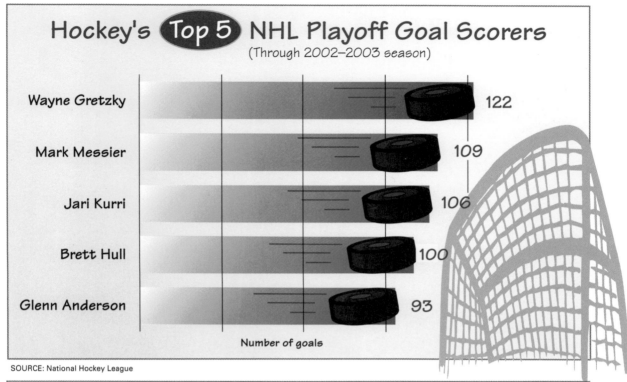

Player	Number of goals
Wayne Gretzky	122
Mark Messier	109
Jari Kurri	106
Brett Hull	100
Glenn Anderson	93

Number of goals

SOURCE: National Hockey League

Hockey's Top 5 Points Scorers in Stanley Cup Playoff Games
(Through 2002–2003 season)

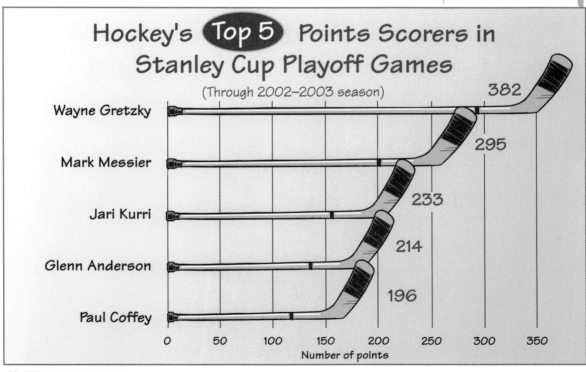

Player	Number of points
Wayne Gretzky	382
Mark Messier	295
Jari Kurri	233
Glenn Anderson	214
Paul Coffey	196

Number of points

SOURCE: National Hockey League

Pro Sports

NHL Teams with Highest Payroll
(2003–2004 season)

$80M	
$70M	
$60M	
$50M	
$40M	
$30M	
$20M	
$10M	
$0	

$77,856,109 $76,488,716 $68,578,885

Detroit Red Wings   New York Rangers   Dallas Stars

SOURCE: *USA Today* salaries database

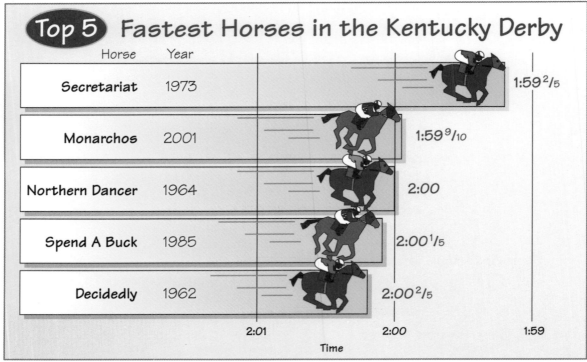

Top 5 Fastest Horses in the Kentucky Derby

Horse	Year	Time
Secretariat	1973	1:59 $^2/_5$
Monarchos	2001	1:59 $^9/_{10}$
Northern Dancer	1964	2:00
Spend A Buck	1985	2:00 $^1/_5$
Decidedly	1962	2:00 $^2/_5$

2:01   2:00   1:59

Time

SOURCE: *USA Today*

Pro Sports

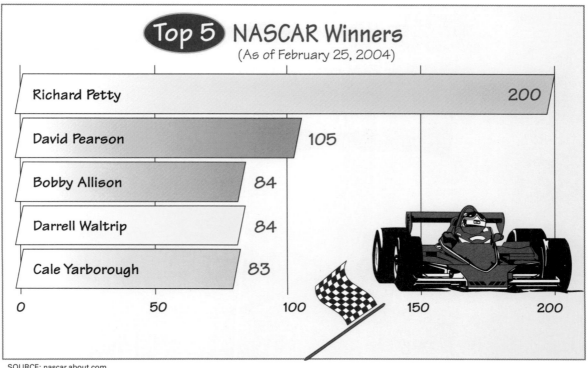

Top 5 NASCAR Winners
(As of February 25, 2004)

Driver	Wins
Richard Petty	200
David Pearson	105
Bobby Allison	84
Darrell Waltrip	84
Cale Yarborough	83

0   50   100   150   200

SOURCE: nascar.about.com

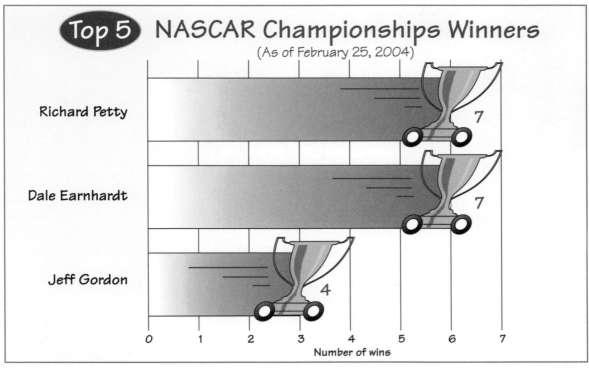

Top 5 NASCAR Championships Winners
(As of February 25, 2004)

Driver	Number of wins
Richard Petty	7
Dale Earnhardt	7
Jeff Gordon	4

0   1   2   3   4   5   6   7
Number of wins

SOURCE: nascar.about.com

Pro Sports

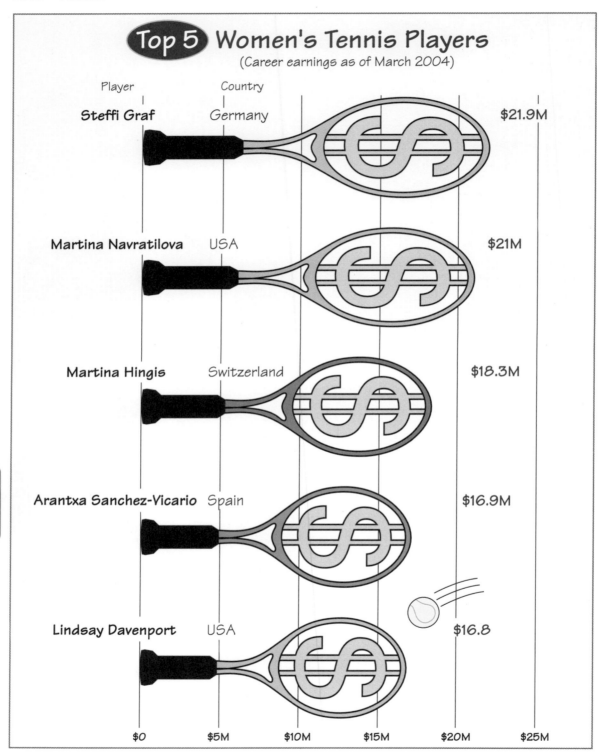

Top 5 Women's Tennis Players

(Career earnings as of March 2004)

Player	Country	Earnings
Steffi Graf	Germany	$21.9M
Martina Navratilova	USA	$21M
Martina Hingis	Switzerland	$18.3M
Arantxa Sanchez-Vicario	Spain	$16.9M
Lindsay Davenport	USA	$16.8

$0 $5M $10M $15M $20M $25M

SOURCE: sportsillustrated.cnn.com

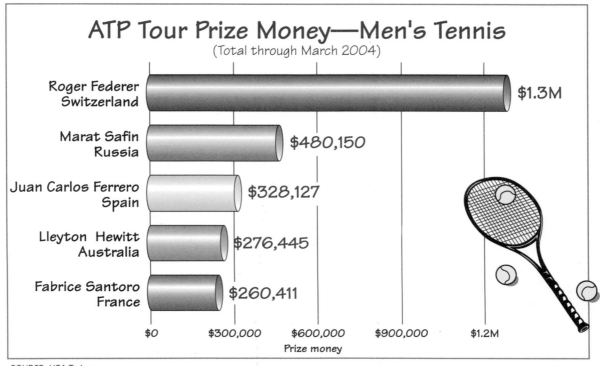

ATP Tour Prize Money—Men's Tennis
(Total through March 2004)

Player	Prize money
Roger Federer, Switzerland	$1.3M
Marat Safin, Russia	$480,150
Juan Carlos Ferrero, Spain	$328,127
Lleyton Hewitt, Australia	$276,445
Fabrice Santoro, France	$260,411

Prize money: $0 $300,000 $600,000 $900,000 $1.2M

SOURCE: *USA Today*

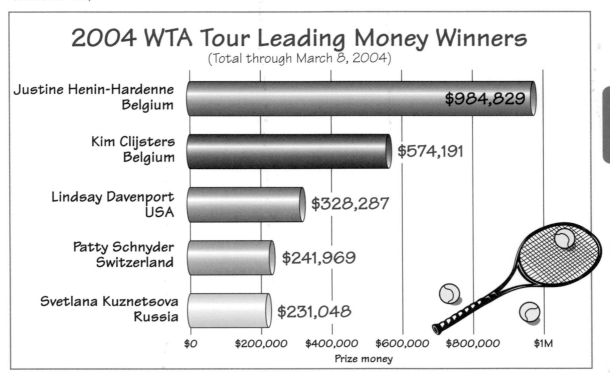

2004 WTA Tour Leading Money Winners
(Total through March 8, 2004)

Player	Prize money
Justine Henin-Hardenne, Belgium	$984,829
Kim Clijsters, Belgium	$574,191
Lindsay Davenport, USA	$328,287
Patty Schnyder, Switzerland	$241,969
Svetlana Kuznetsova, Russia	$231,048

Prize money: $0 $200,000 $400,000 $600,000 $800,000 $1M

Pro Sports

SOURCE: *USA Today*

Top U.S. Open Singles Champions—Men

Player	Number of titles	Years earned
William A. Larned	8	1901–1902, 1906–1911
Richard D. Sears	7	1881–1887
Bill Tilden	6	1920–1925, 1929
Jimmy Connors	5	1974, 1976, 1978 1982–1983
Robert D. Wrenn	4	1893–1894, 1896–1897
John McEnroe	4	1979–1981, 1984

SOURCE: usopen.org

Top U.S. Open Singles Champions—Women

Player	Number of titles	Years earned
Molla Bjurstedt Mallory	8	1915–1918, 1920–1922, 1926
Helen Wills Moody	7	1923–1925, 1927–1929, 1931
Chris Evert Lloyd	6	1975–1978, 1980, 1982
Margaret Smith Court	5	1962, 1965, 1969, 1970, 1973
Steffi Graf	5	1988–1989, 1993, 1995–1996

SOURCE: usopen.org

Pro Sports

2003 PGA Tour Total Birdies

Player	Total birdies
Robert Garnez	466
Vijay Singh	450
Steve Flesch	433
Charles Howell III	428
Skip Kendall	427

SOURCE: Professional Golfers' Association

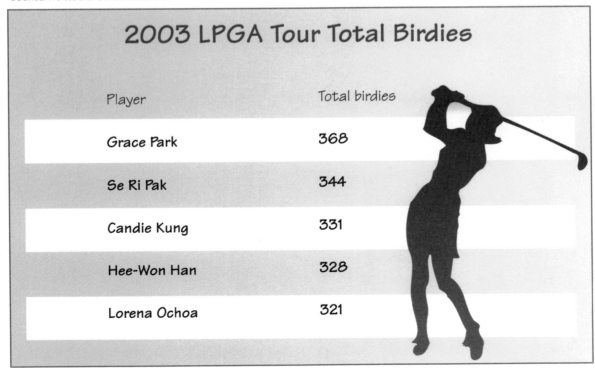

2003 LPGA Tour Total Birdies

Player	Total birdies
Grace Park	368
Se Ri Pak	344
Candie Kung	331
Hee-Won Han	328
Lorena Ochoa	321

SOURCE: Professional Golfers' Association

Pro Sports

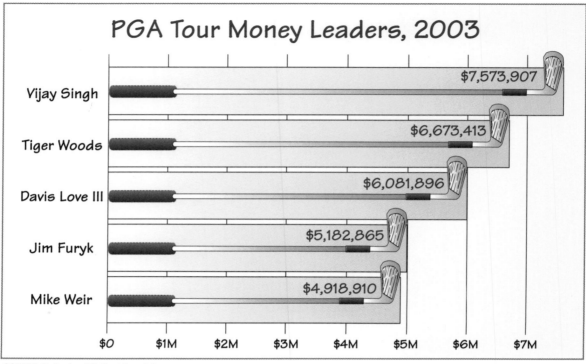

PGA Tour Money Leaders, 2003

Vijay Singh — $7,573,907
Tiger Woods — $6,673,413
Davis Love III — $6,081,896
Jim Furyk — $5,182,865
Mike Weir — $4,918,910

$0 $1M $2M $3M $4M $5M $6M $7M

SOURCE: Professional Golfers' Association

LPGA Tour Money Leaders, 2003

Annika Sorenstam — $1,914,506
Se Ri Pak — $1,543,893
Grace Park — $1,339,217
Hee-Won Han — $1,025,560
Juli Inkster — $997,145

$0 $500,000 $1M $1.5M

SOURCE: Professional Golfers' Association

Pro Sports

America's Favorite Sports Stars, 2004

Men

1.	Michael Jordan
2.	Tiger Woods
3.	Brett Favre
4.	Shaquille O'Neal
5.	Dale Earnhardt Jr.

Women

1.	Venus Williams*
2.	Serena Williams*
3.	Mia Hamm
4.	Michelle Kwan
5.	Anika Sorenstam

* The gap between the two Williams sister is statistically insignificant

Pro Sports

SOURCE: Harris Poll, March 3, 2004

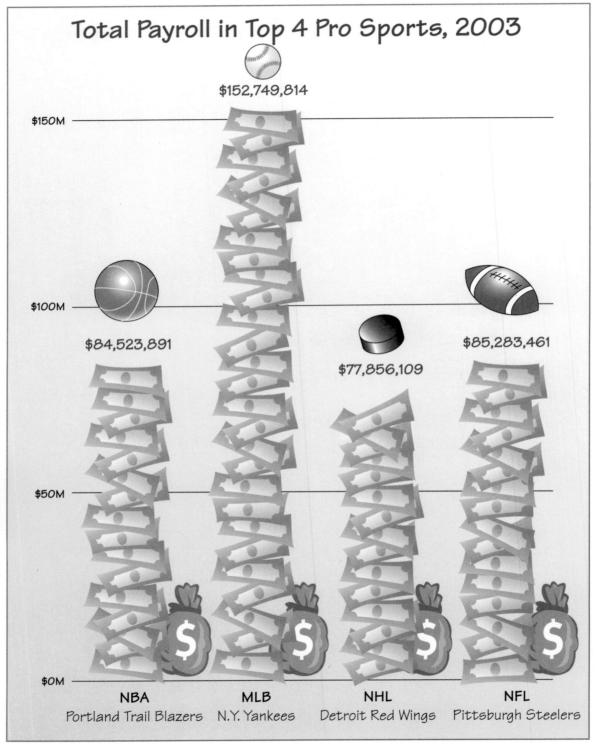

Total Payroll in Top 4 Pro Sports, 2003

$152,749,814

$150M

$100M

$84,523,891

$77,856,109

$85,283,461

$50M

$0M

NBA	MLB	NHL	NFL
Portland Trail Blazers	N.Y. Yankees	Detroit Red Wings	Pittsburgh Steelers

Pro Sports

SOURCE: *USA Today* salaries database

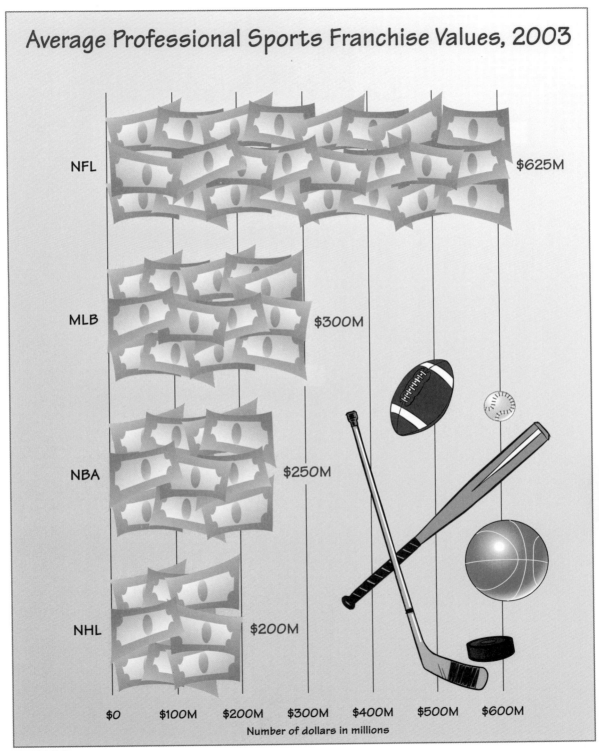

Average Professional Sports Franchise Values, 2003

NFL $625M

MLB $300M

NBA $250M

NHL $200M

$0 $100M $200M $300M $400M $500M $600M
Number of dollars in millions

Pro Sports

SOURCE: *Forbes*

Pets

Look in an American home and you're likely to see a cat snoozing on a couch or a dog sleeping on the carpet. More than half of all households in America include at least one pet. Most of these homes have either dogs or cats—or both dogs and cats. But many other kinds of animals are also kept as pets, including birds, fish, rabbits, guinea pigs, hamsters, gerbils, ferrets, horses— even potbellied pigs!

More homes have dogs than cats. But there are more pet cats than any other kind of pet—more than 70 million felines were counted at the end of 2001. Most cat-owning homes—66%—have only one cat, while about 30% of dog owners have more than one dog. If you live in the south, chances are good you own a dog; on average that region has 37% of all households owning dogs. If you live in the Midwest or West, about a quarter of all households in those areas own at least one cat.

Kidbits Tidbits
- Almost 14 million households in the United States have at least one pet.
- About 20% of U.S. homes include both dogs and cats.
- Dogs have been the #1 pet in the White House; four presidents have had a goat.
- "First Pet" Millie, an English springer spaniel that lived with President George H.W. and Barbara Bush, made almost $1 million for charity by "authoring" *Millie's Book* with Mrs. Bush in 1990.
- The last president to have a pet reptile was John Quincy Adams, who owned an alligator.

Though it's often the children in a home who eagerly want a pet, it's most often the mother who has the main responsibility for caring for the animals, including taking them to veterinarians for vaccinations and other health care. The average cost for veterinary care depends on the type of pet. In 2001, the average yearly veterinary medical expenditure for a dog was $261, compared with $160 for a cat and under $20 for a bird.

Veterinary bills are only part of the cost of owning a pet. Other costs include food, grooming, toys, housing, and so on. For example, Americans spend about $4 billion on dog food each year, and $2.5 billion on cat food.

Many people obtain their pets for little or no cost, often from neighbors or animal shelters. Other people pay hundreds or even thousands of dollars for pedigreed animals—that is, animals that have been carefully bred and for whom there is a written record of parents, grandparents, etc. These animals are often shown professionally— they compete in judged events, such as dog shows and cat shows.

Ask a pet owner if the costs of owning an animal are worth it, and the answer is most likely to be a loud "yes!" Pets add fun, companionship, and love to people's lives. They are even beneficial to people's health. For example, research shows that owning a pet can lower a person's blood pressure and decrease chances of having a heart attack.

Kidbits Tidbits
- The great majority of Americans believe that pets play a positive role in people's lives.
- About 90% of cat and dog owners consider the animals to be members of the family.
- Labrador retrievers rank #1 in registrations with the American Kennel Club, followed by golden retrievers and beagles.
- The Cat Fanciers Association recognizes 36 breeds, of which Persians are #1 in number of registrations.

Pets

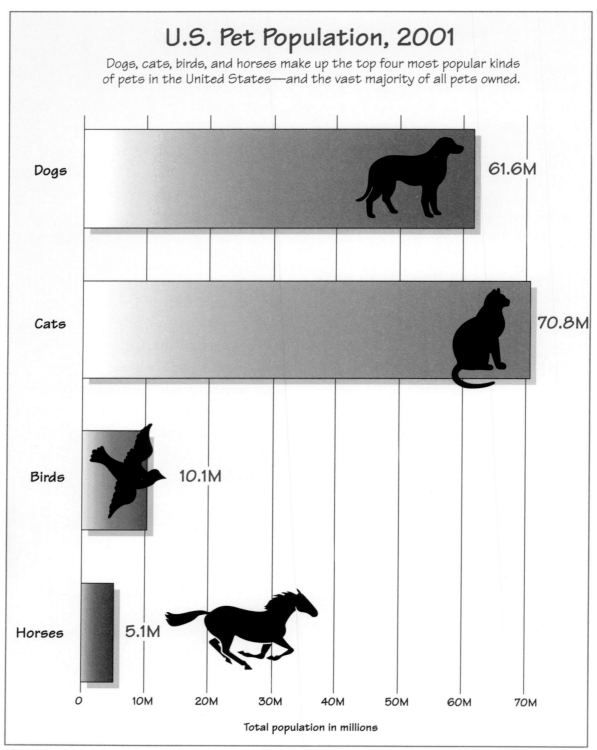

U.S. Pet Population, 2001

Dogs, cats, birds, and horses make up the top four most popular kinds of pets in the United States—and the vast majority of all pets owned.

Dogs — 61.6M

Cats — 70.8M

Birds — 10.1M

Horses — 5.1M

Total population in millions

SOURCE: American Veterinary Medical Association

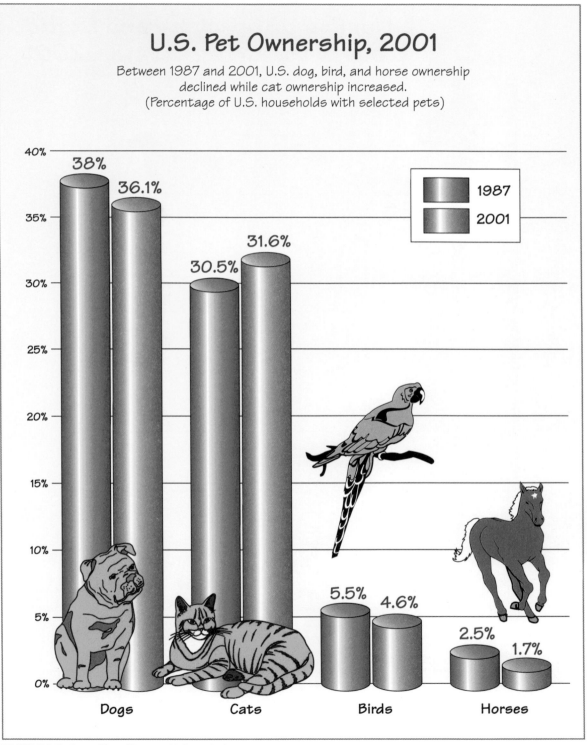

U.S. Pet Ownership, 2001

Between 1987 and 2001, U.S. dog, bird, and horse ownership
declined while cat ownership increased.
(Percentage of U.S. households with selected pets)

1987
2001

38%
36.1%
31.6%
30.5%
5.5%
4.6%
2.5%
1.7%

Dogs
Cats
Birds
Horses

Pets

SOURCE: U.S. Pet Ownership and Demographic Sourcebook

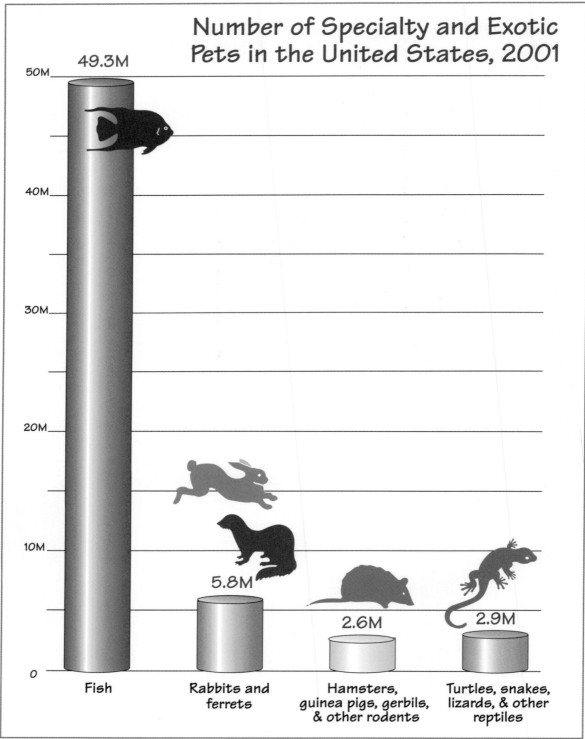

Number of Specialty and Exotic Pets in the United States, 2001

49.3M

50M

40M

30M

20M

10M

5.8M

2.6M

2.9M

0

Fish

Rabbits and ferrets

Hamsters, guinea pigs, gerbils, & other rodents

Turtles, snakes, lizards, & other reptiles

Pets

SOURCE: U.S. Pet Ownership and Demographic Sourcebook

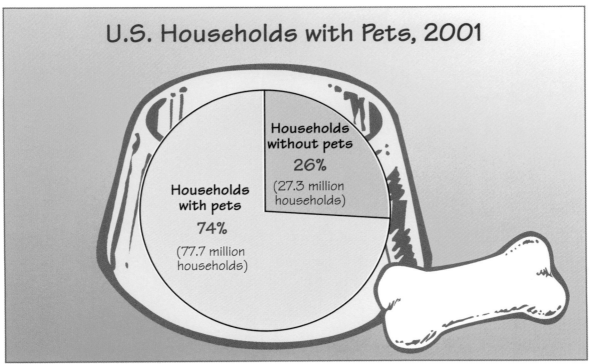

U.S. Households with Pets, 2001

Households without pets
26%
(27.3 million households)

Households with pets
74%
(77.7 million households)

SOURCE: U.S. Pet Ownership and Demographic Sourcebook

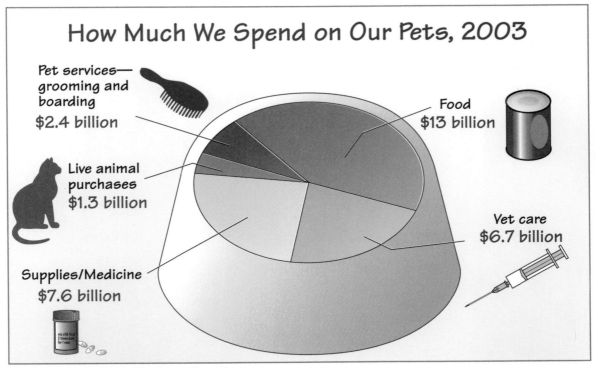

How Much We Spend on Our Pets, 2003

Pet services—grooming and boarding
$2.4 billion

Food
$13 billion

Live animal purchases
$1.3 billion

Vet care
$6.7 billion

Supplies/Medicine
$7.6 billion

Pets

SOURCE: American Pet Products Manufacturing Association

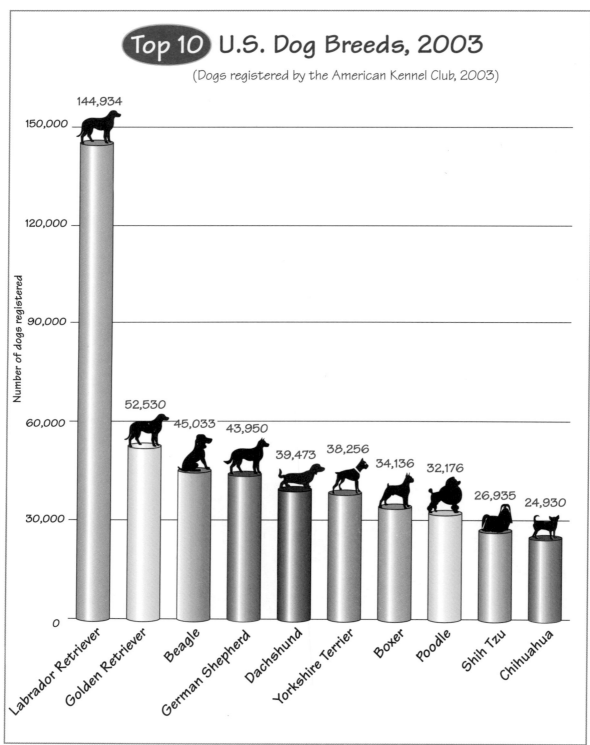

Top 10 U.S. Dog Breeds, 2003

(Dogs registered by the American Kennel Club, 2003)

Number of dogs registered

Labrador Retriever	144,934
Golden Retriever	52,530
Beagle	45,033
German Shepherd	43,950
Dachshund	39,473
Yorkshire Terrier	38,256
Boxer	34,136
Poodle	32,176
Shih Tzu	26,935
Chihuahua	24,930

Pets

SOURCE: American Kennel Club

Who Owns Dogs?

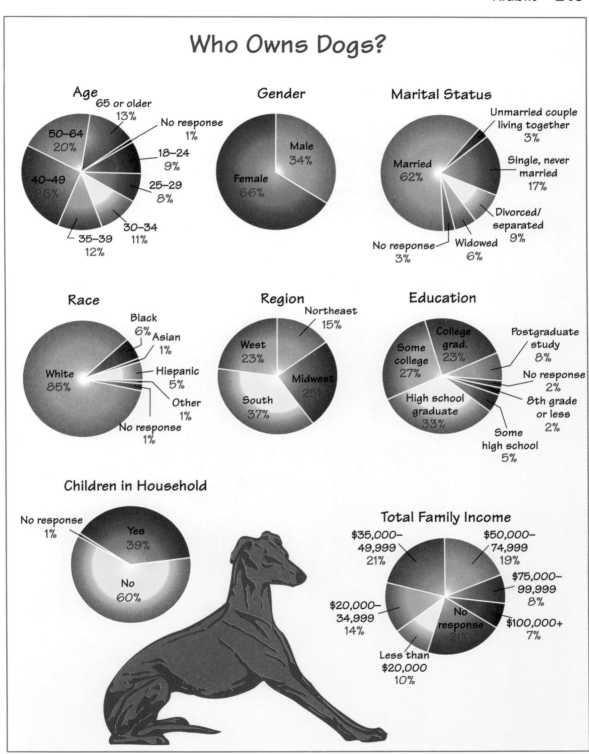

Age

- 65 or older 13%
- No response 1%
- 18–24 9%
- 50–64 20%
- 40–49 26%
- 25–29 8%
- 35–39 12%
- 30–34 11%

Gender

- Male 34%
- Female 66%

Marital Status

- Unmarried couple living together 3%
- Single, never married 17%
- Married 62%
- Divorced/separated 9%
- No response 3%
- Widowed 6%

Race

- Black 6%
- Asian 1%
- White 85%
- Hispanic 5%
- Other 1%
- No response 1%

Region

- Northeast 15%
- West 23%
- Midwest 25%
- South 37%

Education

- College grad. 23%
- Postgraduate study 8%
- Some college 27%
- No response 2%
- High school graduate 33%
- 8th grade or less 2%
- Some high school 5%

Children in Household

- No response 1%
- Yes 39%
- No 60%

Total Family Income

- $35,000–49,999 21%
- $50,000–74,999 19%
- $75,000–99,999 8%
- $20,000–34,999 14%
- No response 21%
- $100,000+ 7%
- Less than $20,000 10%

SOURCE: Purina, State of the American Pet Survey

Pets

Types of Cats We Own

Sixty-six percent of cat owners own only one cat.

Pure or Mixed Breed

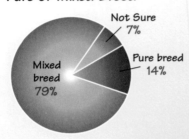

Not Sure
7%

Pure breed
14%

Mixed breed
79%

Age

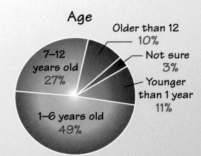

Older than 12
10%

Not sure
3%

Younger than 1 year
11%

7–12 years old
27%

1–6 years old
49%

Gender

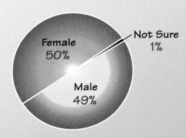

Female
50%

Not Sure
1%

Male
49%

Where We Got Our Cats

Pet Store
6%

Animal Shelter
16%

Breeder
4%

Other
5%

Stray
24%

Family, friend, neighbor

Spayed or Neutered

No
15%

Yes
85%

SOURCE: Purina, State of the American Pet Survey

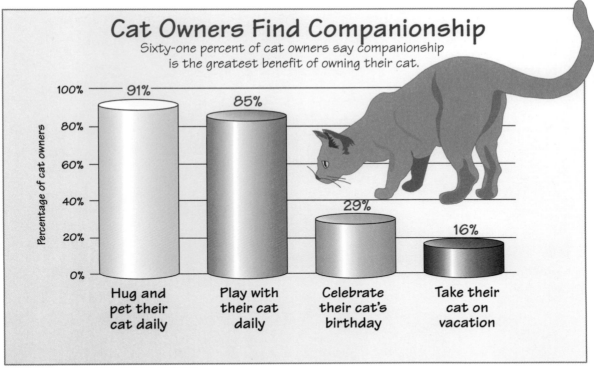

Cat Owners Find Companionship

Sixty-one percent of cat owners say companionship
is the greatest benefit of owning their cat.

SOURCE: Purina, State of the American Pet Survey

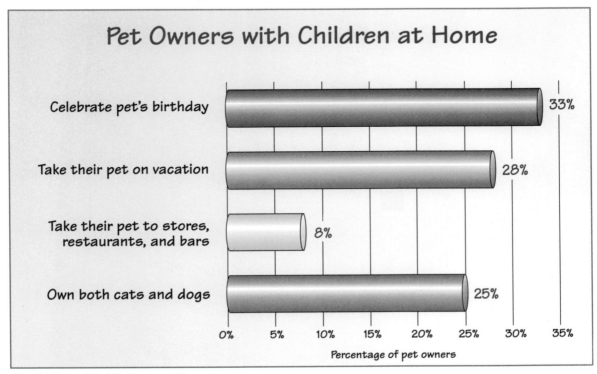

Pet Owners with Children at Home

SOURCE: Purina, State of the American Pet Survey

Healthiest Cities for Cats and Dogs, 2003

(Based on 30 criteria such as weight, preventative care, and air quality)

3. Portland, OR
10. Salt Lake City, UT
9. Philadelphia, PA
2. Oakland, CA
7. Minneapolis-St. Paul, MN
5. San Francisco, CA
8. Columbus, OH
6. Washington, D.C.
4. Anaheim, CA
1. Denver, CO

SOURCE: *USA Today* and data from Purina Pet Institute

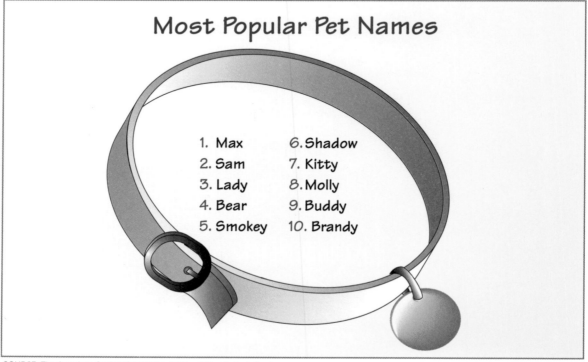

Most Popular Pet Names

1. Max
2. Sam
3. Lady
4. Bear
5. Smokey
6. Shadow
7. Kitty
8. Molly
9. Buddy
10. Brandy

Pets

SOURCE: The American Society for the Prevention of Cruelty to Animals

Who Owns Pets?

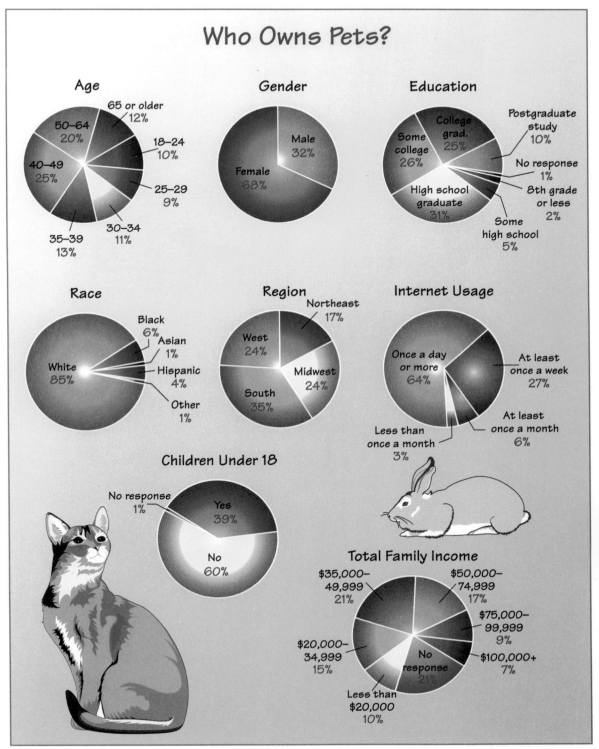

Age
- 65 or older 12%
- 50–64 20%
- 18–24 10%
- 40–49 25%
- 25–29 9%
- 35–39 13%
- 30–34 11%

Gender
- Male 32%
- Female 68%

Education
- College grad. 25%
- Some college 26%
- Postgraduate study 10%
- No response 1%
- 8th grade or less 2%
- High school graduate 31%
- Some high school 5%

Race
- Black 6%
- Asian 1%
- White 85%
- Hispanic 4%
- Other 1%

Region
- Northeast 17%
- West 24%
- Midwest 24%
- South 35%

Internet Usage
- Once a day or more 64%
- At least once a week 27%
- Less than once a month 3%
- At least once a month 6%

Children Under 18
- No response 1%
- Yes 39%
- No 60%

Total Family Income
- $35,000–49,999 21%
- $50,000–74,999 17%
- $75,000–99,999 9%
- $100,000+ 7%
- No response 21%
- $20,000–34,999 15%
- Less than $20,000 10%

SOURCE: Purina, State of the American Pet Survey

Pets

Percentage of Pet Owners Who Own Cats, Dogs or Both

Own dogs
48%

Own both
20%

Own cats
32%

SOURCE: Purina, State of the American Pet Survey

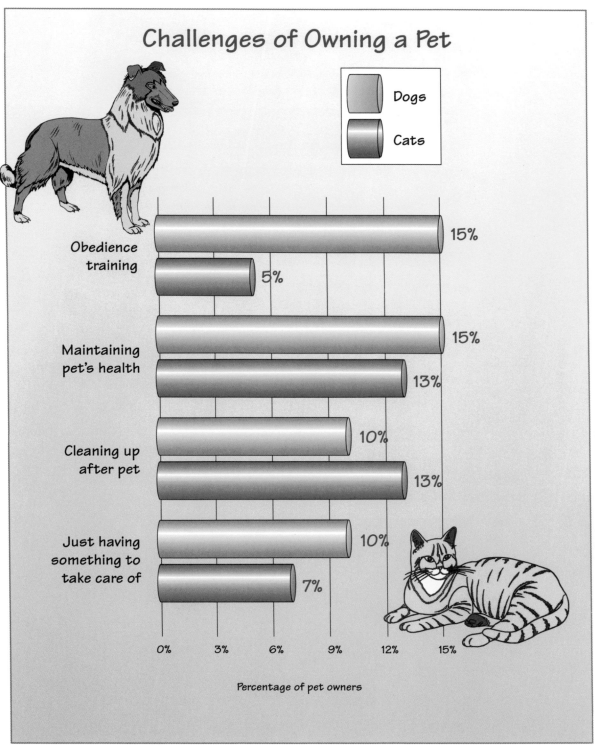

Challenges of Owning a Pet

| | Dogs |
| | Cats |

Obedience training
- Dogs: 15%
- Cats: 5%

Maintaining pet's health
- Dogs: 15%
- Cats: 13%

Cleaning up after pet
- Dogs: 10%
- Cats: 13%

Just having something to take care of
- Dogs: 10%
- Cats: 7%

0%   3%   6%   9%   12%   15%

Percentage of pet owners

Pets

SOURCE: Purina, State of the American Pet Survey

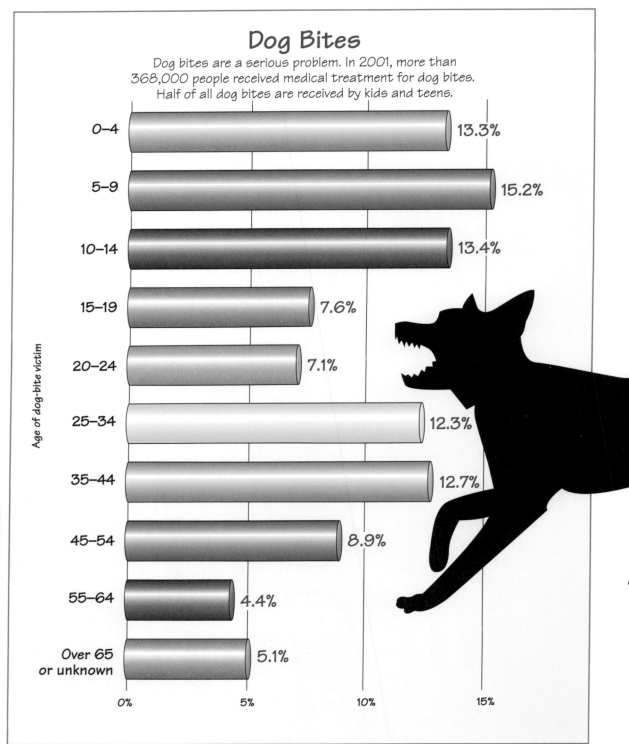

Dog Bites

Dog bites are a serious problem. In 2001, more than 368,000 people received medical treatment for dog bites. Half of all dog bites are received by kids and teens.

Age of dog-bite victim

Age	Percent
0–4	13.3%
5–9	15.2%
10–14	13.4%
15–19	7.6%
20–24	7.1%
25–34	12.3%
35–44	12.7%
45–54	8.9%
55–64	4.4%
Over 65 or unknown	5.1%

Pets

SOURCE: Centers for Disease Control and Prevention, MMWR July 4, 2003

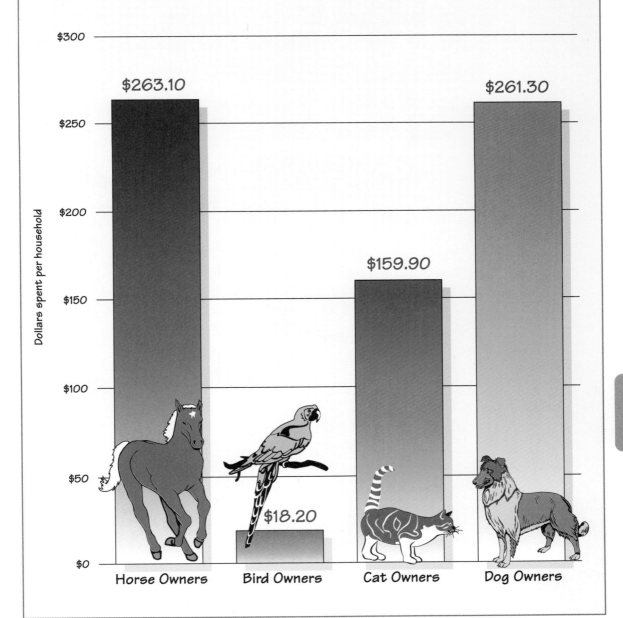

Average Yearly Cost for Veterinary Care, per Animal-Owning Household, 2001

(By selected animal)

Dollars spent per household

$300

$263.10

$261.30

$250

$200

$159.90

$150

$100

$50

$18.20

$0

Horse Owners   Bird Owners   Cat Owners   Dog Owners

Pets

SOURCE: 2002 U.S. Pet Ownership and Demographic Sourcebook

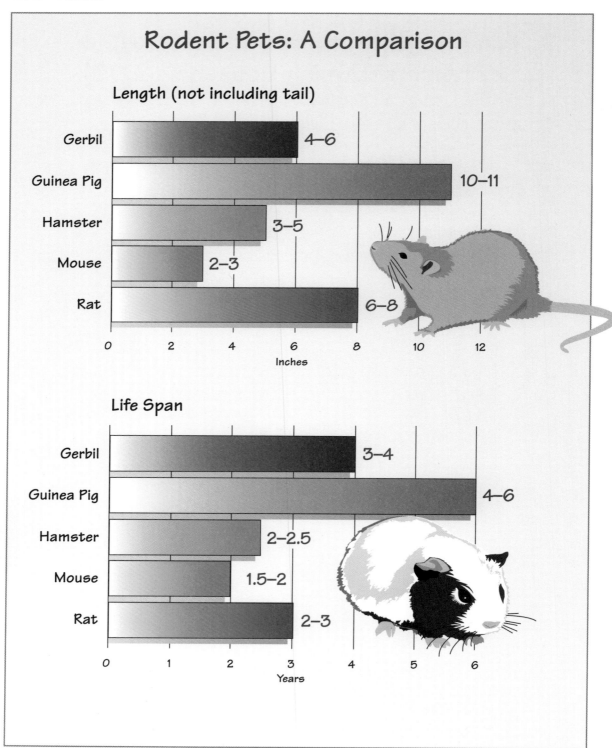

Rodent Pets: A Comparison

Length (not including tail)

Rodent	Inches
Gerbil	4–6
Guinea Pig	10–11
Hamster	3–5
Mouse	2–3
Rat	6–8

Life Span

Rodent	Years
Gerbil	3–4
Guinea Pig	4–6
Hamster	2–2.5
Mouse	1.5–2
Rat	2–3

Pets

SOURCE: factmonster.com

Average Yearly Cost for Veterinary Care, per Animal, 2001

Dogs cost the most—about 37% more than
horses and almost 53% more than cats
(By selected animal)

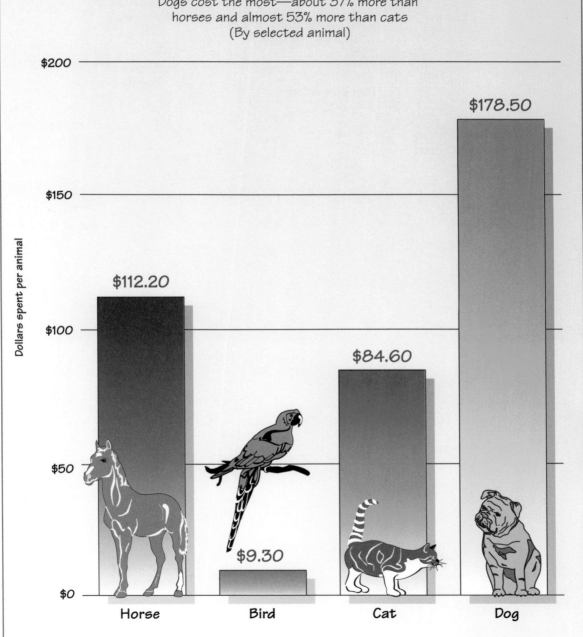

Dollars spent per animal

$200

$178.50

$150

$112.20

$100

$84.60

$50

$9.30

$0

Horse   Bird   Cat   Dog

Pets

SOURCE: 2002 U.S. Pet Ownership and Demographic Sourcebook

Pets

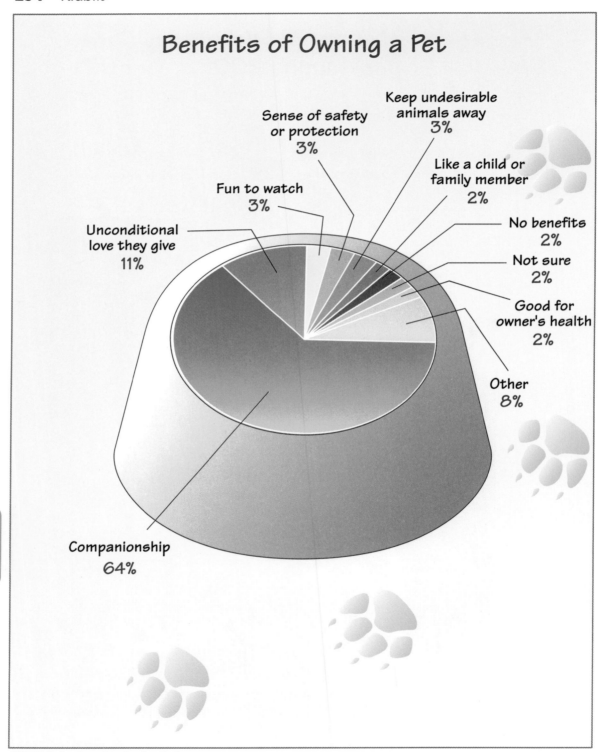

Benefits of Owning a Pet

Sense of safety
or protection
3%

Keep undesirable
animals away
3%

Like a child or
family member
2%

Fun to watch
3%

No benefits
2%

Unconditional
love they give
11%

Not sure
2%

Good for
owner's health
2%

Other
8%

Companionship
64%

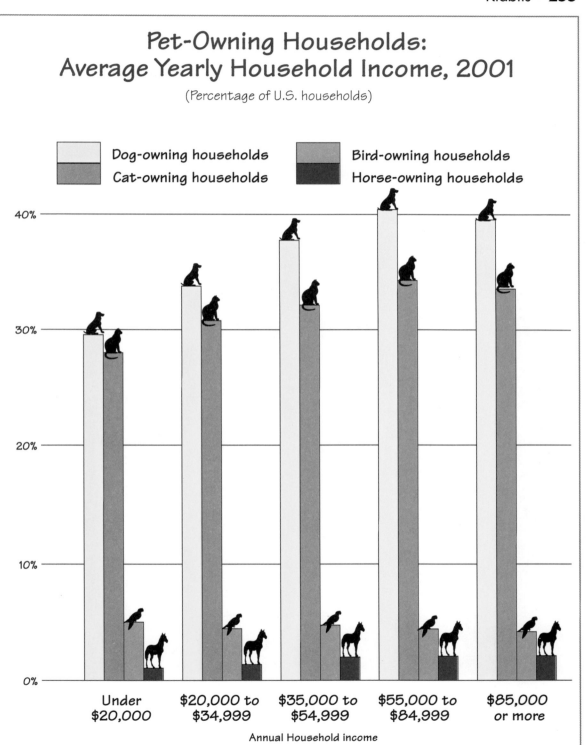

Pet-Owning Households:
Average Yearly Household Income, 2001

(Percentage of U.S. households)

Dog-owning households
Cat-owning households
Bird-owning households
Horse-owning households

40%

30%

20%

10%

0%

Under
$20,000

$20,000 to
$34,999

$35,000 to
$54,999

$55,000 to
$84,999

$85,000
or more

Annual Household income

Pets

SOURCE: infoplease.com

How Much Will That Dog Really Cost?

There's no such thing as a free puppy. Depending on the breed and size,
a new puppy can easily cost between $300 and $900 the first year.

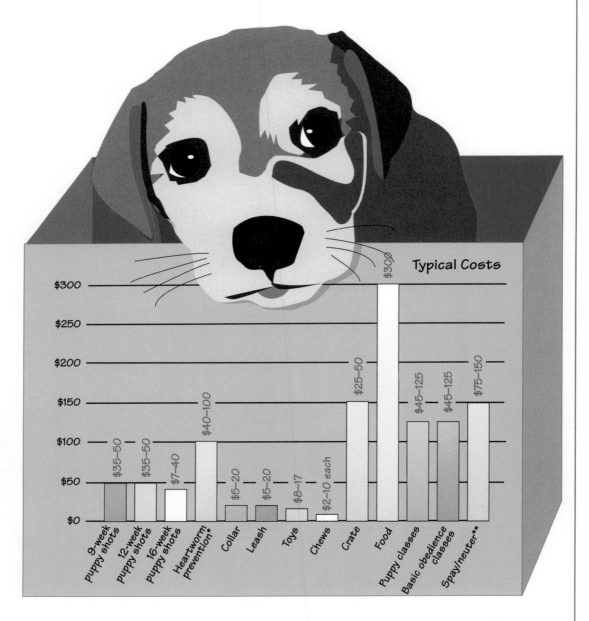

Typical Costs

9-week puppy shots	$35–50
12-week puppy shots	$35–50
16-week puppy shots	$7–40
Heartworm prevention*	$40–100
Collar	$5–20
Leash	$5–20
Toys	$8–17
Chews	$2–10 each
Crate	$25–50
Food	$300
Puppy classes	$45–125
Basic obedience classes	$45–125
Spay/neuter**	$75–150

* Depending on size of dog

** Depending on gender and size of dog

SOURCE: petpeoplesplace.com

Pets

Why People Bring Their Pets to Shelters

1. Moving
2. Landlord Issues
3. Cost of pet maintenance
4. No time for pet
5. Inadequate facilities

1. Too many cats in house
2. Allergies
3. Moving
4. Cost of pet maintenance
5. Landlord Issues

Pets

SOURCE: National Council on Pet Population Study and Policy

The Environment

The world around us constantly changes. Many of the changes result from human activities. All too often, these changes are harmful. Oil spills from giant ships kill birds and mess up beaches. Gases from cars and factories dirty the air and blacken people's lungs. Cutting down forests and draining wetlands destroys the homes and food supplies of endangered animals.

One problem of great concern to many scientists is the gradual warming of earth's atmosphere. This occurs as certain gases in the atmosphere prevent sunlight from being reflected from earth's surface back out into space. As the amount of these "greenhouse gases" increases, the atmosphere traps more and more heat—like a greenhouse traps heat. Most scientists believe that carbon dioxide and other gases released by vehicles and factories are the main cause for the temperature increase. The United States accounts for more than 20% of the world's greenhouse gas emissions. As temperatures continue to rise, climates will change, the sea level will rise, and many plants and animals will have difficulty surviving in their current homes.

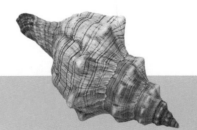

Kidbits Tidbits

- The first Earth Day was held in 1970.
- 1998 was the warmest year on record for the planet since records were first kept in the mid-1800s. 2002 was the second warmest and 2003 was the third warmest.
- In 2002, carbon dioxide emissions accounted for about 85% of greenhouse gas emissions.
- Microscopic organisms in tap water cause 900,000 illnesses in the U.S. each year.
- More than 1 billion of the world's people do not have access to safe drinking water.

Another serious problem is the effect of air pollution on people's health. People with lung and heart disease are very sensitive to air pollution. So, too, are children and elderly people. The U.S. government measures air quality in approximately 3,000 places. Between 1999 and 2001, Riverside, California, had 248 days when there was so much pollution that the air was classified as unhealthy. (California cities consistently rate the worst in this regard.) Los Angeles, California, had 106 unhealthy days and Fresno, California, had 256 unhealthy days.

Some people are taking action to solve environmental problems. Engineers have designed cars and home appliances that use less energy. Homes are better insulated, so that less energy is needed for heating and cooling. Parks around the world have been established, where wild animals and their homes are protected. Communities have recycling programs that enable us to reuse paper, plastic, glass, and other materials. This all saves energy and other valuable natural resources. It also limits pollution.

Many kids take part in projects that improve the environment. They clean up local parks and start school recycling programs. Most importantly, they spread the word about the environment's three R's: reduce, reuse, and recycle.

Kidbits Tidbits

- More than 1 million acres of U.S. wetlands were destroyed from 1985 to 1995.
- A car gets up to 20% better gas mileage at 55 miles per hour than at 70 miles per hour.
- Each year, Americans create 230 million tons of wastes—4.6 pounds per person per day. In 2001, 68% of the wastes were recycled. Americans recycled about 45% of their paper and paperboard wastes and about 49% of the aluminum containers they used.
- By 2004, a total of 1,409 U.S. animal and plant species were classified as endangered or threatened.
- Recycled plastic soda bottles can be made into sweaters. Recycled telephone books can be made into book covers.

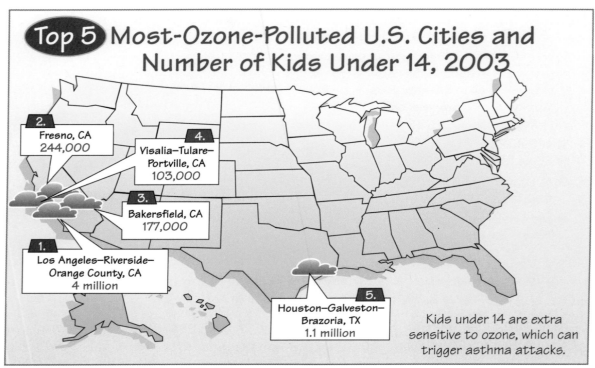

Top 5 Most-Ozone-Polluted U.S. Cities and Number of Kids Under 14, 2003

2.
Fresno, CA
244,000

4.
Visalia–Tulare–Portville, CA
103,000

3.
Bakersfield, CA
177,000

1.
Los Angeles–Riverside–Orange County, CA
4 million

5.
Houston–Galveston–Brazoria, TX
1.1 million

Kids under 14 are extra sensitive to ozone, which can trigger asthma attacks.

SOURCE: American Lung Association, *State of the Air: 2003*

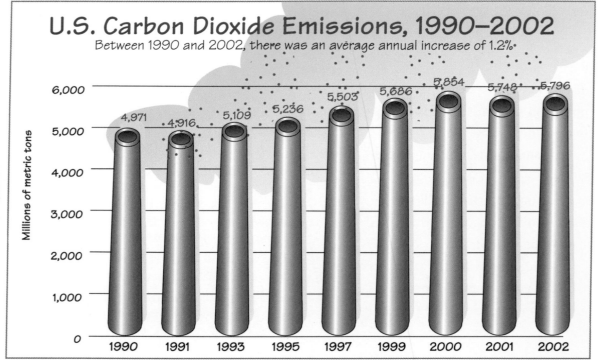

U.S. Carbon Dioxide Emissions, 1990–2002

Between 1990 and 2002, there was an average annual increase of 1.2%

Millions of metric tons

1990	1991	1993	1995	1997	1999	2000	2001	2002
4,971	4,916	5,109	5,236	5,503	5,686	5,854	5,748	5,796

SOURCE: United States Environmental Protection Agency Energy Information Administration

The Environment

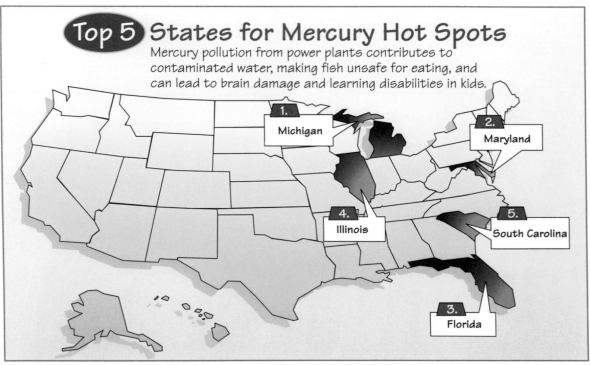

Top 5 States for Mercury Hot Spots

Mercury pollution from power plants contributes to contaminated water, making fish unsafe for eating, and can lead to brain damage and learning disabilities in kids.

1. Michigan
2. Maryland
4. Illinois
5. South Carolina
3. Florida

SOURCE: Environmental Defense

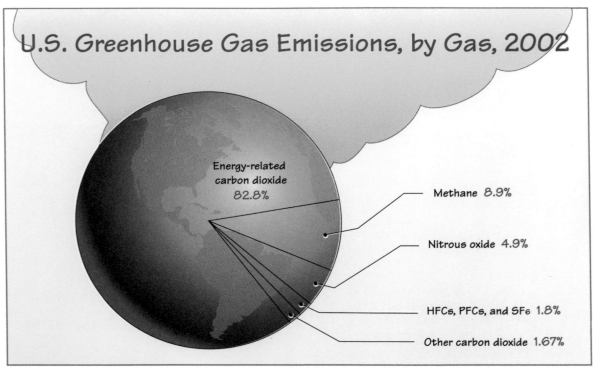

U.S. Greenhouse Gas Emissions, by Gas, 2002

Energy-related carbon dioxide 82.8%

Methane 8.9%

Nitrous oxide 4.9%

HFCs, PFCs, and SF$_6$ 1.8%

Other carbon dioxide 1.67%

SOURCE: U.S. Environmental Protection Agency Energy Information Administration

The Environment

America's 10 Most Endangered Rivers

6. Spokane River

3. Snake River

5. Allegheny and Monongahela Rivers

7. Housatonic River

10. Mississippi River

1. Colorado River

9. Big Darby Creek

2. Big Sunflower River

4. Tennessee River

8. Peace River

SOURCE: American Rivers, *America's Most Endangered Rivers of 2004*

America's 10 Most Endangered National Parks

10. Yellowstone National Park

8. *Underground Railroad

5. Joshua Tree National Park

4. Great Smoky Mountains

7. Shenandoah National Park

6. Organ Pipe Cactus National Park

3. Everglades National Park

9. Wrangell–St. Elias National Park & Preserve

1. Big Thicket National Preserve

2. Biscayne National Park
mostly underwater

*The Underground Railroad National Park is made up of over 100 sites. A selection are marked on this map (●).

SOURCE: National Park Service

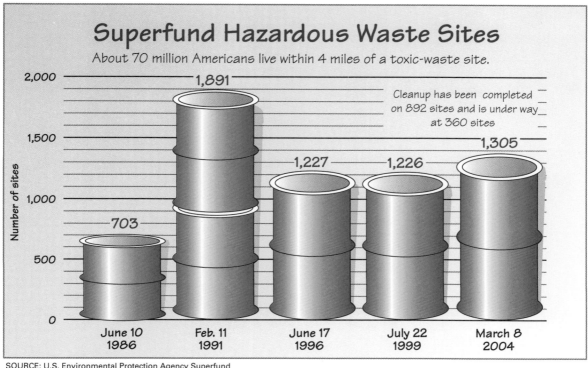

Superfund Hazardous Waste Sites

About 70 million Americans live within 4 miles of a toxic-waste site.

Number of sites

Cleanup has been completed on 892 sites and is under way at 360 sites

1,891

1,305

1,227

1,226

703

| June 10 1986 | Feb. 11 1991 | June 17 1996 | July 22 1999 | March 8 2004 |

SOURCE: U.S. Environmental Protection Agency Superfund

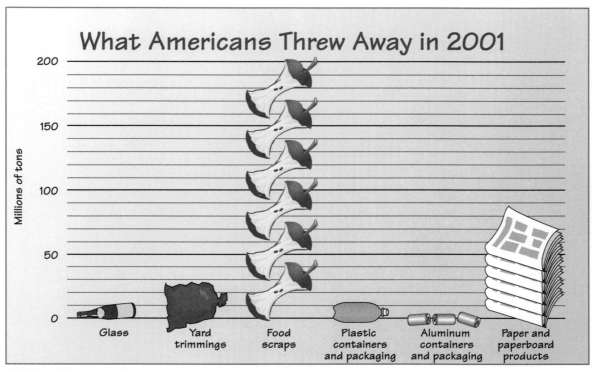

What Americans Threw Away in 2001

Millions of tons

Glass | Yard trimmings | Food scraps | Plastic containers and packaging | Aluminum containers and packaging | Paper and paperboard products

SOURCE: U.S. Environmental Protection Agency Municipal Solid Waste Division

Paper Recycling

We use paper and paperboard products every day—tissues, paper plates, food bags, packaging, newspapers, and cardboard boxes. Paper and paperboard products make up the largest proportion of municipal solid waste.
(Recycling rates, 2001)

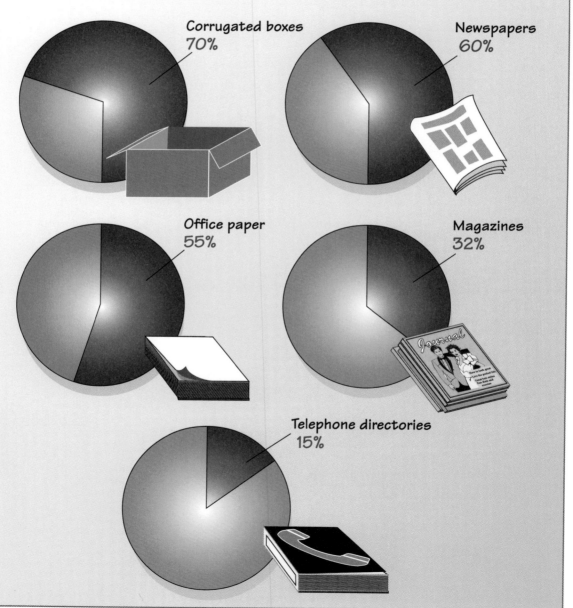

Corrugated boxes
70%

Newspapers
60%

Office paper
55%

Magazines
32%

Telephone directories
15%

SOURCE: U.S. Environmental Protection Agency Municipal Solid Waste Division

The Environment

How Much Trash Gets Recycled? 2001

On average, Americans create about 208 million tons of trash each year. That averages out to about 4.6 pounds of garbage created per person, per day.

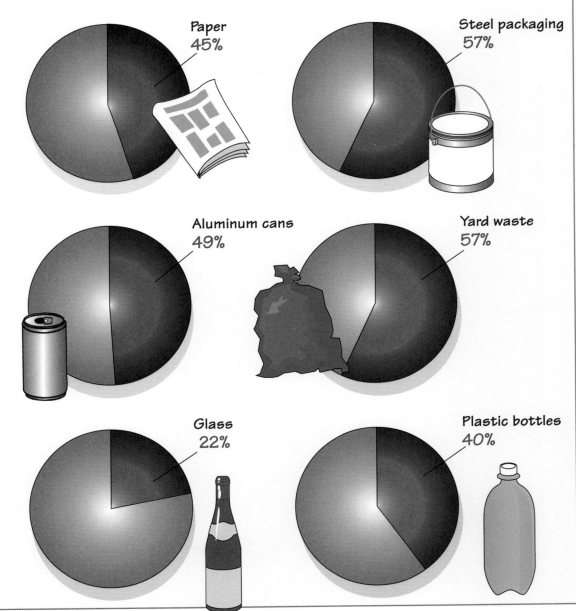

Paper
45%

Steel packaging
57%

Aluminum cans
49%

Yard waste
57%

Glass
22%

Plastic bottles
40%

The Environment

SOURCE: U.S. Environmental Protection Agency Municipal Solid Waste Division

Top 5 U.S. States with Most Hazardous Waste Sites, 2002

2. California 96 Sites

4. New York 90 Sites

5. Michigan 67 Sites

3. Pennsylvania 92 Sites

1. New Jersey 113 Sites

SOURCE: U.S. Environmental Protection Agency Superfund

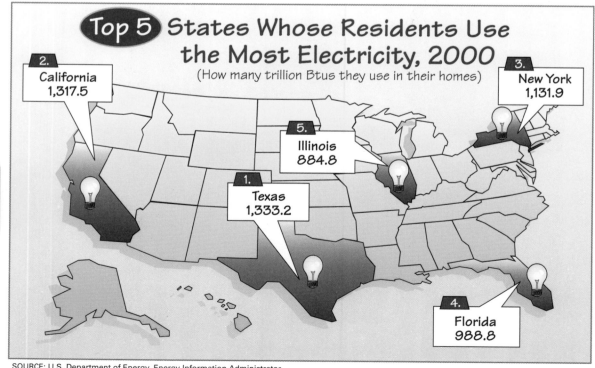

Top 5 States Whose Residents Use the Most Electricity, 2000
(How many trillion Btus they use in their homes)

2. California 1,317.5

3. New York 1,131.9

5. Illinois 884.8

1. Texas 1,333.2

4. Florida 988.8

SOURCE: U.S. Department of Energy, Energy Information Administrator

The Environment

Top 10 Industries in Toxic-Chemical Releases, 2001

Total on- and off-site releases (in millions and billions of pounds)

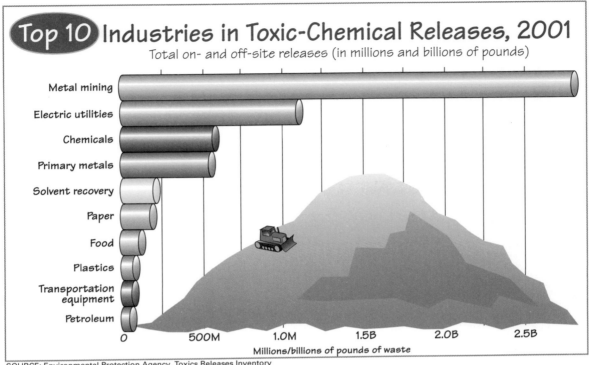

Millions/billions of pounds of waste

SOURCE: Environmental Protection Agency, Toxics Releases Inventory

Plant Species in Trouble as of March 2004

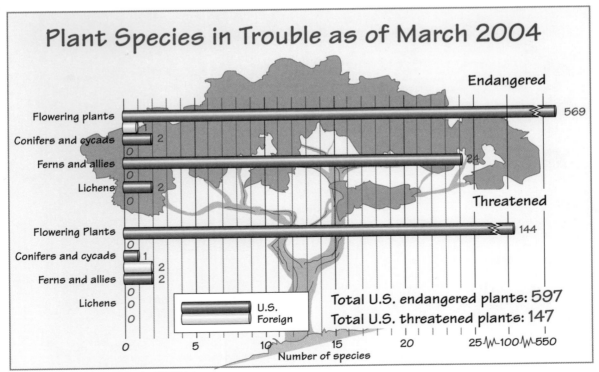

Number of species

Total U.S. endangered plants: 597
Total U.S. threatened plants: 147

SOURCE: U.S. Fish and Wildlife Service TESS Database

Animal Species in Trouble as of March 2004

Endangered Species

Animal	U.S.	Foreign
Mammals	69	251
Birds	76	175
Reptiles	14	64
Amphibians	12	8
Fish	71	11
Snails	21	1
Clams	62	2
Crustaceans	18	0
Insects	35	4
Arachnids	12	0

Legend: U.S. / Foreign

Number of species endangered

Total U.S. endangered: 390

Threatened Species

Animal	U.S.	Foreign
Mammals	9	17
Birds	14	6
Reptiles	22	15
Amphibians	9	1
Fish	43	0
Snails	11	0
Clams	8	0
Crustaceans	3	0
Insects	9	0
Arachnids	0	0

Legend: U.S. / Foreign

Number of species threatened

Total U.S. threatened: 128

The Environment

SOURCE: U.S. Fish and Wildlife Service, TESS Database

Life Span of Wildlife
(In the wild)

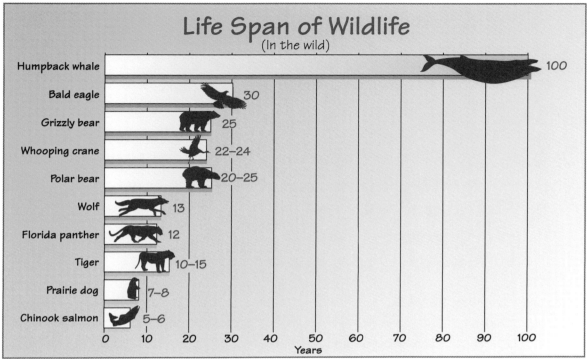

Humpback whale	100
Bald eagle	30
Grizzly bear	25
Whooping crane	22–24
Polar bear	20–25
Wolf	13
Florida panther	12
Tiger	10–15
Prairie dog	7–8
Chinook salmon	5–6

Years

SOURCE: National Wildlife Federation

Tigers in Trouble

Only five of the eight original subspecies of tigers are left in the world. Three have become extinct in the last 60 years.

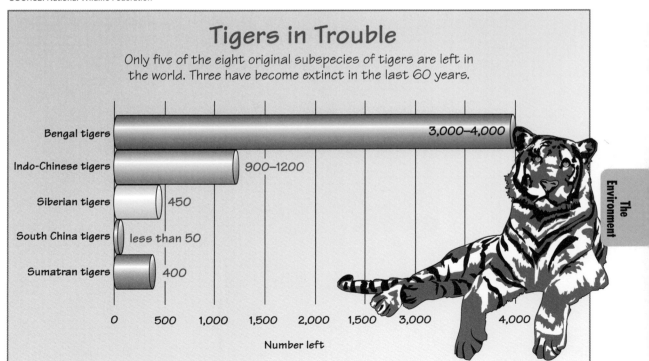

Bengal tigers	3,000–4,000
Indo-Chinese tigers	900–1200
Siberian tigers	450
South China tigers	less than 50
Sumatran tigers	400

Number left

SOURCE: tigersincrisis.com

Attitudes

So what do you think about fashion, politics, religion, dating, music, drinking, and a zillion other things? What's your favorite cereal, hobby, TV show? What are your attitudes toward people who cheat, people of different races, elderly people?

Who—and what—influences your opinions? Your parents, teachers, or friends? What you see on television or read in books?

How quickly do you form opinions? What does it take to make you change your attitude toward something, or someone? Are you willing to consider the facts and listen to reason?

Everyone has opinions on a wide range of issues. These opinions are important. Town officials want to know what issues are important to taxpayers. Jacket manufacturers want to know what brands are "in" with teenage buyers. Politicians want to know for whom people of different ages are planning to vote—and why.

Research companies are constantly taking surveys to find out what people think about everything, what they like, and what they

Kidbits
Tidbits

● Nine out of ten Americans find Internet spam annoying.

●Twenty-nine percent of Americans say professional football is their favorite sport. Only 13% say baseball is theirs.

● In 2003, about 74% of American teens thought that downloading music files without paying should be legal.

● In 2003, 89% of Americans felt good about their lives, down from 95% in 1998.

● In 1997, about one-third of Americans felt good about the morals and values of Americans but that number went up to 47% by 2003.

plan to do in the future. For instance, one survey of teenagers ages 15 through 18 found that their main concern was getting a good job. A survey of preteens found that more 7- to 12-year-olds preferred to play outside than to go to a sports event. Another survey found that kids think playing sports is more fun that going to the movies—and much, much more fun than watching TV!

Opinions can differ widely depending on age, sex, education, economic status, and other factors. For example, romance books are more popular with girls than with boys, but science fiction tales are favorites of more boys than girls. Men say a person's eyes are the first thing they notice when they meet someone; women are most likely to notice a person's smile and teeth when they're first introduced. College graduates are more likely than high school dropouts to support women's rights to have abortions.

Many surveys suggest that young people are more tolerant than older people. For example, there are indications that teenagers are more tolerant than adults of racial diversity. Young adults also seem to be more accepting than older adults of single parenthood.

Kidbits
Tidbits

● According to a Harris Poll, America's favorite college football team was Notre Dame's Fighting Irish every year from 1997 to 2003.

● If people could stop time and live forever in good health, most Americans would choose 41 as the ideal age.

● Forty-two percent of Americans think God is male, 1% think God is female, 38% believe God is neither and 11% think God is both.

● The great majority of Americans believes that pets play a positive role in people's lives.

● About 90% of cat and dog owners consider the animals to be members of the family.

● Americans think scientists, firemen, doctors, teachers, and nurses are the professions with the most prestige. The lowest ratings go to real estate agents (6%), stockbrokers (8%), and actors (13%).

Attitudes

Attitudes

Top 10 Teen Goals for the Future, 2003

To enjoy life
- Total: 88%
- Boys: 84%
- Girls: 92%

Go to college
- Total: 84%
- Boys: 81%
- Girls: 88%

Buy a house
- Total: 84%
- Boys: 82%
- Girls: 87%

Have good relationship with family
- Total: 84%
- Boys: 80%
- Girls: 88%

Have good relationship with friend
- Total: 84%
- Boys: 79%
- Girls: 89%

Have successful career
- Total: 83%
- Boys: 80%
- Girls: 85%

Get married
- Total: 81%
- Boys: 77%
- Girls: 85%

Make lots of money
- Total: 76%
- Boys: 77%
- Girls: 74%

Have children
- Total: 74%
- Boys: 71%
- Girls: 78%

Give back to community
- Total: 42%
- Boys: 37%
- Girls: 46%

Legend: Total, Boys, Girls

X-axis: 0%, 20%, 40%, 60%, 80%

SOURCE: Mediamark Research, Inc., *Survey of the American Consumer*

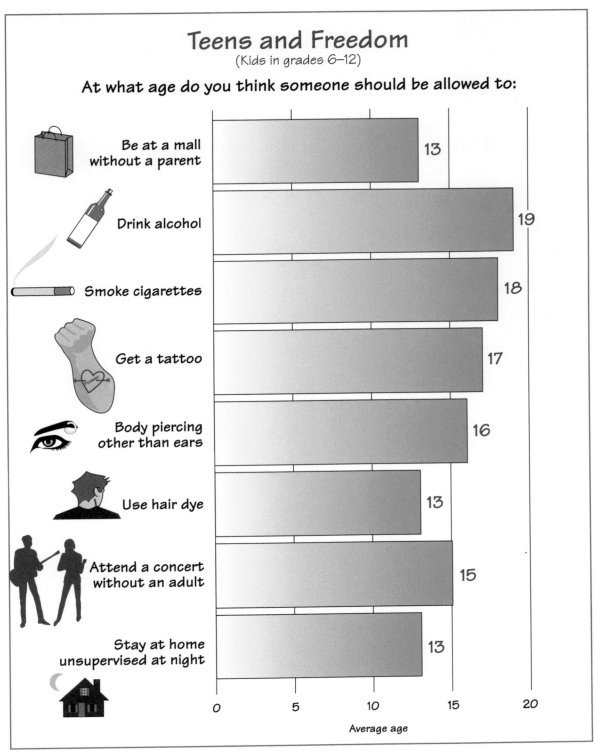

Teens and Freedom
(Kids in grades 6–12)

At what age do you think someone should be allowed to:

Be at a mall without a parent — 13

Drink alcohol — 19

Smoke cigarettes — 18

Get a tattoo — 17

Body piercing other than ears — 16

Use hair dye — 13

Attend a concert without an adult — 15

Stay at home unsupervised at night — 13

Average age
(0, 5, 10, 15, 20)

Attitudes

SOURCE: *USA Weekend*, "Teens and Freedom Survey"

Top Concerns for Teens
(Kids in grades 6–12)

Economy

Not at all concerned 9%

Not very concerned 29%

Very concerned 62%

Not very concerned 10%

War/terrorism

Not at all concerned 4%

Very concerned 86%

Drugs

Not at all concerned 13%

Not very concerned 22%

Very concerned 65%

Acceptance by others

Not at all concerned 14%

Not very concerned 24%

Very concerned 62%

Family

Not at all concerned 5%

Very concerned 87%

Not very concerned 8%

School

Not at all concerned 5%

Very concerned 84%

Not very concerned 11%

Violence

Not at all concerned 9%

Very concerned 71%

Not very concerned 20%

Money

Not at all concerned 5%

Not very concerned 15%

Very concerned 80%

Sexual issues

Not at all concerned 13%

Not very concerned 26%

Very concerned 61%

Attitudes

SOURCE: *USA Weekend*, "Teens & the Opposite Sex Survey"

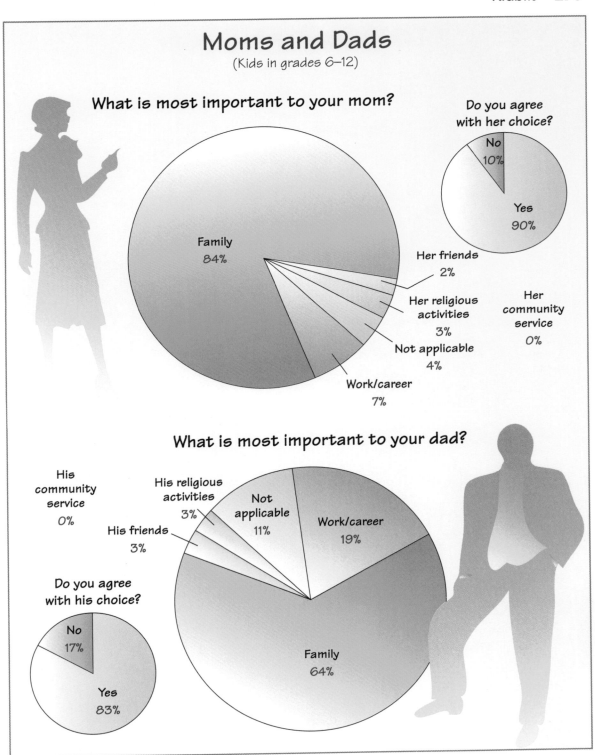

Moms and Dads
(Kids in grades 6–12)

What is most important to your mom?

Family 84%

Her friends 2%

Her religious activities 3%

Not applicable 4%

Work/career 7%

Her community service 0%

Do you agree with her choice?

No 10%

Yes 90%

What is most important to your dad?

His community service 0%

His religious activities 3%

His friends 3%

Not applicable 11%

Work/career 19%

Family 64%

Do you agree with his choice?

No 17%

Yes 83%

Attitudes

SOURCE: *USA Weekend,* "Teens and Parents Survey 2001"

Girls and Guys

(Kids in grades 6–12)

Is it OK for girls in your grade to call guys?

Boys

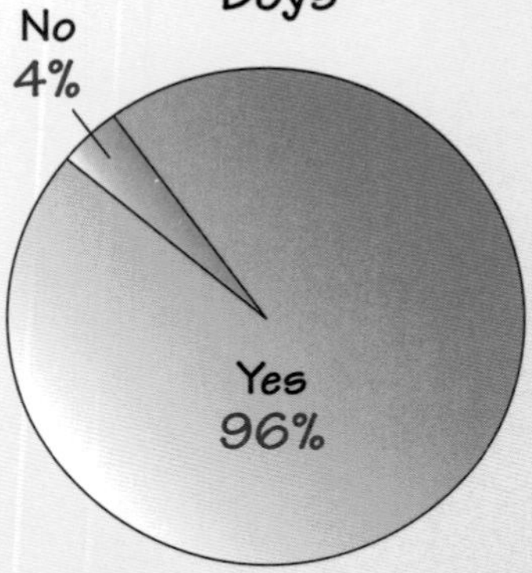

No
4%

Yes
96%

Girls

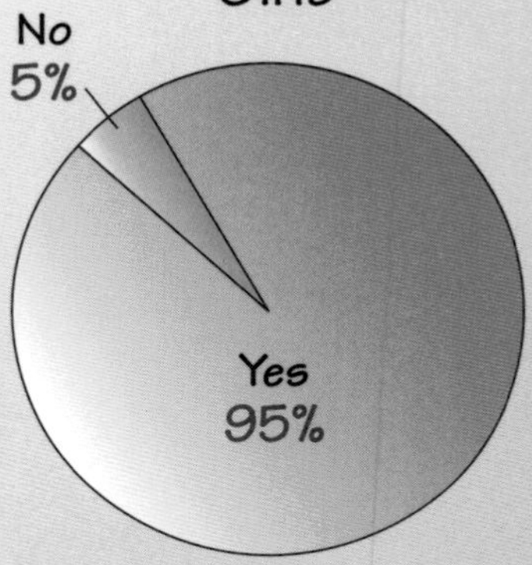

No
5%

Yes
95%

Is it OK for girls in your grade to ask guys out?

Boys

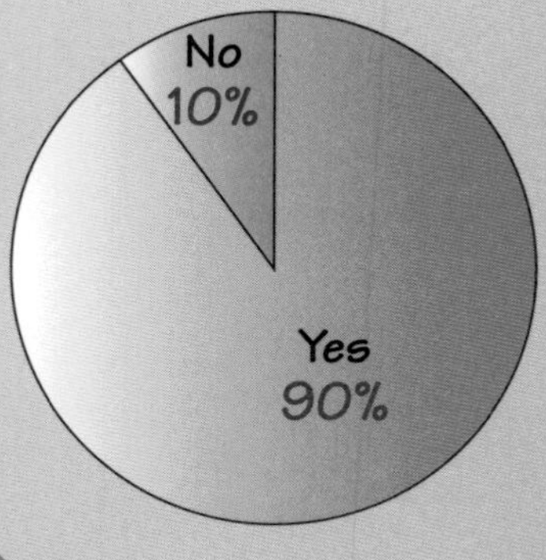

No
10%

Yes
90%

Girls

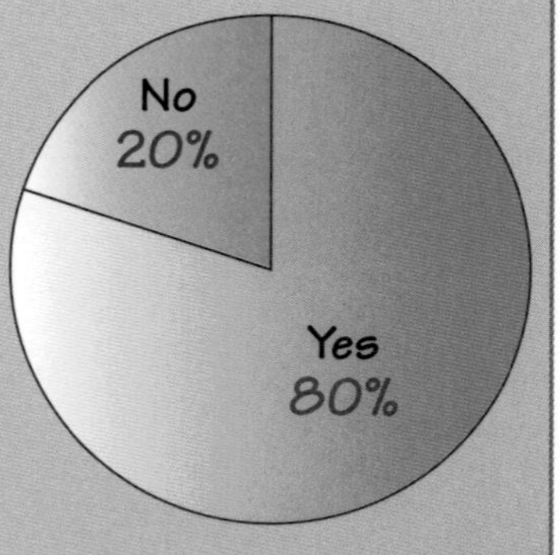

No
20%

Yes
80%

Attitudes

SOURCE: *USA Weekend*, "Teens & the Opposite Sex Survey"

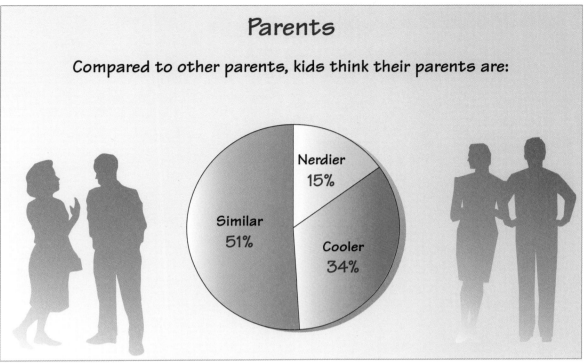

Parents

Compared to other parents, kids think their parents are:

- Nerdier 15%
- Similar 51%
- Cooler 34%

SOURCE: *USA Weekend,* "Teens and Parents Survey 2001"

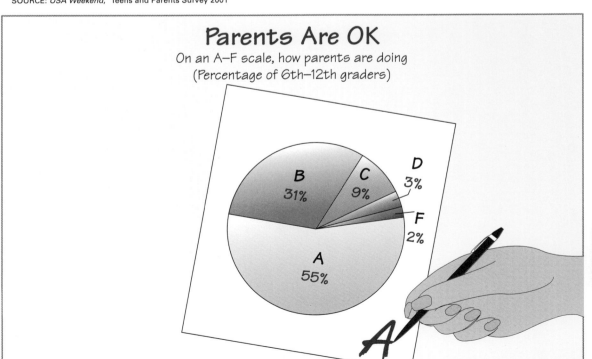

Parents Are OK

On an A–F scale, how parents are doing
(Percentage of 6th–12th graders)

- B 31%
- C 9%
- D 3%
- F 2%
- A 55%

SOURCE: *USA Weekend,* "Teens and Parents Survey 2001"

Attitudes

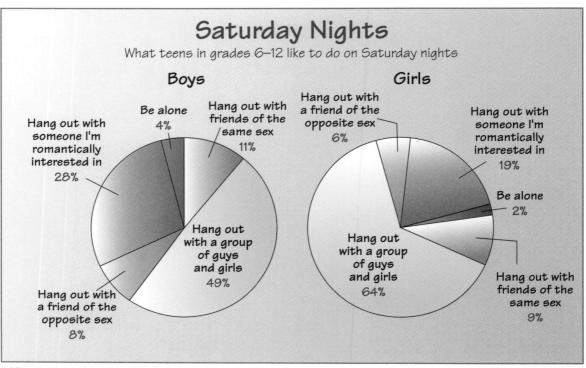

Saturday Nights
What teens in grades 6–12 like to do on Saturday nights

Boys

- Be alone 4%
- Hang out with friends of the same sex 11%
- Hang out with someone I'm romantically interested in 28%
- Hang out with a friend of the opposite sex 8%
- Hang out with a group of guys and girls 49%

Girls

- Hang out with a friend of the opposite sex 6%
- Hang out with someone I'm romantically interested in 19%
- Be alone 2%
- Hang out with friends of the same sex 9%
- Hang out with a group of guys and girls 64%

SOURCE: *USA Weekend,* "Teens & the Opposite Sex Survey"

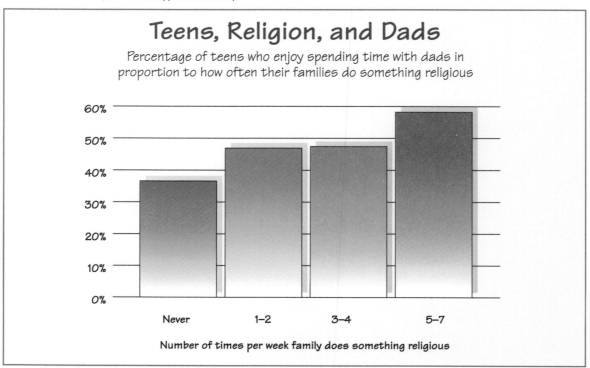

Teens, Religion, and Dads
Percentage of teens who enjoy spending time with dads in proportion to how often their families do something religious

Number of times per week family does something religious

| Never | 1–2 | 3–4 | 5–7 |

SOURCE: National Longitudinal Survey of Youth

Attitudes

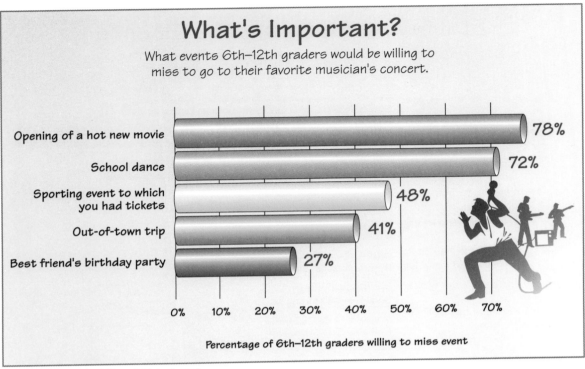

What's Important?

What events 6th–12th graders would be willing to miss to go to their favorite musician's concert.

- Opening of a hot new movie — **78%**
- School dance — **72%**
- Sporting event to which you had tickets — **48%**
- Out-of-town trip — **41%**
- Best friend's birthday party — **27%**

0% 10% 20% 30% 40% 50% 60% 70%

Percentage of 6th–12th graders willing to miss event

SOURCE: *USA Weekend*, "Tunes & 'Tudes Survey"

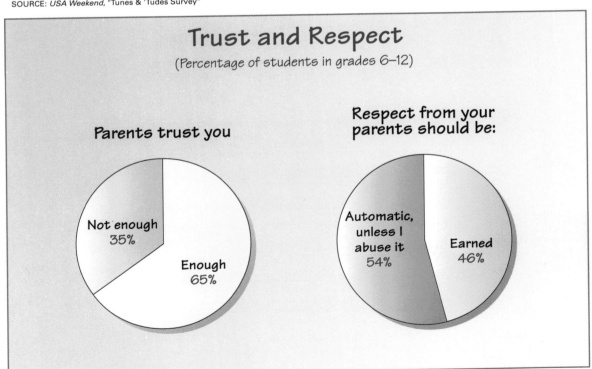

Trust and Respect

(Percentage of students in grades 6–12)

Parents trust you

- Not enough 35%
- Enough 65%

Respect from your parents should be:

- Automatic, unless I abuse it 54%
- Earned 46%

SOURCE: *USA Weekend*, "Teens and Freedom Survey"

Attitudes

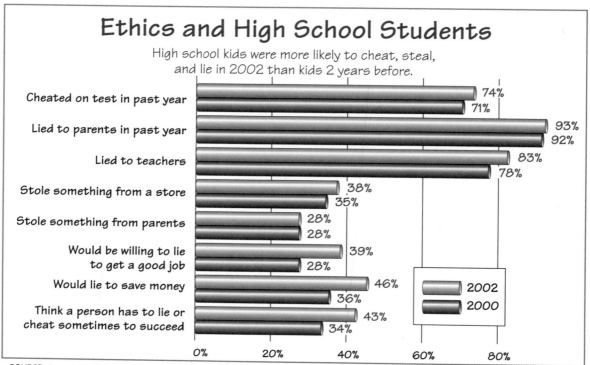

Ethics and High School Students

High school kids were more likely to cheat, steal, and lie in 2002 than kids 2 years before.

- Cheated on test in past year: 74% / 71%
- Lied to parents in past year: 93% / 92%
- Lied to teachers: 83% / 78%
- Stole something from a store: 38% / 35%
- Stole something from parents: 28% / 28%
- Would be willing to lie to get a good job: 39% / 28%
- Would lie to save money: 46% / 36%
- Think a person has to lie or cheat sometimes to succeed: 43% / 34%

Legend: 2002, 2000

SOURCE: Josephson Institute of Ethics, "The Ethics of American Youth: 2002 Report Card"

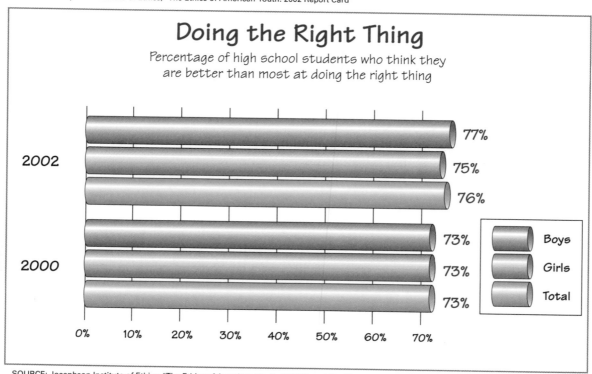

Doing the Right Thing

Percentage of high school students who think they are better than most at doing the right thing

2002
- Boys: 77%
- Girls: 75%
- Total: 76%

2000
- Boys: 73%
- Girls: 73%
- Total: 73%

SOURCE: Josephson Institute of Ethics, "The Ethics of American Youth: 2002 Report Card"

Attitudes

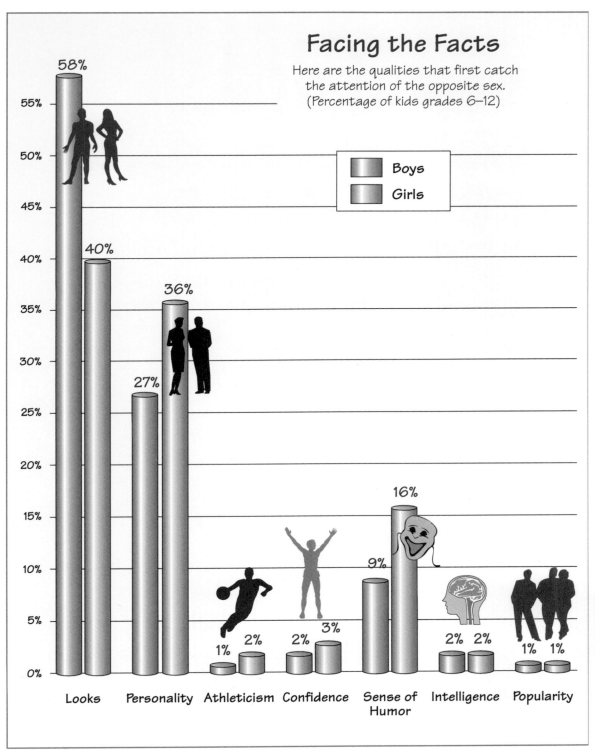

Facing the Facts

Here are the qualities that first catch
the attention of the opposite sex.
(Percentage of kids grades 6–12)

Boys
Girls

- Looks — 58%, 40%
- Personality — 27%, 36%
- Athleticism — 1%, 2%
- Confidence — 2%, 3%
- Sense of Humor — 9%, 16%
- Intelligence — 2%, 2%
- Popularity — 1%, 1%

SOURCE: *USA Weekend*, "Teens & the Opposite Sex Survey"

Attitudes

Food

Food gives you energy, helps you grow, and keeps you healthy. It can also give you lots of pleasure. A meal of your favorite foods is always a treat. So, too, are those after-school snacks!

It's important to eat lots of fruit, veggies, and whole-grain starchy foods, such as bread and pasta. You should eat meat only in moderation. And, by proportion, you should eat very little fat. Many Americans do not follow this advice. They eat more cheese than lettuce, more fatty beef than lean chicken, more pepperoni pizzas than pizzas topped with vegetables. A diagram called a food pyramid shows which foods make up a healthy diet (look on page 297—or you can usually find one on your favorite cereal box or loaf of bread). But a recent study found that only 1% of American children met the food pyramid's guidelines.

Many factors influence what we eat. These include where we live, our religious beliefs, the amount of money we have, and how much time we have to prepare and eat meals.

People in different places have different food favorites. People in Philadelphia, for example, like pepper pot soup. In New

Kidbits Tidbits

- On average, Americans eat 350 slices of pizza every second.
- Dunkin' Donuts sells about 1 billion cups of coffee a year.
- Restaurant dinner orders often include a soft drink (25.2%), French fries (24.8%), pizza (24.1%), hamburger (16.7%), and side salad (16.3%).
- Coca-Cola sold 4.5 billion cases of soda in the United States in 2002. Each case equaled 24 twelve-ounce servings.
- An average American eats 1,400 chickens, 21 cows, 14 sheep, and 12 pigs during his or her lifetime.
- Americans eat about 10 pounds of breakfast cereal a year.

Orleans, French onion soup is the favorite. In New York and New England people prefer white cheddar cheese. Elsewhere in the United States, yellow cheddar is the hands-down favorite. The popularity of brands also varies from region to region. For example, people who live in the South prefer one brand of peanut butter. On the West Coast, another brand is much more popular.

People in different countries also have different eating habits. Rice is the basic starchy food in Asia, while potatoes fill this role in northern Europe. Fish is the main source of protein in Japan, but in Argentina—which has broad plains for raising live-stock—beef is the main source of protein.

Cow milk is drunk in Canada, sheep and goat milk in Turkey, and reindeer milk is a staple in Finland.

Advertising plays a role in food preferences, too. A large supermarket may carry 20,000 different items, including dozens of brands of bread, breakfast cereal, cookies, and frozen desserts. Advertising helps per-suade buyers to select a certain brand or item. The food indus-try spends $30 billion a year, but only 2% of that goes to promote fruits, veg-etables, whole grains, and beans.

Kidbits Tidbits

- Each day, an average of about 1 million boxes of Jell-O are bought in the United States. People in Salt Lake City eat more lime jello than people in any other city in the United States.
- In 2002, Americans consumed 24 pounds of candy per person—up from 18.4 pounds in 1986. On average, each American ate about 12 pounds of chocolate in 2002.
- Americans' favorite grain food is bread, followed by cereal, rice, and pasta.
- Each year more than 10 billion doughnuts are made in the United States.
- Vanilla is the most popular ice cream flavor. On average, each American consumes about 47 pints of ice cream each year.

Food

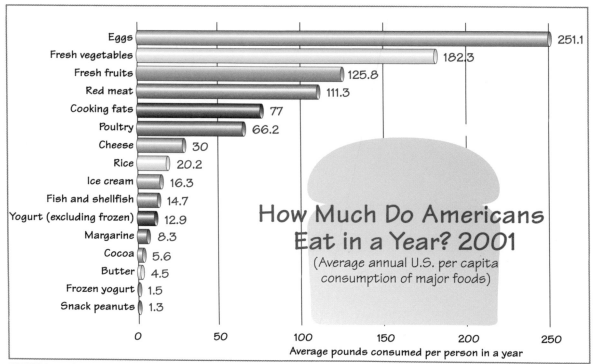

How Much Do Americans Eat in a Year? 2001
(Average annual U.S. per capita consumption of major foods)

Food	Average pounds consumed per person in a year
Eggs	251.1
Fresh vegetables	182.3
Fresh fruits	125.8
Red meat	111.3
Cooking fats	77
Poultry	66.2
Cheese	30
Rice	20.2
Ice cream	16.3
Fish and shellfish	14.7
Yogurt (excluding frozen)	12.9
Margarine	8.3
Cocoa	5.6
Butter	4.5
Frozen yogurt	1.5
Snack peanuts	1.3

SOURCE: United States Department of Agriculture Economic Research Service

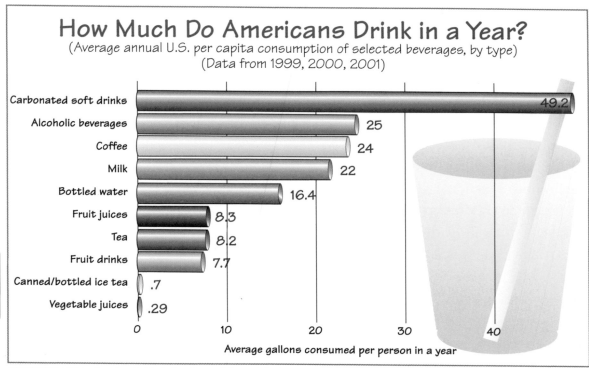

How Much Do Americans Drink in a Year?
(Average annual U.S. per capita consumption of selected beverages, by type)
(Data from 1999, 2000, 2001)

Beverage	Average gallons consumed per person in a year
Carbonated soft drinks	49.2
Alcoholic beverages	25
Coffee	24
Milk	22
Bottled water	16.4
Fruit juices	8.3
Tea	8.2
Fruit drinks	7.7
Canned/bottled ice tea	.7
Vegetable juices	.29

SOURCE: United States Department of Agriculture Economic Research Service

Food

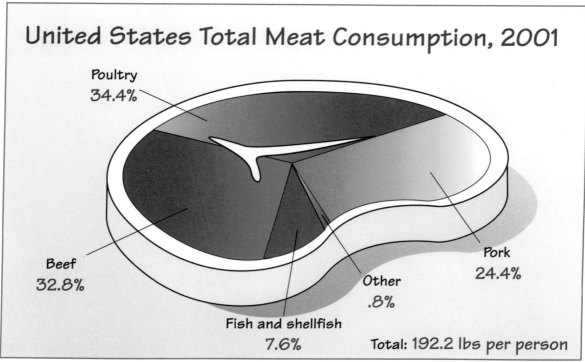

United States Total Meat Consumption, 2001

Poultry
34.4%

Beef
32.8%

Fish and shellfish
7.6%

Other
.8%

Pork
24.4%

Total: 192.2 lbs per person

SOURCE: United States Department of Agriculture Economic Research Service

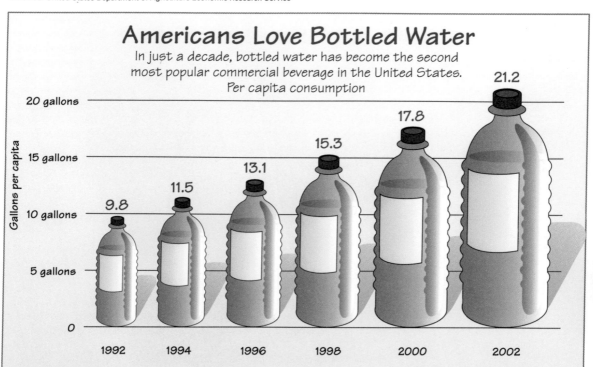

Americans Love Bottled Water

In just a decade, bottled water has become the second
most popular commercial beverage in the United States.
Per capita consumption

Gallons per capita

20 gallons

15 gallons

10 gallons

5 gallons

0

9.8 — 1992
11.5 — 1994
13.1 — 1996
15.3 — 1998
17.8 — 2000
21.2 — 2002

SOURCE: Beverage Marketing Corporation

Food

America's Top 5 Soft Drinks, 2003

Billions of cans (12 oz)

35B
30B — 30.3
25B
20B — 20.3
15B — 15.3
10B — 10.3 — 9.6
5B
0

Coke Classic   Pepsi   Diet Coke   Mountain Dew   Sprite

SOURCE: Beverage Marketing Corporation

Soft Drink Serving Sizes

Soft drink consumption increased by 300% in the last 20 years.
Average serving sizes have also increased.

Average serving size

20 oz
15 oz
10 oz
5 oz
0

6.5 oz   12 oz   20 oz

1950s   1960s   2000

SOURCE: American Academy of Pediatrics

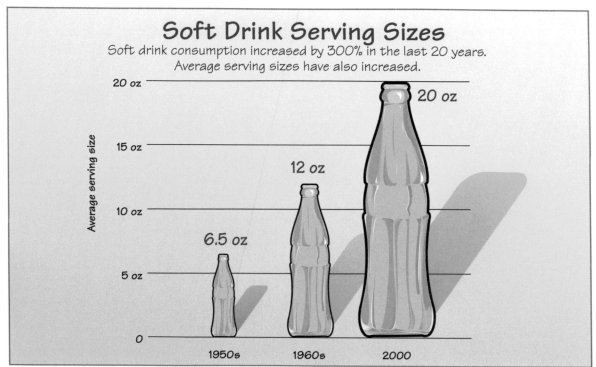

Top 5 Favorite Snack-Size Halloween Candy, 2002

In 2002, Americans ate almost 24 pounds of candy each and chewed an average of 1.7 pounds of gum. They spent $2.3 billion on Halloween candy

Percentage of market share

	14%	13%	11%	6%	6%
	Snickers	Reese's Cups	Kit Kat	Milky Way	M&Ms

15% — 12% — 9% — 6% — 3% — 0%

SOURCE: *USA Today* and Industry Resources, Inc.

America's Favorite Salty Snack Sensations, 2002

(Percentage of total salty snack industry sales)

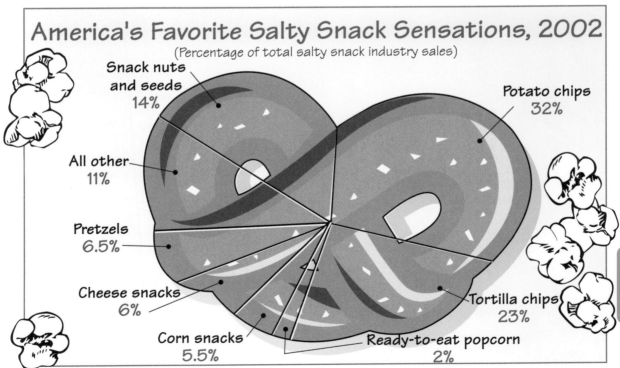

Snack nuts and seeds
14%

Potato chips
32%

All other
11%

Pretzels
6.5%

Cheese snacks
6%

Corn snacks
5.5%

Ready-to-eat popcorn
2%

Tortilla chips
23%

Food

SOURCE: Mintel International Group, "The Salty Snacks Market"

Top 5 Sources of Calcium

Only 19% of teen girls and 52% of teen boys get the recommended amounts of calcium.

	Serving size	Mg of calcium	Percent recommended value
1. Plain yogurt	1 cup	450	45%
2. American cheese	2 oz	350	35%
3. Ricotta cheese	1/2 cup	340	34%
4. Fruit yogurt	1 cup	315	31%
5. Milk	1 cup	300	30%

SOURCE: National Institute of Child Health and Human Development

What Americans Eat for Breakfast on the Go

Top 10 carried breakfast foods

SOURCE: NPD Group

Food

Top 5 Ice Cream Producing States, 2002

5. Minnesota
46.1M gallons

3. Pennsylvania
56M gallons

1. California
131.2M gallons

3. Texas
53.1M gallons

2. Indiana
79.3M gallons

SOURCE: United States Department of Agriculture

1. Cherry Garcia
2. Chocolate Chip Cookie Dough
3. Chocolate Fudge Brownie
4. New York Super Fudge Chunk
5. Chunky Monkey
6. Half Baked!
7. Phish Food
8. Cherry Garcia Frozen Yogurt
9. Peanut Butter Cup
10. Chocolate Fudge Brownie Frozen Yogurt

Ben & Jerry's Top 10 Ice Cream/ Frozen Yogurt Flavors, 2004

(By annual sales)

Food

SOURCE: Ben & Jerry's Homemade

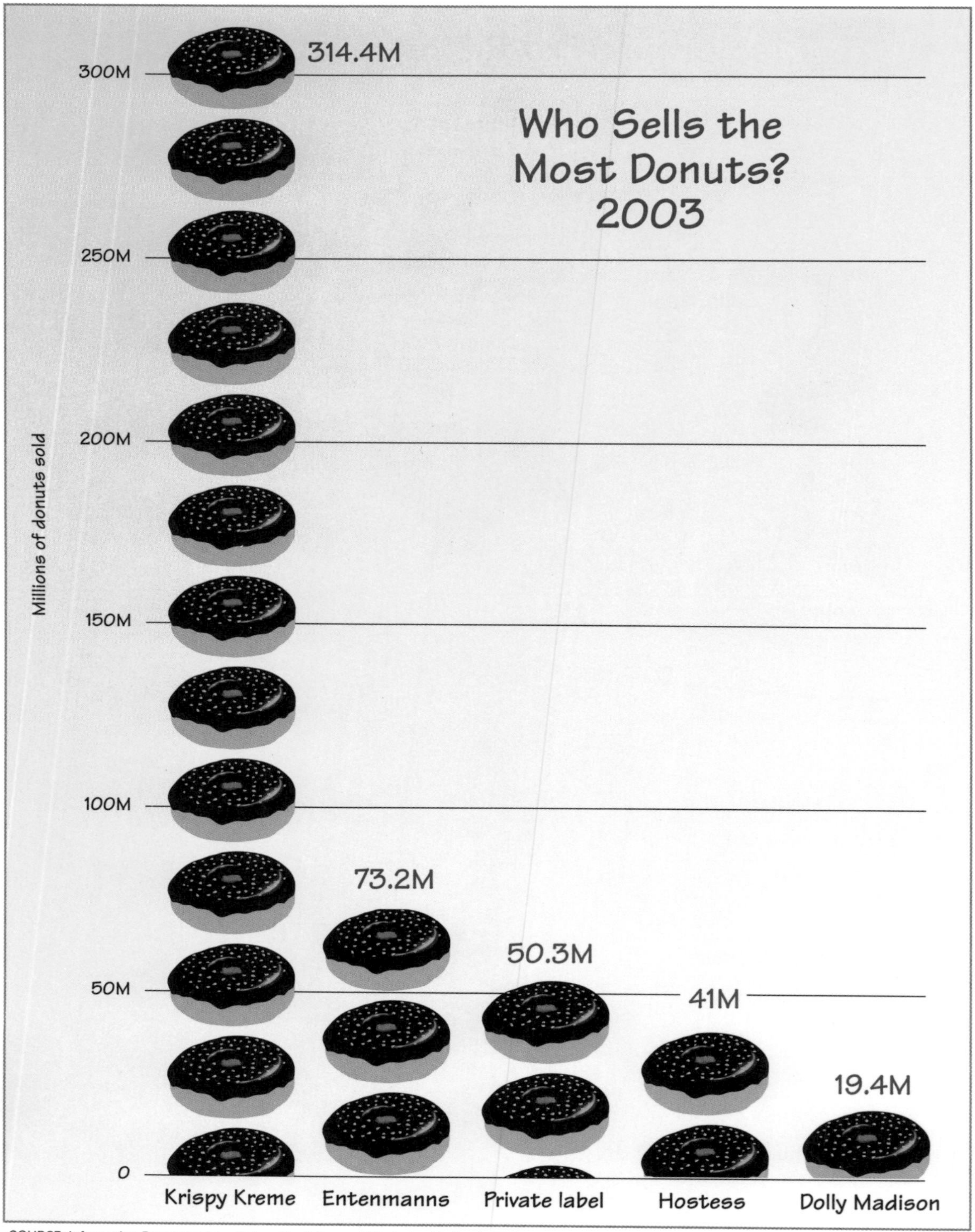

Millions of donuts sold

300M — 314.4M

Who Sells the Most Donuts? 2003

250M

200M

150M

100M

73.2M

50.3M

50M — 41M

19.4M

0

| Krispy Kreme | Entenmanns | Private label | Hostess | Dolly Madison |

Food

SOURCE: Information Resources Inc., *Bakery Prodution and Marketing Redbook, 2003*

Fast-Food Frenzy

There are more than 11,285 Burger King restaurants in 58 countries.

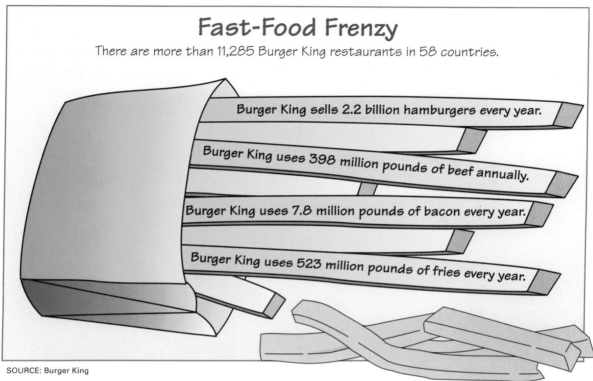

Burger King sells 2.2 billion hamburgers every year.

Burger King uses 398 million pounds of beef annually.

Burger King uses 7.8 million pounds of bacon every year.

Burger King uses 523 million pounds of fries every year.

SOURCE: Burger King

When We Order Pizza, 2003

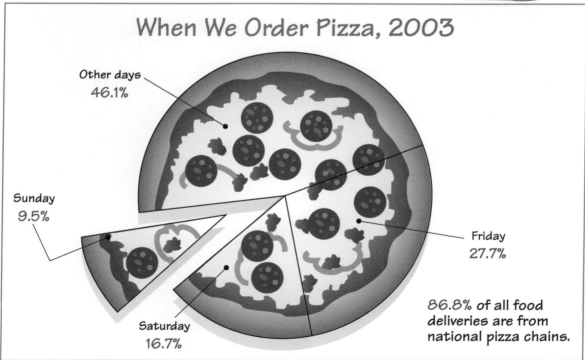

Other days
46.1%

Sunday
9.5%

Saturday
16.7%

Friday
27.7%

86.8% of all food deliveries are from national pizza chains.

SOURCE: Sandelman & Associates

Food

Top 5 Hot dog Eating Cities, 2003

More than one-third of all hot dogs are sold between Memorial Day and Labor Day.

5. Philadelphia, PA
17.5M

2. New York City, NY
35.2M

1. Los Angeles, CA
44.7M

3. Chicago, IL
19.6M

4. Baltimore, MD/ Washington, DC
19.6M

SOURCE: National Hot Dog & Sausage Council

Top 5 Foods Kids Eat at Home

Top 5 foods eaten at home by 13- to 17-year-olds

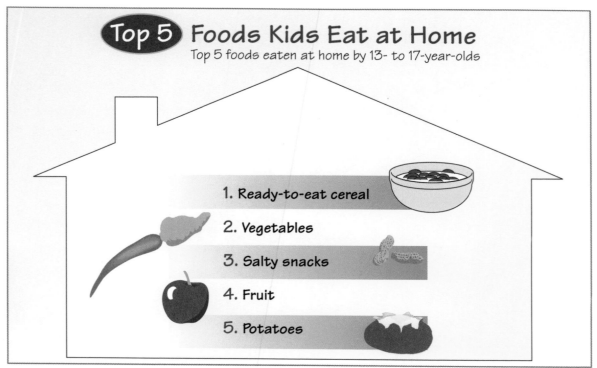

1. Ready-to-eat cereal
2. Vegetables
3. Salty snacks
4. Fruit
5. Potatoes

SOURCE: The NPD Group/NPD Foodworld/National Eating Trends

Food

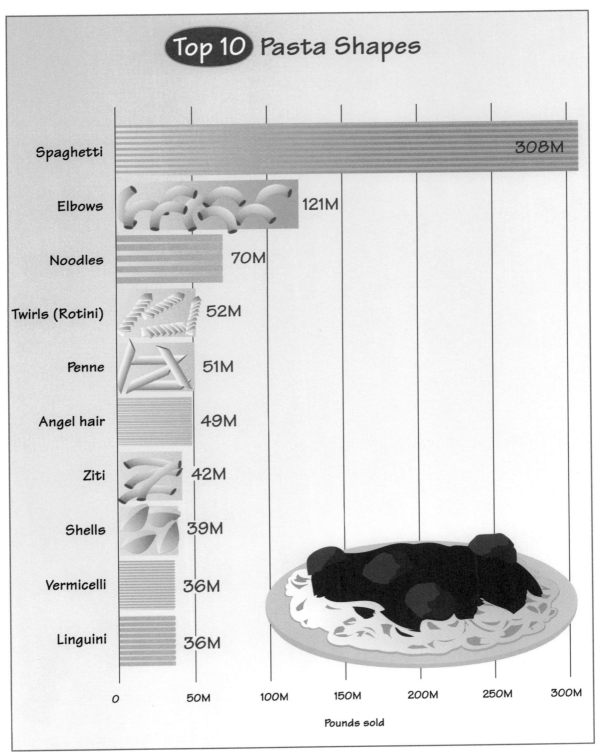

Top 10 Pasta Shapes

Pasta Shape	Pounds sold
Spaghetti	308M
Elbows	121M
Noodles	70M
Twirls (Rotini)	52M
Penne	51M
Angel hair	49M
Ziti	42M
Shells	39M
Vermicelli	36M
Linguini	36M

Pounds sold

0   50M   100M   150M   200M   250M   300M

Food

SOURCE: National Pasta Association

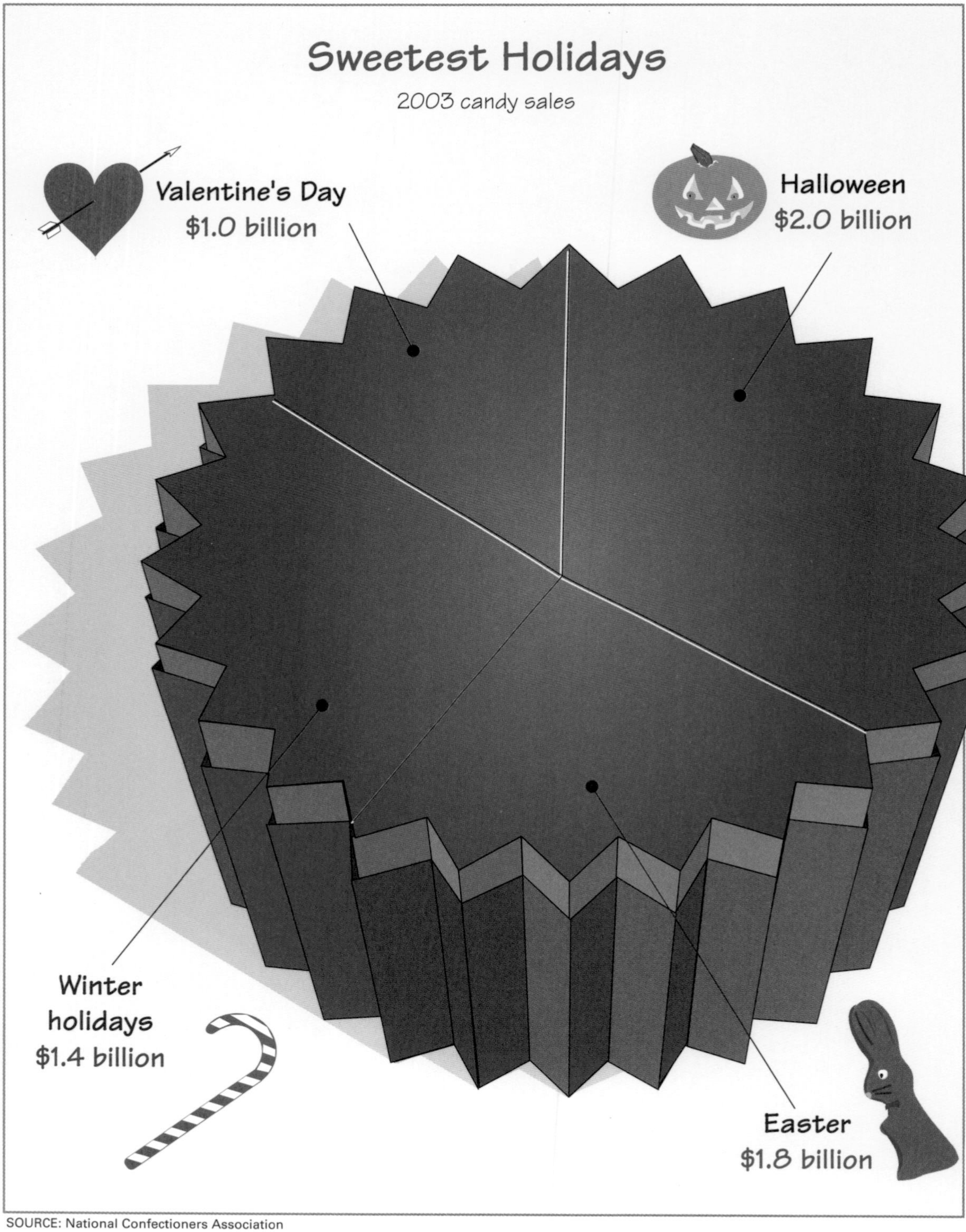

Sweetest Holidays

2003 candy sales

Valentine's Day
$1.0 billion

Halloween
$2.0 billion

Winter holidays
$1.4 billion

Easter
$1.8 billion

SOURCE: National Confectioners Association

Food

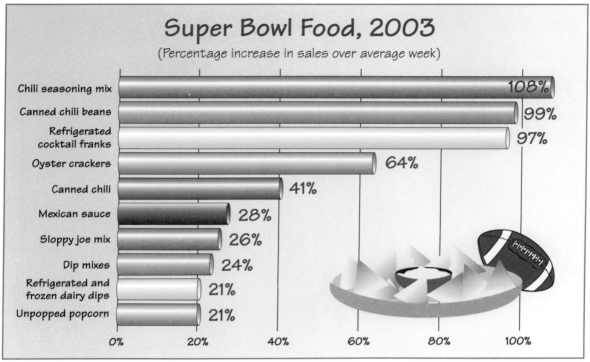

Super Bowl Food, 2003
(Percentage increase in sales over average week)

Food	Percentage
Chili seasoning mix	108%
Canned chili beans	99%
Refrigerated cocktail franks	97%
Oyster crackers	64%
Canned chili	41%
Mexican sauce	28%
Sloppy joe mix	26%
Dip mixes	24%
Refrigerated and frozen dairy dips	21%
Unpopped popcorn	21%

SOURCE: AC Nielsen

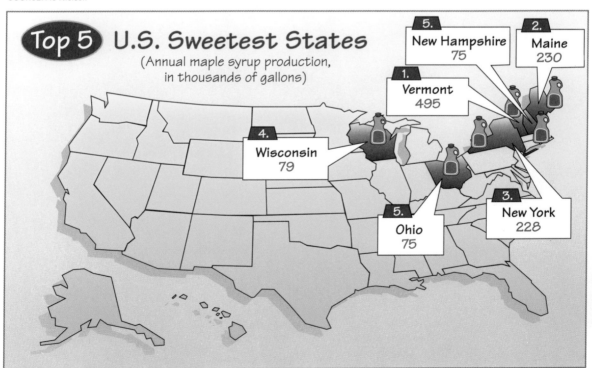

Top 5 U.S. Sweetest States
(Annual maple syrup production, in thousands of gallons)

5. New Hampshire 75
2. Maine 230
1. Vermont 495
4. Wisconsin 79
3. New York 228
5. Ohio 75

SOURCE: New England Agricultural Statistics Service

Food

When We Buy Our Food

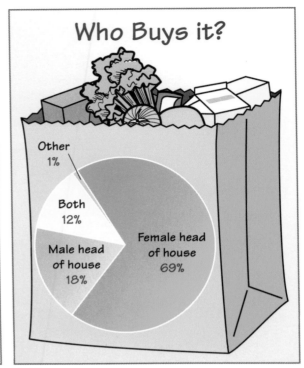

Saturday 22%
Friday 16%
Thursday 12%
Wednesday 13%
Tuesday 9%
Monday 12%
Sunday 16%

Who Buys it?

Other 1%
Both 12%
Male head of house 18%
Female head of house 69%

SOURCE: Progressive Grocer, "70th Annual Report of the Grocery Industry, April 2003"

How $100 Is Spent at the Grocery Store

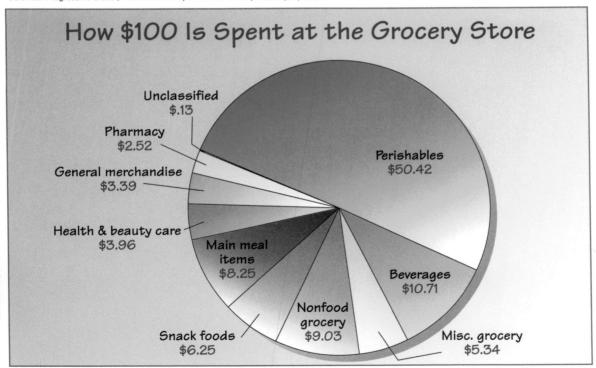

Unclassified $.13
Pharmacy $2.52
General merchandise $3.39
Health & beauty care $3.96
Main meal items $8.25
Snack foods $6.25
Nonfood grocery $9.03
Misc. grocery $5.34
Beverages $10.71
Perishables $50.42

SOURCE: Progressive Grocer, "70th Annual Report of the Grocery Industry, April 2003"

Food

The Food Pyramid

The U.S. Department of Agriculture (USDA) has created this recommended balance of food groups for good nutrition.

Fats, Oils, & Sweets
USE SPARINGLY

Milk, Yogurt, & Cheese Group
2–3 SERVINGS DAILY

Meat, Poultry, Fish, Dry Beans, Eggs, & Nuts Group
2–3 SERVINGS DAILY

Vegetable Group
3–5 SERVINGS DAILY

Fruit Group
2–4 SERVINGS DAILY

Bread, Cereal, Rice, & Pasta Group
6–11 SERVINGS DAILY

Number of servings eaten per day

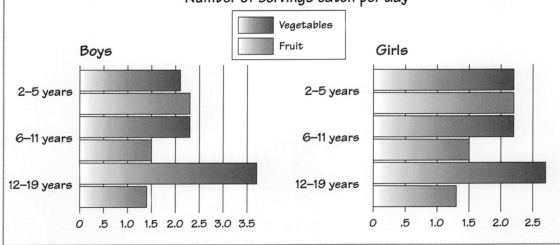

Vegetables
Fruit

Boys

Girls

SOURCE: BRFSS, "Fruit and Vegetable Intake in the U.S. 2000"

Computers

It's hard to believe that digital computers have only been around since 1946. And, considering where we are with laptops and PDAs (personal digital assistants), it's hard to imagine that the first computer was a huge monster that weighed 30 tons!

It didn't have transistors, integrated circuits, disk drives, not even a keyboard or a monitor. Those things hadn't been invented yet! It couldn't do word processing or play games or send e-mail. In fact, a $40 calculator today has more total computer power than that first computer!

Today, computers are everywhere. In only a short period of time, they have become as much a part of everday American life as televisions, microwaves, and telephone answering machines. PCs sit on desktops and are carried in briefcases and backpacks. Tiny computers are installed in cars, stoves, and hundreds of other products. People of every age, and in every kind of job, use computers. In general, young people are more comfortable with using computers than are older people. Today's kids have grown up with computers. In fact, many young people are finding that their computer skills can be a great source of extra money. Lots of teens make money

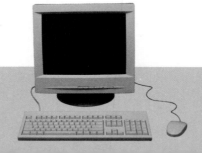

Kidbits Tidbits

- The first computer, named ENIAC, weighed 30 tons and filled a room. Today's laptop computers are 1,000 times faster than ENIAC.
- The most popular things for teens to do online are to send e-mail and do schoolwork.
- By 2003, 204.3 million Americans were using the Internet. Seventy-seven percent of kids ages 2–17 used the Web either at home or at school.
- The largest online service provider in 2003 was America Online, or AOL, with 24.7 million subscribers.
- In 2003, women 35–54 years old used the Internet the most. Eighty-two percent of them went online regularly compared with 80% of men in that age group. In the over 55 age group, 63% used the Internet regularly.

writing computer programs, maintaining computer bulletin boards, repairing computers, even teaching old folks how to zip around the World Wide Web!

One of the most popular uses of computers is to go "online." Surfing the Net, you can visit people and places all over the world, including sports teams, museums, parks, and schools. You can search encyclopedias, dictionaries, newspapers, and other reference sources (a great way to do research for school and business reports). You can "chat" with friends, movie stars, musicians, and politicians.

The best way to explore the Internet is via the World Wide Web. The Web is a collection of standards that make it easier to navigate the Internet and access information. The Web displays information in interconnected "pages" that are linked to one another by key words or phrases that are highlighted. Point to a highlighted word, click the mouse, and you instantly jump to another page. Each page has an address. For example, the Web address for the White House is: *www.whitehouse.gov*.

Going online also lets you send e-mail from your computer to someone else's computer. You can shop for everything from candy to Cadillacs. You can make plane reservations and find recipes. You can download games and other programs to your own computer. You can even take a virtual tour of Mars, go inside the eye of a hurricane, or "chat" with some of the world's most famous people!

Kidbits Tidbits

- It's expected that by 2005, 6 million American kids between the ages of 8 and 12 will have their own Web site.
- The top online destinations for kids 12–17 in September 2003 were Originalicons.com and Blunt Truth.
- Bill Gates, one of the two guys who started Microsoft, is the richest person in the world. In 2003 he was worth $46.6 billion.

Computers

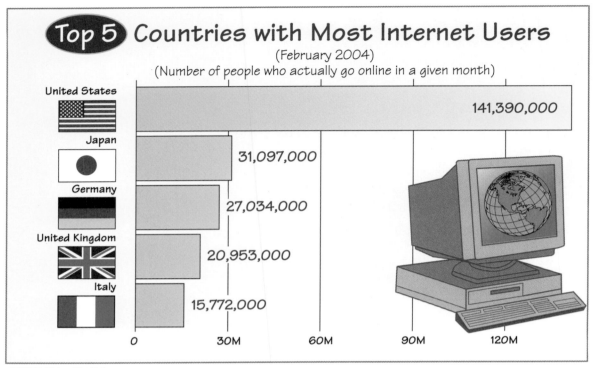

Top 5 Countries with Most Internet Users

(February 2004)
(Number of people who actually go online in a given month)

United States — 141,390,000
Japan — 31,097,000
Germany — 27,034,000
United Kingdom — 20,953,000
Italy — 15,772,000

0   30M   60M   90M   120M

SOURCE: Nielsen/Net Ratings

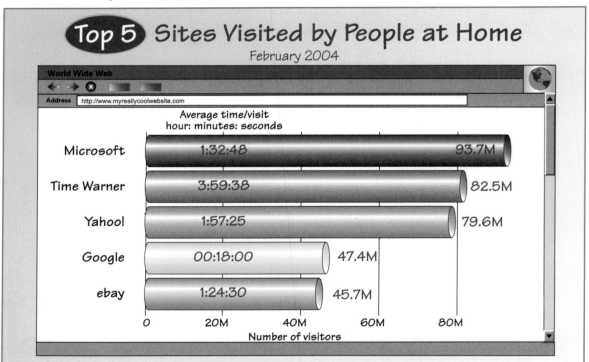

Top 5 Sites Visited by People at Home

February 2004

World Wide Web

Address http://www.myreallycoolwebsite.com

Average time/visit
hour: minutes: seconds

Site	Average time/visit	Number of visitors
Microsoft	1:32:48	93.7M
Time Warner	3:59:38	82.5M
Yahoo!	1:57:25	79.6M
Google	00:18:00	47.4M
ebay	1:24:30	45.7M

0   20M   40M   60M   80M
Number of visitors

SOURCE: Nielsen/Net Ratings

Do I Really Need...

Percentage of young people who say it would be very hard to live without

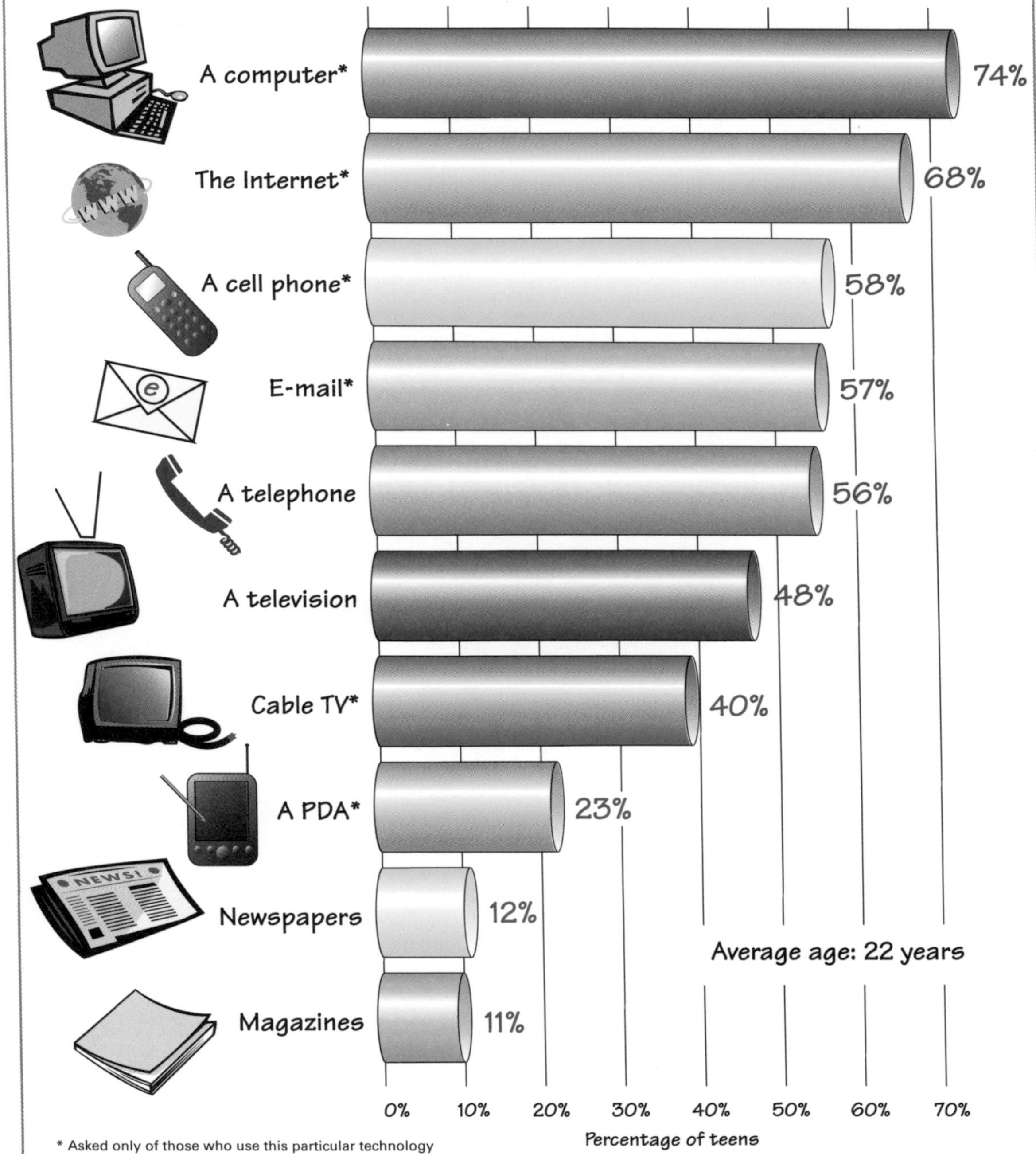

Item	Percentage
A computer*	74%
The Internet*	68%
A cell phone*	58%
E-mail*	57%
A telephone	56%
A television	48%
Cable TV*	40%
A PDA*	23%
Newspapers	12%
Magazines	11%

Average age: 22 years

Percentage of teens

0%   10%   20%   30%   40%   50%   60%   70%

* Asked only of those who use this particular technology

SOURCE: Pew Research Center, "Internet & American Life Project"

Computers

Top 5 High Speed Access Cities, 2004

People who connect to the Internet through a broadband connection say they save about 3.5 hours a week with their high speed connection. (Percentage with broadband connection)

2. Boston, MA 50%

5. Kansas City, KS/MO 46%

1. San Diego, CA 52%

3. New York, NY 49%

4. Providence, RI 47%

SOURCE: comScore Networks

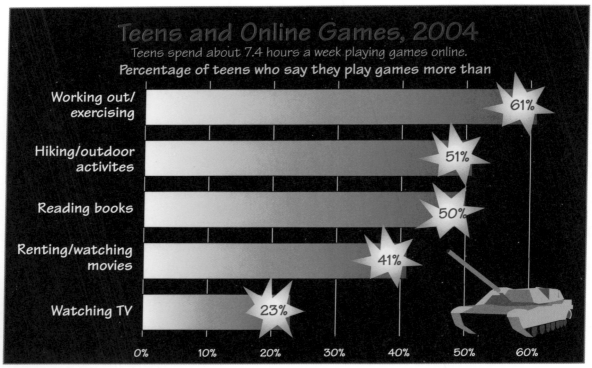

Teens and Online Games, 2004

Teens spend about 7.4 hours a week playing games online.

Percentage of teens who say they play games more than

- Working out/exercising — 61%
- Hiking/outdoor activites — 51%
- Reading books — 50%
- Renting/watching movies — 41%
- Watching TV — 23%

0% 10% 20% 30% 40% 50% 60%

SOURCE: AOL/Digital Marketing Services

Computers

Top 5 Most Popular Google Searches, 2003

SOURCE: Google

1. britney spears
2. harry potter
3. matrix
4. shakira
5. david beckham

Top 5 Most Popular Yahoo! Searches, 2003

1. KaZaA
2. harry potter
3. american idol
4. britney spears
5. 50 cent

SOURCE: Yahoo!

Top 5 Most Popular Lycos Searches, 2003

1. KaZaA
2. britney spears
3. dragonball
4. paris hilton
5. IRS

SOURCE: Lycos

Computers

Spam Is Growing

Americans are becoming fed up with spam and three quarters
of Americans favor a law that would make it illegal.

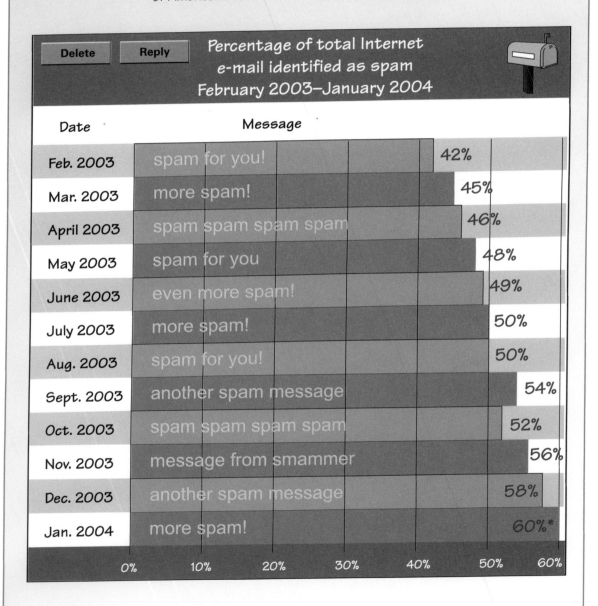

Delete	Reply	Percentage of total Internet e-mail identified as spam February 2003–January 2004

Date	Message					
Feb. 2003	spam for you!				42%	
Mar. 2003	more spam!				45%	
April 2003	spam spam spam spam				46%	
May 2003	spam for you					48%
June 2003	even more spam!					49%
July 2003	more spam!					50%
Aug. 2003	spam for you!					50%
Sept. 2003	another spam message					54%
Oct. 2003	spam spam spam spam					52%
Nov. 2003	message from smammer					56%
Dec. 2003	another spam message					58%
Jan. 2004	more spam!					60%*

0%   10%   20%   30%   40%   50%   60%

* Fifty-one billion messages of the 85 billion filtered by Brightmail's Probe Network

SOURCE: Brightmail Logistics and Operations Center (BLOC)

Computers

Online at Home, 2001

Most common activities of teens, ages 15–17

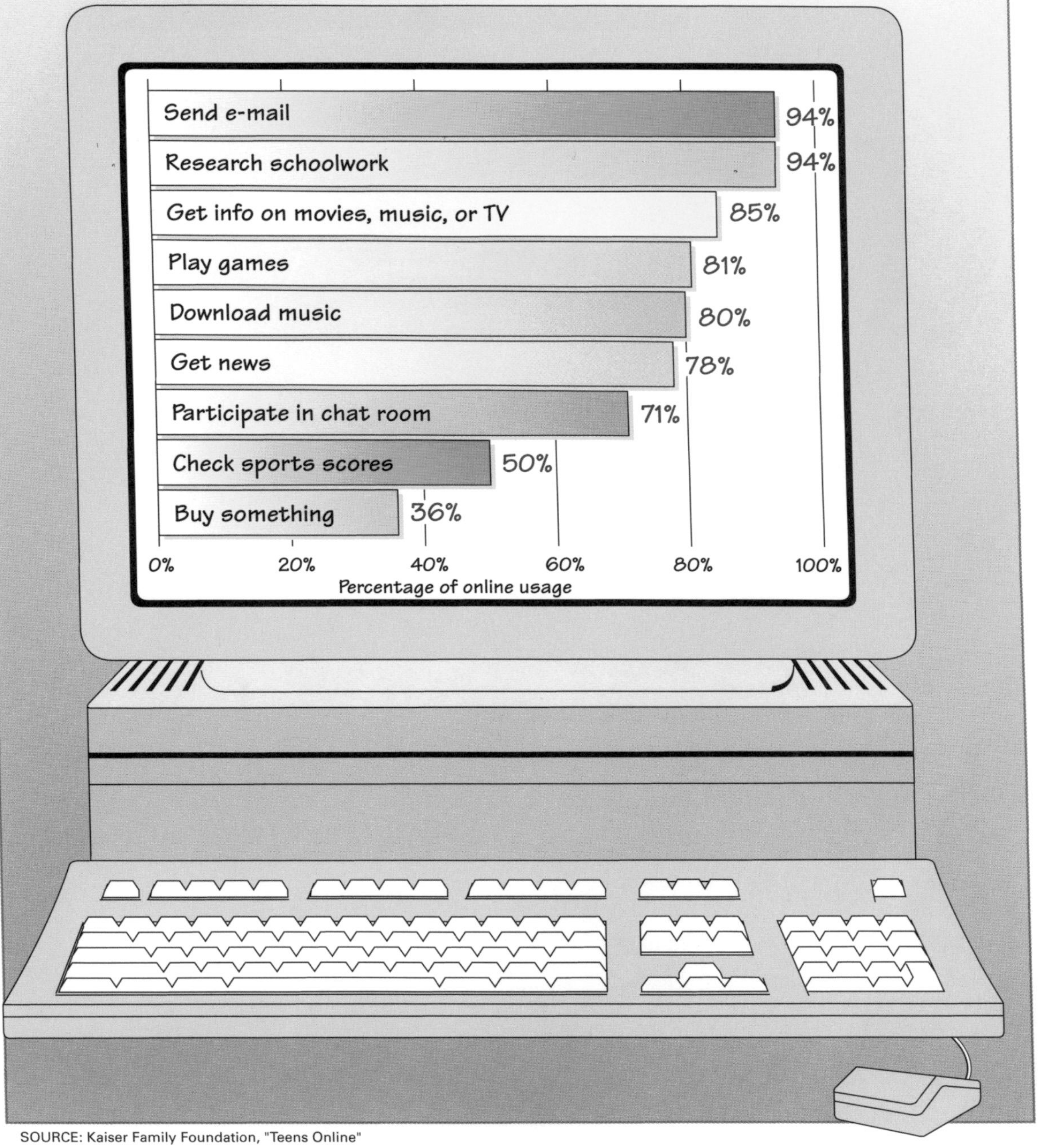

Activity	Percentage
Send e-mail	94%
Research schoolwork	94%
Get info on movies, music, or TV	85%
Play games	81%
Download music	80%
Get news	78%
Participate in chat room	71%
Check sports scores	50%
Buy something	36%

Percentage of online usage

0%   20%   40%   60%   80%   100%

Computers

SOURCE: Kaiser Family Foundation, "Teens Online"

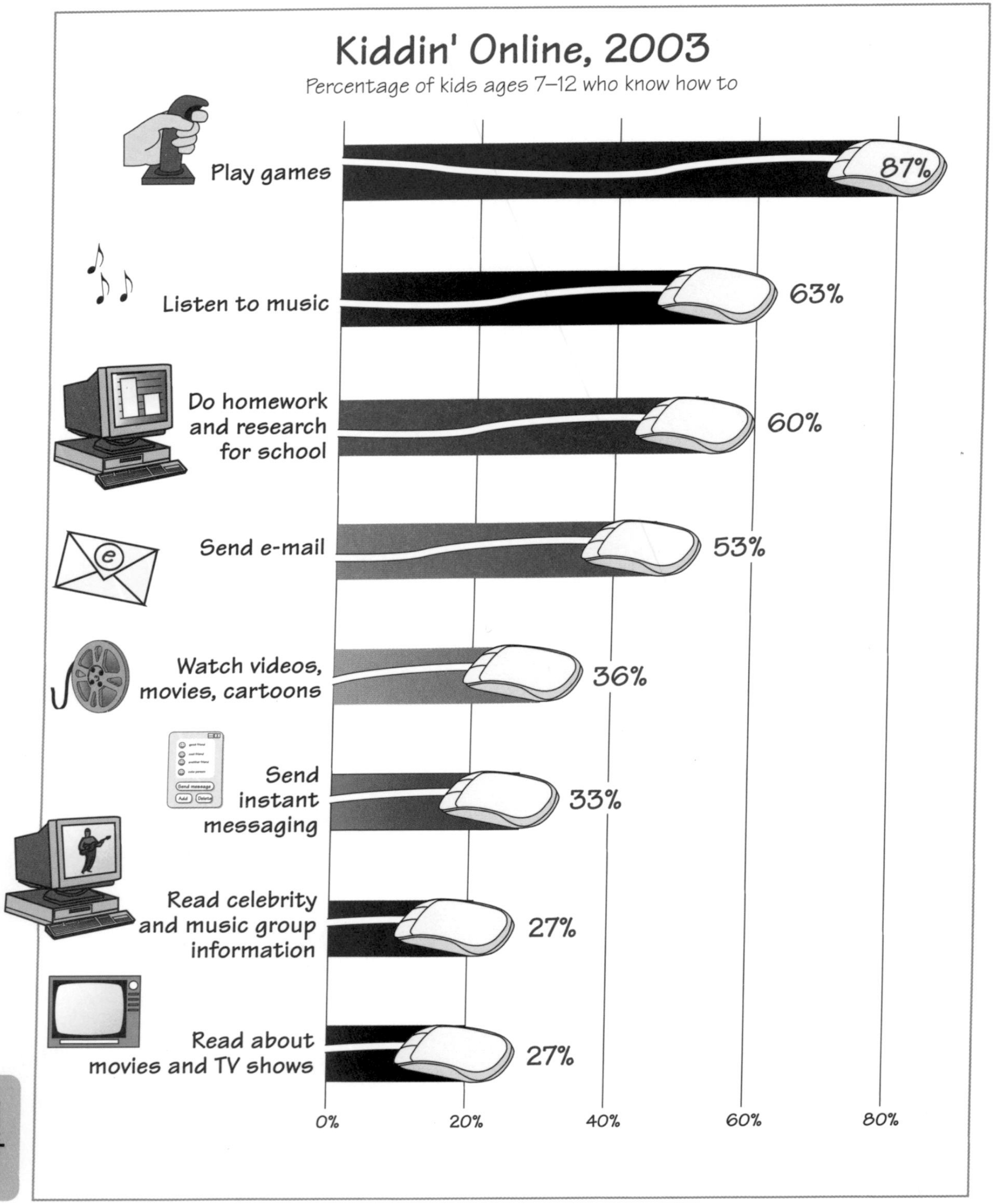

Kiddin' Online, 2003

Percentage of kids ages 7–12 who know how to

Activity	Percentage
Play games	87%
Listen to music	63%
Do homework and research for school	60%
Send e-mail	53%
Watch videos, movies, cartoons	36%
Send instant messaging	33%
Read celebrity and music group information	27%
Read about movies and TV shows	27%

0% 20% 40% 60% 80%

Computers

SOURCE: AOL/Digital Marketing Services

How Kids Find Out About Web Sites

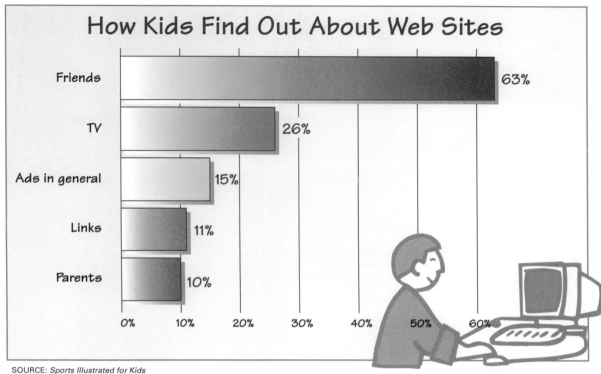

- Friends 63%
- TV 26%
- Ads in general 15%
- Links 11%
- Parents 10%

0% 10% 20% 30% 40% 50% 60%

SOURCE: *Sports Illustrated for Kids*

Computers at Home, 1990–2002

Between 1990 and 2002, there was a 232% increase in the number of U. S. households with computers.

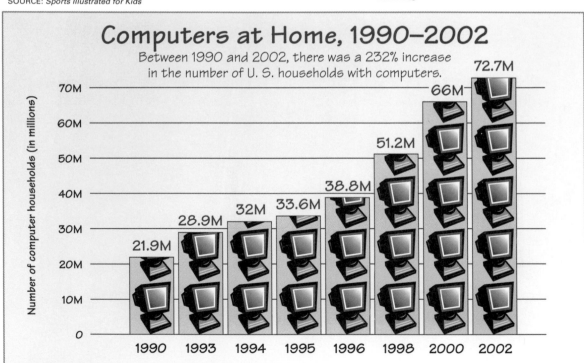

Number of computer households (in millions)

70M
60M
50M
40M
30M
20M
10M
0

- 1990 — 21.9M
- 1993 — 28.9M
- 1994 — 32M
- 1995 — 33.6M
- 1996 — 38.8M
- 1998 — 51.2M
- 2000 — 66M
- 2002 — 72.7M

Computers

SOURCE: Motion Picture Association, "U.S. Entertainment Industry: 2002 MPA Market Statistics"

Parents, Kids, and the Internet, 2003

How parents monitor their child's Internet activities

Activity	Percentage
Keep computer in common room	79%
Occasionally watch over shoulder	75%
Check Internet history	60%
Use blocking software	32%
Read child's e-mail	25%
Always sit with child	19%
Use monitoring software	17%

0% 10% 20% 30% 40% 50% 60% 70% 80%

How much attention kids think parents pay to sites kids visit

Kids 12–15 say

A lot 47%
A little 49%
None 4%

How much attention parents pay to sites kids visit

Parents say

A lot 66%
A little 33%
None 1%

SOURCE: Taylor Kids Pulse

Computers

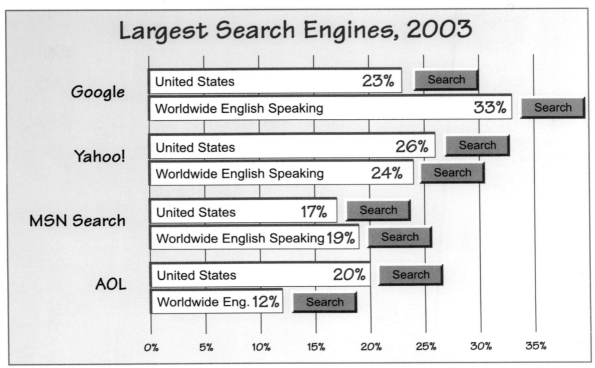

Largest Search Engines, 2003

Google
| United States | 23% | Search |
| Worldwide English Speaking | 33% | Search |

Yahoo!
| United States | 26% | Search |
| Worldwide English Speaking | 24% | Search |

MSN Search
| United States | 17% | Search |
| Worldwide English Speaking | 19% | Search |

AOL
| United States | 20% | Search |
| Worldwide Eng. | 12% | Search |

0% 5% 10% 15% 20% 25% 30% 35%

SOURCE: comScore Networks

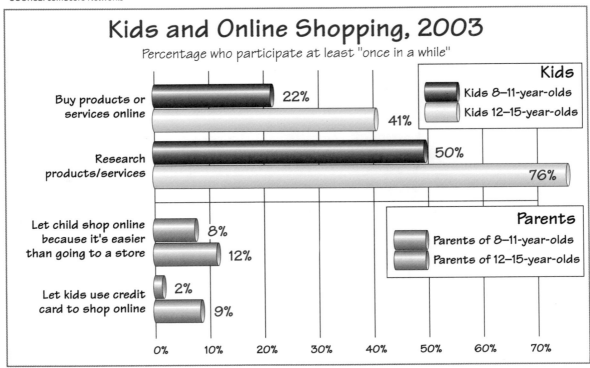

Kids and Online Shopping, 2003

Percentage who participate at least "once in a while"

Kids
Kids 8–11-year-olds
Kids 12–15-year-olds

Parents
Parents of 8–11-year-olds
Parents of 12–15-year-olds

Buy products or services online — 22% / 41%

Research products/services — 50% / 76%

Let child shop online because it's easier than going to a store — 8% / 12%

Let kids use credit card to shop online — 2% / 9%

0% 10% 20% 30% 40% 50% 60% 70%

SOURCE: Taylor Kids Pulse

Computers

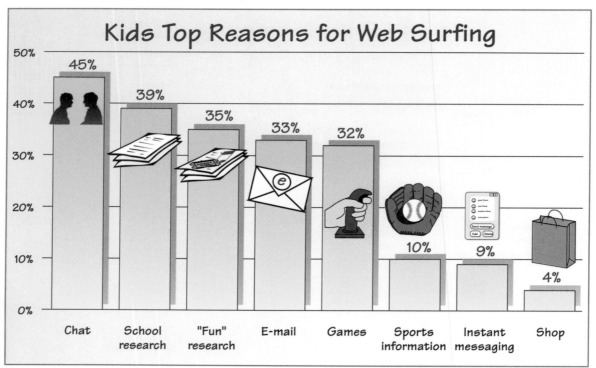

Top 10 "Youth Wired" Cities, 2003

Cities which have the highest percentage of kids ages 7–12 online between 5 and 7 days a week

8. San Francisco 37%

2. Philadelphia 45.5%

3. New York 44.6%

7. Boston 37%

9. Detroit 36%

6. Chicago 38.6%

4. Washington, DC 41%

10. Houston 34%

1. Tampa/St. Petersburg 47%

5. Miami/Ft. Lauderdale 39%

SOURCE: AOL/Digital Marketing Services

Kids Top Reasons for Web Surfing

Reason	Percentage
Chat	45%
School research	39%
"Fun" research	35%
E-mail	33%
Games	32%
Sports information	10%
Instant messaging	9%
Shop	4%

SOURCE: *Sports Illustrated for Kids*

Computers

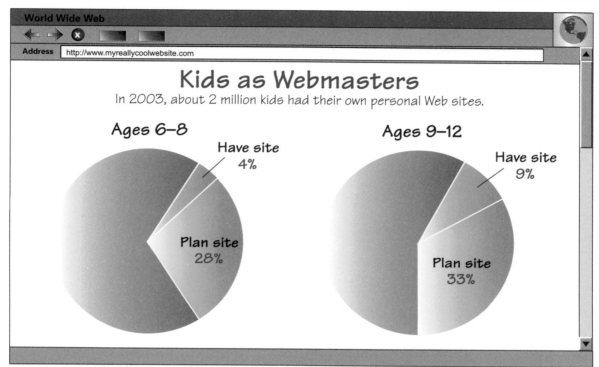

World Wide Web

Address http://www.myreallycoolwebsite.com

Kids as Webmasters

In 2003, about 2 million kids had their own personal Web sites.

Ages 6–8

Have site
4%

Plan site
28%

Ages 9–12

Have site
9%

Plan site
33%

SOURCE: Grunwald Associates

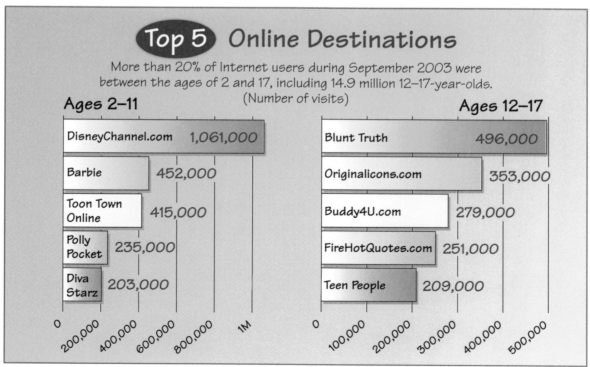

Top 5 Online Destinations

More than 20% of Internet users during September 2003 were
between the ages of 2 and 17, including 14.9 million 12–17-year-olds.
(Number of visits)

Ages 2–11

DisneyChannel.com	1,061,000
Barbie	452,000
Toon Town Online	415,000
Polly Pocket	235,000
Diva Starz	203,000

0 200,000 400,000 600,000 800,000 1M

Ages 12–17

Blunt Truth	496,000
Originalicons.com	353,000
Buddy4U.com	279,000
FireHotQuotes.com	251,000
Teen People	209,000

0 100,000 200,000 300,000 400,000 500,000

SOURCE: Nielsen/Net Ratings

Computers

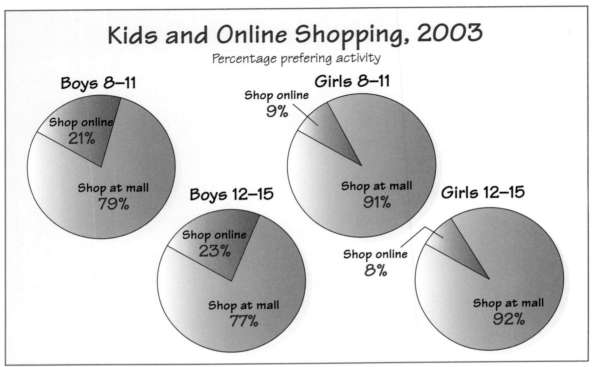

Kids and Online Shopping, 2003
Percentage prefering activity

Boys 8–11
Shop online 21%
Shop at mall 79%

Girls 8–11
Shop online 9%
Shop at mall 91%

Boys 12–15
Shop online 23%
Shop at mall 77%

Girls 12–15
Shop online 8%
Shop at mall 92%

SOURCE: Taylor Kids Pulse

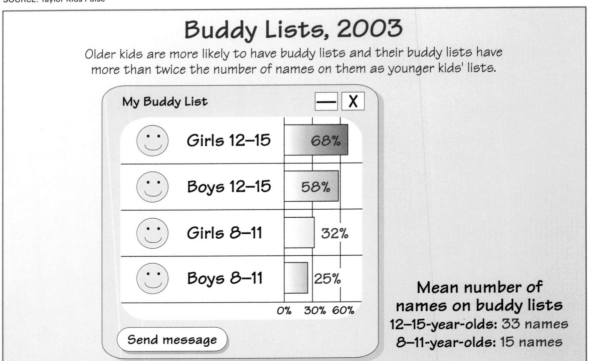

Buddy Lists, 2003

Older kids are more likely to have buddy lists and their buddy lists have more than twice the number of names on them as younger kids' lists.

My Buddy List

🙂	Girls 12–15	68%
🙂	Boys 12–15	58%
🙂	Girls 8–11	32%
🙂	Boys 8–11	25%

0%   30% 60%

Send message

Mean number of names on buddy lists
12–15-year-olds: 33 names
8–11-year-olds: 15 names

SOURCE: Taylor Kids Pulse

Instant Messaging, 2003

Younger kids primarily IM relatives, but older kids
IM a wider variety of people including strangers.

Legend:
- Kids 8–11
- Kids 12–15

Category	Kids 8–11	Kids 12–15
Relatives	74%	63%
Friends from school	39%	73%
Friends who live far away	31%	53%
Friends in area, but not at school	30%	45%
People from school they don't hang out with	14%	31%
Strangers	11%	21%

SOURCE: Taylor Kids Pulse

Who's Playing Games? 2003

Percentage playing computer and video games

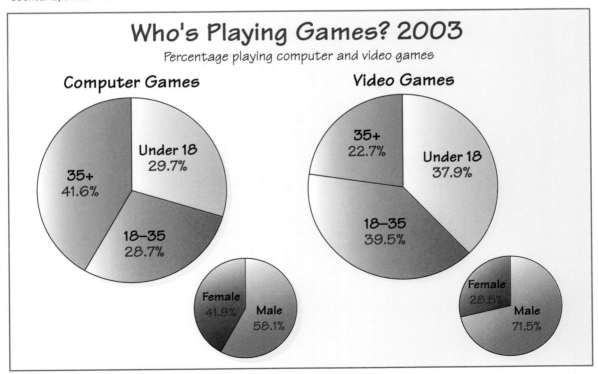

Computer Games
- Under 18: 29.7%
- 18–35: 28.7%
- 35+: 41.6%
- Female: 41.9%
- Male: 58.1%

Video Games
- Under 18: 37.9%
- 18–35: 39.5%
- 35+: 22.7%
- Female: 28.5%
- Male: 71.5%

SOURCE: Entertainment Software Association

Computers

Parents and Internet Shopping, 2003

Parents use the Internet to buy personal items like clothes, makeup, books, etc. for their daughters; and computers, sporting goods, etc. for their sons. Percentage of parents who have bought specific items in past year

Item	For girls	For boys
Clothing	35%	27%
Books	33%	27%
CDs	32%	24%
Downloaded music	22%	18%
Videos/DVDs	21%	24%
Video/computer games	19%	35%
Personal care products	16%	5%
Airline tickets	13%	17%
Electronics	12%	25%
Sporting goods	8%	16%

Computers